Optimise

Student's Book

B1

Preliminary
for Schools

macmillan
education

UNIT	READING	GRAMMAR	VOCABULARY
1 This is me (PERSONAL IDENTITY) p 4–13	*What do they do all day?* Skimming 4-option multiple choice	Present simple, present continuous, stative verbs Quantifiers	Words connected with *personality* Nouns with *-ity* / *-ness* Collocations with adjectives
2 Home sweet home (HOUSE AND HOME) p 14–23	*Accommodation available* Understanding text type 3-option multiple choice	Past simple and past continuous *used to* and *would*	Words connected with *the house and home* Phrasal verbs Word patterns
Progress check Units 1 and 2: Grammar and vocabulary / Exam skills p 24–25			
3 On the road (TRAVEL AND TRANSPORT) p 26–35	*The Hyperloop* Understanding tenses Gapped text	Present perfect simple and continuous Countable and uncountable nouns	Words connected with *holidays* Adjectives with *un-* / *im-* / *il-* / *ir-* / *dis-* Word patterns
4 Give it a go (NEW EXPERIENCES) p 36–45	*Maximum fun!* Scanning Matching	*will* and *be going to* Present simple and present continuous for future	Words connected with *outdoor activities* Phrasal verbs Collocations connected with *free time*
Progress check Units 3 and 4: Grammar and vocabulary / Exam skills p 46–47			
5 In good health (HEALTH) p 48–57	*Teenlife: animal lives* Paraphrasing Matching	Modals (1): ability, obligation, advice, permission Modals (2): possibility, probability, certainty	Words connected with *health and illness* Phrasal verbs Collocations with *have*, *take*, *make* and *do*
6 A piece of cake! (FOOD AND DRINK) p 58–67	*A young star of the kitchen* Identifying synonyms 4-option multiple choice	Relative clauses Articles	Words connected with *food* Phrasal verbs Adjectives/nouns/verbs
Progress check Units 5 and 6: Grammar and vocabulary / Exam skills p 68–69			
7 Shop till you drop! (SHOPPING AND SERVICES) p 70–79	*Teenagers take over the market* Understanding time words and phrases Gapped text	Past perfect simple and continuous Comparatives and superlatives	Words connected with *shopping* Phrasal verbs Idioms for *shopping and spending*
8 A sense of style (FASHION) p 80–89	*Project fashion!* Understanding attitude and opinion Matching	The passive Question tags	Words connected with *clothes and accessories* Phrasal verbs Adjectives/nouns/verbs
Progress check Units 7 and 8: Grammar and vocabulary / Exam skills p 90–91			
9 Playing to win! (SPORT) p 92–101	*Want to play Quidditch?* Understanding implication 4-option multiple choice	Conditionals (1): zero, first and second conditionals Time clauses	Words connected with *people in sport* Phrasal verbs Collocations with *do*, *play* and *go*
10 All in good fun! (ENTERTAINMENT) p 102–111	*We love Hollywood* Understanding linking words and phrases Gapped text	Conditionals (2): third conditional The causative	Words connected with *people in the media* Phrasal verbs Word patterns
Progress check Units 9 and 10: Grammar and vocabulary / Exam skills p 112–113			
11 Curious minds (EDUCATION) p 114–123	*Summer camp* Understanding specific information Matching	Reported speech Reported questions	Words connected with *studying* Phrasal verbs Idioms for *education and learning*
12 Our wonderful world (THE NATURAL WORLD) p 124–133	*River clean-up!* Understanding instructions 3-option multiple choice	Future perfect Modal perfect	Words connected with *natural habitats* Phrasal verbs Adjectives and nouns
Progress check Units 11 and 12: Grammar and vocabulary / Exam skills p 134–135			
OPTIMISE YOUR EXAMS	▶ **READING** p 136–139	▶ **WRITING** p 140–141	▶ **LISTENING** p 142–143
Grammar reference p 148–160	Vocabulary reference p 161–168	Writing reference p 169–174	Irregular verbs reference p 175

LISTENING	SPEAKING	LANGUAGE IN USE	WRITING
Understanding the situation **3-option multiple choice (pictures)**	Talking about yourself **Questions** Talk2Me	Identifying phrasal verbs **4-option multiple-choice cloze**	Starting and ending an email **An email**
Predicting **3-option multiple choice (interview)**	Saying where things are **Extended turn (photos)** Talk2Me	Result clauses **Open cloze**	Using the right style **An article**
Listening for attitude and opinion **3-option multiple choice (dialogues)**	Making suggestions **Discussion (pictures)** Talk2Me	Using particles to create phrasal verbs **Open cloze**	Choosing positive and negative points **A review**
Listening for the main idea **Multiple matching**	Expressing opinions **General conversation** Talk2Me	Connectors of contrast **Key word transformation**	Giving your opinion **An article**
Recognising synonyms **3-option multiple choice (interview)**	Talking about habits **Questions** Talk2Me	Words formed from verbs **Word formation**	Using narrative tenses **A story**
Recognising similar meaning **Gap fill**	Describing situations and actions **Extended turn (photos)** Talk2Me	Collocations **4-option multiple-choice cloze**	Making suggestions **An email**
Understanding relevant information **3-option multiple choice (pictures)**	Asking questions **General conversation** Talk2Me	Nouns connected with people **Word formation**	Using direct speech **A story**
Knowing what type of information to listen for **Gap fill**	Discussing alternatives **Discussion (pictures)** Talk2Me	*-ing* and infinitives **Key word transformation**	Writing descriptions **A story**
Identifying why answers are incorrect **3-option multiple choice (dialogues)**	Talking about other people **Questions** Talk2Me	Verbs with similar meaning **4-option multiple-choice cloze**	Expressing preferences **An email**
Selecting relevant information **Gap fill**	Listening and responding **General conversation** Talk2Me	*wish* and *if only* **Open cloze**	Describing how to do something **An article**
Understanding implication **3-option multiple choice (pictures)**	Expressing uncertainty **Extended turn (photos)** Talk2Me	Nouns with similar meaning **4-option multiple-choice cloze**	Understanding the notes **An email**
Thinking logically **Multiple choice (single extract)**	Negotiating agreement **Discussion (pictures)** Talk2Me	Auxiliary verbs **Open cloze**	Giving reasons **An essay**

▶ SPEAKING / ▶ SPEAKING TEST VIDEO p 144–147

Student's Resource Centre

- *Talk2Me* videos
- Speaking Test video
- *Optimise your grammar* worksheets
- *Optimise your vocabulary* worksheets
- *Say it right* pronunciation worksheets
- Culture and CLIL worksheets
- Class and Workbook audio

1 This is me

READING | 4-option multiple choice | A magazine interview

1 **In pairs or as a group, add more words and phrases to the categories for describing people.**

Hair and facial hair	*long, dark-haired, moustache*
Face and complexion	*blue eyes, pale skin, freckles*
Height and build	*tall, thin, muscular*
Appearance and personality	*friendly, serious, fashionable*

2 **Which words and phrases in Exercise 1 can you use to describe yourself?**

3 **Read the text quickly and decide if the statements are T (True) or F (False).**

1 Forensic artists usually draw pictures of people they know very well. **T / F**
2 Their pictures often help the police do their job. **T / F**
3 They sometimes draw people from a long time ago. **T / F**
4 Computer programs can help them get the picture right. **T / F**
5 To a forensic artist, 'curly hair' and 'wavy hair' are exactly the same thing. **T / F**
6 Forensic artists rarely draw faces. **T / F**

EXAM SKILL

Skimming

- Skimming is reading quickly to get the general meaning of a text.
- When you skim, move your eyes quickly over the text without going back. Focus on the general idea and don't worry about words you don't understand.

OPTIMISE YOUR EXAM

4-option multiple choice

- When you are not sure of an answer, cross out the answers that are definitely wrong.
- When you are left with two possible answers, read them again carefully and check the relevant part of the text. Then make your final choice.

JOB ZONE

What do they do all day?

This week: forensic artists

Karen Jacobs works as a forensic artist.

Karen, what is a 'forensic artist'? What do you do all day?

In simple words, I draw people! For example, the police contact me when a witness sees someone commit a crime. I listen to the description of the criminal and turn the description into a picture.

So, forensic artists help catch criminals?

In a way, yes! Do you know who Lois Gibson is? She's in the *Guinness Book of World Records* as the world's most successful forensic artist. Her pictures help catch lots of criminals – over 1,300 of them so far!

Do you only draw criminals?

No, I also draw historical figures. I do lots of work for TV programmes and museums. At the moment, I'm working on a TV documentary about ancient Egypt. We're making drawings and 3D models of the pharaohs. It's fascinating!

Do you use a pencil and paper?

Yes, but we also use computers. These days, technology is developing very quickly. It's really useful, and there are some great computer programs we can use. When a witness says that a person wears glasses, for example, we can bring up on screen different styles of glasses for the witness to choose from.

What skills do you need for your job?

Forensic artists do need good drawing skills, of course, but they also need good people skills. We often work with people who are upset, so we help them remember clearly and give us enough detail. Perhaps the witness says the criminal has curly hair. We try to find out exactly what they mean by 'curly'. For example, is 'wavy' a better word? A forensic artist also needs to be an expert in different hairstyles!

What do you know about faces?

Faces obviously change as we get older. But this is interesting: the face of a shy person changes differently to the face of a lively, sociable person! And do you know which part of your face continues to grow all through your life? Your nose!

4 1.01 **Read the text again. For each question, choose the correct answer.**

1 What does Karen Jacobs do regularly?
   - **A** She helps Lois Gibson solve crimes.
   - **B** She meets criminals and draws them.
   - **C** She listens to police officers describing criminals.
   - **D** She draws pictures of criminals and people from the past.

2 Karen says she sometimes uses modern technology to
   - **A** find pictures that match someone's description.
   - **B** find pictures of real people online.
   - **C** design different types of glasses.
   - **D** have video calls with witnesses.

3 Good people skills help a forensic artist to
   - **A** draw more artistic pictures.
   - **B** learn about different hairstyles.
   - **C** communicate better with witnesses.
   - **D** not get upset while they're working.

4 What advice might a forensic artist give to someone interested in the job?

A Find out what criminals often look like, then make all your drawings look like that.

B Make sure you visit a library to read about the history of hairdressing.

C Try to be lively and sociable so that criminals are happy to tell you what they know.

D Learn about how faces change and find out how technology can help you.

5 **Complete the sentences with highlighted words or phrases from the text.**

1 When you ___________ something _______ on a computer screen, you make it appear.
2 A ___________ is someone who sees something happening, such as an accident or a crime.
3 If someone is ___________ , they're very good at something.
4 An ___________ is a person who knows a lot about a subject.
5 When you ___________ something _______ something else, you make the first thing become something different.
6 'To ___________ ' is an informal way of saying 'to become older'.
7 If something is ___________ , it's extremely interesting.
8 Someone who is ___________ is sad, angry or annoyed.

THINK | RESEARCH | CULTURE | LEARN | ME

Choose a person you know and think about how their appearance might change in the future. Describe them as they might be in ten years' time.

▶ **Workbook Unit 1:** Reading, pages 4–5, exercises 1, 2, 3

1

GRAMMAR 1 | Present simple, present continuous, stative verbs

Grammar in context

Find these verbs in the text on page 5 and match each one with a description.

1 I ***draw*** *people!* ____
2 *At the moment, I'm* ***working*** *on a TV documentary about ancient Egypt.* ____
3 *Forensic artists* ***do need*** *good drawing skills, of course …* ____
4 *Perhaps the witness says the criminal* ***has*** *curly hair.* ____
5 *These days, technology* ***is developing*** *very quickly.* ____

a) a situation or action happening at the moment
b) a changing situation
c) a stative verb
d) a habit, routine and permanent situation
e) the emphatic present simple

REMEMBER

- We use the present simple for general truths and facts, habits, routines and permanent situations.
- We use the present continuous for descriptions of pictures, actions happening now and temporary or changing situations.
- Stative verbs are not usually used in the present continuous. Common stative verbs include: *believe, hate, like, need,* etc.
- Some verbs can be stative or action verbs, depending on the meaning: *Sam* ***has*** *red hair.* (state)
  Samia ***is having*** *a haircut at the moment.* (action)

▶ **See Grammar reference, Unit 1,** page 148

1 **Look at the picture and choose the correct word or phrase.**

This is a picture of my friend Emma. She (1) lives / is living near me and (2) we're / we're being in the same class at school. She (3) has / is having short, dark hair and (4) usually wears / is usually wearing glasses. (5) Emma smiles / Emma's smiling in the picture and that's not unusual. She (6) always seems / is always seeming happy and in a good mood. She's very friendly and sociable, but she (7) doesn't speak / isn't speaking much in class. At the moment, I think (8) Emma shops / Emma's shopping with her mum.

2 **Look at the picture and put the verbs into the correct form. Use short forms where possible.**

This is a picture of my friend Paulina. She (1) ______________ (not / look) much like Emma – their hair (2) ______________ (not / be) the same colour or length and Paulina (3) ______________ (not / wear) glasses. Also, Paulina (4) ______________ (not / smile) as much as Emma. She (5) ______________ (often / seem) very serious, but in fact she (6) ______________ (have [emphatic]) a great sense of humour and (7) ______________ (often / tell) really funny jokes! In the picture, she (8) ______________ (wear) a green top. Paulina (9) ______________ (love) cycling, so she (10) ______________ (almost always / arrive) at school wearing her cycling helmet. Paulina's in the same class as Emma and me, but she (11) ______________ (not / live) near me. Right now, I imagine Paulina (12) ______________ (watch) something on YouTube.

3 **Look at the two pictures again and write questions using the words and phrases given.**

Example: Which girl / wear / pink top
Which girl is wearing a pink top?

1 Who / have / long hair
____
2 Emma / smile / in the photo
____
3 either of them / seem / shy
____
4 Paulina / usually / ride / a bike to school
____
5 Your own question:
____

4 **In pairs, ask and answer the questions in Exercise 3. Use your imagination where necessary.**

Words connected with *personality*

1 1.02 **Write a word from the box in each gap to complete the definitions. Listen and check.**

creative | curious | dependable | friendly
generous | negative | polite | popular
serious | shy | unreliable

Someone who is …

1 __________ is not enthusiastic about something.
2 __________ is imaginative, artistic and talented.
3 __________ wants to find out and learn about things.
4 __________ doesn't do what they say they will.
5 __________ is someone you can trust and rely on.
6 __________ is pleasant and helps other people.
7 __________ is liked by lots of people.
8 __________ gives a lot of their time to people.
9 __________ behaves in a very nice way.
10 __________ is very careful and doesn't laugh a lot.
11 __________ is nervous and embarrassed around people.

2 **In pairs or as a group, discuss the difference in meaning between each pair of words in bold.**

1 a **friendly** / **popular** person
2 a **generous** / **polite** person
3 a **serious** / **shy** person

Nouns with *-ity* / *-ness*

3 1.03 **Find four adjectives in the box which do not make nouns ending in *-ity*. Write their nouns in each gap. Listen and check.**

creative | curious | dependable
friendly | generous | negative
personal | polite | popular
reliable | serious | shy

1 __________ , __________ , __________
2 __________
3 __________
4 __________

SAY IT RIGHT

Resource centre: Unit 1
/ə/

4 **Complete the words in the sentences.**

1 I was surprised by my best friend's negativ__________ when I told him I wanted to live abroad when I'm older.
2 I don't find it easy to talk to new people because of my shy__________ .
3 They're twins, but Susie's personal__________ is totally different from Annabel's.
4 My friend__________ with Corey is one of the most important relationships in my life.
5 Thanks to the genero__________ of your parents, we've bought some new equipment for the school's art room.
6 Just out of curio__________ , why did you choose to get that hairstyle?

Collocations with adjectives

5 1.04 **Match 1–6 to a–f to make collocations. Listen and check.**

1 big — **a)** awake
2 fast — **b)** voice
3 feel — **c)** time
4 wide — **d)** asleep
5 long — **e)** trouble
6 deep — **f)** small

6 **Fill the gaps in the text with collocations from Exercise 5.**

My best friend Leah's in (**1**) __________ again! The problem is she's so unreliable. She promised to babysit her neighbours' kids, but turned up half an hour late. Then, when Mr and Mrs Ghadie got home, the kids were (**2**) __________ and playing, and Leah was (**3**) __________ on the sofa! Mr Ghadie shouted at her in his (**4**) __________ , and called her irresponsible. Leah said it made her (**5**) __________ . I hope she's learnt her lesson, but I don't think they'll ask her to babysit again for a very (**6**) __________ !

THINK | RESEARCH | CULTURE | LEARN | ME

Look at the adjectives in Exercise 1 again. Think about which three are the most important qualities in a friend for you.

1 LISTENING | 3-option multiple choice (pictures)

1 **In pairs or as a group, think of different situations where people introduce themselves or other people.**

Example: *Meeting a new teacher for the first time*

EXAM SKILL

Understanding the situation

- When you're doing a listening task, it's important to understand the general situation. This helps you to understand the gist of what you're listening to.
- As you listen, ask yourself these key questions: Who's talking? Who are they talking to? Where are they? What's the general topic/situation?

2 1.05 **Listen to people speaking in four different situations. Make notes to answer the questions for each situation.**

Situation 1:

1 Who's talking? ________________

2 Where are they? ________________

3 What are they talking about? ________________

Situation 2:

4 Where are the boy and the girl? ________________

Situation 3:

5 Where would you hear someone say this?

____

Situation 4:

6 Where would you hear someone say this?

____

OPTIMISE YOUR EXAM

3-option multiple choice (pictures)

- Look at each picture before you listen and think of words and ideas you might hear. For example, in Exercise 3, picture 1A, you might hear *computer* or *internet*, etc.
- Remember that you will probably hear about the ideas in all three pictures. For example, in question 1, you'll hear something about computers, something about dancing and something about being a nurse. But Jared only wants to do one of those jobs.

3 1.06 **Listen to longer extracts of the conversations. For each question, choose the correct answer.**

1 What job does Jared want to do when he's older?

A B C

2 What does Samantha agree to?

A B C

3 What does Robert have at the moment?

A B C

4 What is Josephine studying?

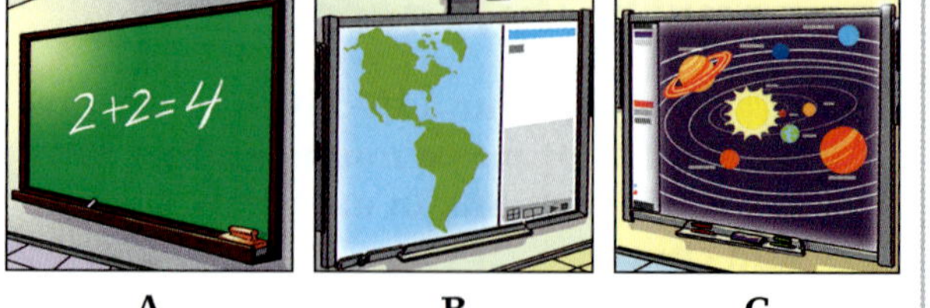

A B C

4 1.06 **Listen again and check your answers.**

THINK | **RESEARCH** | CULTURE | LEARN | ME

Do a class survey. Find out:

- what job each person wants to do when they're older.
- what job their parents/guardians do.
- what pets they have.
- if they like going to parties.
- if they like watching videos online.

▶ **Workbook Unit 1:** Listening, page 8, exercises 1, 2, 3

Grammar in context

Look at these sentences from the audio in the listening lesson on page 8. Decide if the word or phrase in capitals can replace the word or phrase in bold. Write 'yes' or 'no'.

1 ***Both*** *my parents work.*

(BOTH OF) __________

2 *I don't know* ***most*** *people here.*

(MOST OF) __________

3 *You can win a lot of money on* ***every*** *question – if you're clever!*

(EACH OF THE) __________

4 ***Not all of*** *you will know who Josephine is.*

(NOT ALL) __________

REMEMBER

- We use quantifiers to talk about numbers and amounts.
- Common quantifiers include: *all, both, each, enough, every, little, lots of, many, most, much, some,* etc.
- After *each* and *every* (but NOT *each of the*), we can use a singular countable noun: *Every* ***student*** *in my class is 14 years old.*
- After some quantifiers, including *all* (*of the*), *both* (*of the*), *each of the*, *lots of* (*the*), *many* (*of the*), and *most* (*of the*), we can use a plural countable noun: *Many* ***teenagers*** *are shy.*
- After some quantifiers, including *little* and *much*, we can use an uncountable noun: *I haven't got much* ***money*** *on me.*
- Quantifiers with *of the* take a plural verb: *Most of the boys* ***have*** *short hair.* The exception is *each of the*, which takes a singular verb: *Each of the girls* ***has*** *long hair.*
- With some quantifiers, you need to use a different grammatical structure depending on the meaning. For example, *all* = generally (***All*** *people breathe air.*), *all (of) + the* = specific (***All of the*** *people in my class have a mobile phone.*).

▶ See Grammar reference, Unit 1, page 148

1 Choose the correct word or phrase to complete the sentences.

1 Every **girl** / **girls** in our class **have** / **has** a sister or brother.

2 Each of the **student** / **students** in our class **have** / **has** a social media profile.

3 Sue's got an earring in **each** / **every** ear.

4 **Most** / **Most of** artists are very creative people.

5 My cousins are visiting us at the moment! We're taking **both** / **both of** them to the zoo tomorrow.

2 Write sentences about the cartoon using the words and phrases.

Example: all of / man / look / very serious

All of the men look very serious.

1 both / police officer / wear / uniform

____

2 all / man / stand up

____

3 most / man / tall

____

4 woman / look carefully at / every / man

____

5 woman / look carefully at / each of / man

____

6 woman / talk to / both of / police officer

____

3 Write a word or phrase from the box in each gap.

all	all of	both	enough	every	of	others	some

When you see someone's face, do you know who that person is?

(**1**) __________ face is different. And (**2**) __________ us can recognise someone from their face. Well, no – not if you've got 'prosopagnosia', which is also called 'face blindness'.

Most (**3**) __________ the people with face blindness have a problem in a particular part of their brain. (**4**) __________ of them have it from birth, and (**5**) __________ develop it after an accident or illness. But they (**6**) __________ have the same disability: they can't tell who someone is by looking at their face. For example, a woman goes to meet her friend. There are two people waiting – and they (**7**) __________ look exactly the same to her!

There's no medical treatment for the condition, but there are things people with face blindness can do. These include trying to memorise everyone's voice, body language and body shape. That usually gives them (**8**) __________ information to work out who someone is.

▶ Workbook Unit 1: Grammar 2, page 7, exercises 1, 2, 3

1 SPEAKING | Questions

Talk2Me — Well, she's ...

Flipped classroom

1 ▷ **Watch the *Talk2Me* video and answer the questions.**

1 What is Jamie's favourite drink?
2 How long have Angus and Jamie been friends?
3 Is Maddy's drink bigger than Jamie's?

2 ▷ **Watch the video again. Underline the phrases in the *Phrase expert* box that you hear on the video.**

> **PHRASE EXPERT**
>
> Yes, I've (studied English) for … | My favourite (subject/sport) is definitely/probably … | Well, (s)he's/it's … | I don't have a lot of free time, but … | I'd say I'm (friendly/quite tall)

3 **In pairs or as a group, answer the questions.**

1 How much personal information do you put on social media, such as Facebook?
2 How do you feel about answering personal questions about yourself?

> **EXAM SKILL**
>
> **Talking about yourself**
>
> - Speaking exams often include personal questions, so you need to be able to talk about yourself and your life, family, friends, studies, etc.
> - At the start of the speaking exam, the examiner will ask you about facts such as *What's your name?, How old are you?* and *Where do you live?* You can give short answers to these questions: *My name is Sam Lopez. / I'm 14. / I live in Moscow.*
> - For other questions, you need to say more and give full answers. For example, if the question is *How would you describe your personality?*, don't just say *I'm friendly*. You have to give longer answers to show you can speak English well.

4 🔊 1.07 **Listen to two students answering these questions. Tick the answers which give enough detail.**

	Nisha	Alfie
1 What's your name?		
2 How old are you?		
3 Where do you live?		
4 Do you study English at school?		
5 Do you like it?		
6 What's your favourite school subject?		
7 What do you enjoy doing in your free time?		
8 Tell me about your best friend.		

5 **Look at the questions in Exercise 4 and think about your answers. Make notes if necessary.**

> **OPTIMISE YOUR EXAM**
>
> **Questions**
>
> - Don't memorise long answers because you might not answer the examiner's questions correctly. However, it's fine to learn one or two sentences to talk about typical subjects.

6 **In pairs or groups, use your notes in Exercise 5 to ask and answer the questions.**

▶ **Workbook Unit 1:** Speaking, pages 8–9, exercises 1, 2, 3

LANGUAGE IN USE | 4-option multiple-choice cloze

1 **In pairs or as a group, ask and answer the questions.**

1 What jobs do robots help us do?

2 Do you think machines or robots can be cleverer than a human? Do they have feelings?

REMEMBER

- Phrasal verbs consist of a main verb followed by a particle – an adverb (*look* ***up***), or a preposition (*look* ***into***), or both (*look* ***up to***).
- The meaning of a phrasal verb is often different from the meaning of the individual words, e.g. you *look up into the sky*, but when you *look up a word in a dictionary*, the phrasal verb '*look up*' means '*find*' or '*try to find*', not '*put your eyes up*'.
- Think of each phrasal verb as one piece of vocabulary, e.g. you might write in your notebook: *look up* = (*try to*) *find*.
- Phrasal verbs with *turn* are often connected to a changing situation.
- Phrasal verbs with *look* are often connected to seeing something – literally or metaphorically.

2 **Write the correct form of *turn* or *look* in each gap. Use the words in italics to help you. If you aren't sure, ask yourself if the action is connected to *a changing situation* or *seeing something*.**

1 You can ___________ *up* curious facts about body language/human personalities online.

2 ___________ *off* the TV and do something creative!

3 If you ___________ *over*, there's a brilliant short story on the next page.

4 As a babysitter, you're responsible for ___________ *after* someone else's kids.

5 How do caterpillars ___________ *into* butterflies?

6 ___________ *on* the TV! *CSI: New York* is starting.

7 I'm really ___________ *forward to* going to Nadine's party next week.

8 Scientists are ___________ *into* what causes face blindness in the brain.

3 **Quickly read the text in Exercise 5, ignoring the gaps and answer choices. Which question best summarises the main points of the text?**

a) Are machines and robots cleverer than humans?

b) What do most people think about modern technology?

c) Is it possible for machines and robots to think and feel?

4 **Read the text again. Which gaps test your knowledge of phrasal verbs?**

OPTIMISE YOUR EXAM

4-option multiple-choice cloze

- Before you look at the possible answers, quickly read the whole text to get a general idea of what it's about.
- Fill the gaps you're sure about first. Then go back to the gaps where you're not so sure.
- If you're not 100% sure, make a guess. Don't leave any gaps blank.

5 **Choose the correct word to fill each gap.**

Do computers have personalities?

Think about your computer, or your mobile phone. It is definitely 'clever' in some ways, but it doesn't feel sad when you **(1)** ____ it off. It doesn't **(2)** ____ forward to you using it. It can't feel any emotions when you start using it. In other words, it doesn't have a **(3)** ____ .

Humans have 'consciousness'. This **(4)** ____ that we can think and feel, but what about computers? Scientists are looking into this, and **(5)** ____ think that technology can become 'conscious'. They say: 'Maybe the internet can already think. How would we know?' Others believe that only things that are alive can have consciousness.

In the future, if our computers **(6)** ____ into conscious machines, will they end up being more creative than humans? No one knows. But it makes you think, doesn't it?

	A	B	C	D
1	**A** make	**B** turn	**C** close	**D** change
2	**A** look	**B** see	**C** watch	**D** notice
3	**A** reliability	**B** negativity	**C** popularity	**D** personality
4	**A** believes	**B** recognises	**C** means	**D** seems
5	**A** all	**B** each	**C** both	**D** some
6	**A** come	**B** turn	**C** become	**D** improve

1 **In pairs or groups, answer the questions.**

1 What's your family like?
2 How are some families different from others?

EXAM SKILL

Starting and ending an email

- It's important to start and end your email in the right way. This depends on who you are writing to. For example we can use *Hi …* and *Can't wait to see you!* (informal) or *Dear …* and *All the best,* (formal) at the beginning and end of an email.
- In your first paragraph, remember to thank the person for their email.

2 **Read part of an email from Claire's English teacher and the notes Claire has made. Answer the questions.**

From: Mr Jones
Subject: Class project

Dear Class,

I'd like each person in our class to do a project on their family. — *Interesting!*

What's your family like? Who do you live with? — *Explain*

Do you think it's better to have a large or small family? — *Say which you prefer*

How should we present our projects to the rest of the school? — *Suggest …* Don't forget to include some photos!

1 Which of these is a good first paragraph for Claire's email?
 a) Thank you for your email. A school project on families sounds really interesting!
 b) Thanks for your email. Interesting!
2 What information should Claire give in paragraph 2?
 a) the people she lives with and what personalities they have
 b) whether she likes her family or not
3 In paragraph 3, what does Claire need to decide?
4 In paragraph 4, should Claire give a fact or an opinion?

3 **Choose the best option to complete Claire's reply. You can use your answers from Exercise 2 to help you.**

From: Claire
Subject: RE: Class project

(1) **Hi** / **Dear** Mr Jones,

(2) **Thank you for your email. A school project on families sounds really interesting.** / **Thanks for your email. Interesting!**

I live with my parents, two brothers and a sister.
(3) **My brothers are really messy and noisy, but my sister is very cute!** / **I really like them.**

(4) **Personally** / **Definitely**, I think having a large family is great. It's often crazy, but it's never boring! We sometimes argue and fight, but we also have lots of fun together.
I wouldn't want to have a small family.

I think we should organise an exhibition in the school hall. The other students could see it during break time and learn more about us and our families.

(5) **It's great to hear from you!** / **I look forward to starting this project.**

(6) **Speak soon!** / **All the best,**

Claire

4 **Answer the questions.**

1 Do you think Claire has a traditional family? Explain why / why not?
2 Why does Claire prefer to have a large family?
3 Why does Claire think an exhibition is a good idea?

OPTIMISE YOUR EXAM

An email

- Read the exam question carefully and take time to understand the notes.
- Use the notes when planning and writing your first draft. Add a few sentences to each note to develop the idea. Make sure you answer all four notes.
- Check your draft carefully thinking about grammar, punctuation, spelling and the information included in each paragraph.
- Correct any mistakes and write your final email.

5 Look at this writing task and answer the questions.

Read this email from your English teacher Mrs Fairfax and the notes you have made.

From: Mrs Fairfax

Subject: End-of-year project

Dear Class,

For our end-of-year project I'd like you to write about the important people in your lives and how you spend time with them. *(Interesting!)*

What different groups of people do you often spend time with? Think about your family, close friends and members of a sports team or a club. *(Tell Mrs Fairfax)*

Which group do you like being with the most? Why? *(Explain)*

It would be great to present your projects to the school. Would you prefer to prepare a poster or write an article on the school blog? *(Say which you prefer)*

Reply soon!

Emma Fairfax

1 What is interesting in the first paragraph?

2 What do you have to explain to Mrs Fairfax?

Write your **email** to Mrs Fairfax using **all the notes**.

6 Plan Make a paragraph plan.

Part	Purpose	Useful phrases	My notes
First line	greet the person you are writing to	*Dear …*	
Paragraph 1	thank the other person for their email and write about the first note on the email	*Thanks for …* *The project sounds …*	
Paragraph 2	write about the second note on the email	*I belong to many groups …, but …, I think the group I feel most part of is …*	
Paragraph 3	write about the third note on the email	*I love … most because …,* *I love being part of all of them, but …*	
Paragraph 4	write about the fourth note on the email	*I think … is a good idea because …* *I would prefer to … because …*	
Closing expression & your name	say goodbye first name	*All the best,* *Best wishes,*	

7 Write Write your email to Mrs Fairfax in an appropriate style. Use all the notes. Write about 100 words.

8 Check Before you hand in your email, complete this checklist.

Checklist

- ◯ I've started and ended my email the right way.
- ◯ I've written about all four notes in the exam task and developed them further.
- ◯ I've written about 100 words.
- ◯ I've checked my spelling, grammar and punctuation.

▶ **Writing reference,** page 173 ▶ Workbook Unit 1: Writing, page 10, exercises 1, 2, 3, 4 and Progress check 1, page 11

2 Home sweet home

READING | 3-option multiple choice | A short message

1 In pairs or groups, answer the questions. Use the words in the box to help you.

apartment/flat (on the ground/first/second/etc. floor) | block of flats | cottage terraced/semi-detached/detached house

1 What kind of place do you live in? What's your neighbourhood like?

____

2 What do you like and dislike most about where you live?

____

EXAM SKILL

Understanding text type

- If you understand what type of text you are reading (a notice, an advertisement, etc.), it helps you understand what the text says.
- Look at the design of the text to help you choose the correct type. Does it look like something on a noticeboard or something on a phone screen, etc.?

2 Look at the texts in Exercise 4 and match them to the text types. There are two text types you don't need.

Text 1 ____
Text 2 ____
Text 3 ____
Text 4 ____
Text 5 ____

a) an email
b) an invitation
c) a magazine advert
d) a note
e) a reminder
f) a notice
g) a text message

3 Read the texts in Exercise 4 quickly and answer these questions.

1 How did Natasha and Adriana hear about the rooms?
2 Do they decide to rent the rooms?

OPTIMISE YOUR EXAM

3-option multiple choice

- With multiple-choice questions, you often need to recognise different ways of saying the same thing.
- Read through the answers A–C first and underline the key words. Think of ways they could be written differently, then read through the texts to check.

1

ACCOMMODATION AVAILABLE

Two furnished bedrooms in local family flat available. All meals and cleaning, but not laundry, included.

2

Natasha,
I was walking past the noticeboard when I saw the perfect accommodation advert! When are you free to see the rooms?
Adriana

4 1.08 **Read the texts. For each question, choose the correct answer.**

1
- **A** People who rent these rooms must wash their own clothes.
- **B** People who rent these rooms have to cook their own food.
- **C** People who rent these rooms have to buy their own furniture.

2
- **A** Natasha must make an appointment to see the rooms.
- **B** Natasha should tell Adriana when she can see the rooms.
- **C** Natasha needs to go and read the advertisement for the rooms.

3
- **A** Natasha wants to tell Adriana which bedroom lamps to buy for the rooms.
- **B** Natasha wants to check if she needs to buy bedroom lamps for the rooms.
- **C** Natasha wants to ask Adriana to see if there are any bedroom lamps in the rooms.

4
- **A** Adriana wants her mum to send something to her.
- **B** Adriana wants her mum to buy something for her.
- **C** Adriana wants her mum to keep something for her.

5
- **A** Guests have to bring food to the party.
- **B** Guests should say if they are coming to the party.
- **C** Guests can invite other friends too.

3

16:12 82%
Online **Flatmates**

Hi Adriana. 😃 When we saw the rooms, did you notice any bedroom lamps? I'm in the supermarket and can buy some if not.
Natasha

4

From: Adriana To: Mum

I don't need the cooking things you were planning to send as all meals are included. Please look after them for me for the future!

5 **Follow the instructions and find the secret word.**

Secret word: _ _ _ _ _ _ _ _
1 2 3 4 5 6 7 8

1. Find a word that means places to live or stay: ___________
   Take the fourth and fifth letters and write them above 3 and 4.
2. Find a word that means with all furniture provided: ___________
   Take the third and the eighth letters and write them above 1 and 8.
3. Find a word that means dirty clothes that need washing: ___________
   Take the second letter and write it above 6.
4. Find a word that means someone you live with in the same flat: ___________
   Take the seventh letter and write it above 7.
5. Find a word that means things to eat and drink: ___________
   Take the eighth letter and write it above 5.
6. Find a word that means a kind of party you have when you move into a new place to live: ___________
   Take the second letter and write it above 2.

What do you think the secret word means?

5

House-warming Party

7:30 pm Thursday!

Refreshments provided but numbers are limited because of space, so please let us know if you can make it.

Natasha & Adriana

THINK | RESEARCH | CULTURE | LEARN | ME

What do you think makes some people easy to live with and some people difficult to live with?

▶ **Workbook Unit 2:** Reading, pages 12–13, exercises 1, 2, 3, 4

2 GRAMMAR 1 | Past simple and past continuous

Grammar in context

Choose the correct words to complete this sentence. Then find the sentence in the note on page 15 to check your answer. Explain your choice.

I ______ past the noticeboard when I ______ the perfect accommodation advert!

a) walked, saw
b) was walking, was seeing
c) walked, was seeing
d) was walking, saw

REMEMBER

- We use the past simple to talk about single actions, permanent situations, habits and facts in the past.
- We use the past continuous to talk about actions in progress and temporary and changing situations in the past.
- When an action in progress is interrupted by another action, we use the past continuous for the first and the past simple for the second: *I **was watching** TV when my friend **phoned** me.*
- In stories, we use the past continuous for background information: *The sun **was shining**. The birds **were singing**.* We use the past simple for the main events: *I **opened** the door and **left** the house.*

▶ **See Grammar reference, Unit 2,** page 149

1 Choose the correct word or phrase.

1 We **moved** / **were moving** house last year and I really like our new neighbourhood.
2 I looked through the window. It **rained** / **was raining** hard and I didn't have an umbrella!
3 In the 19th century, most houses **didn't have** / **weren't having** bathrooms.
4 My parents **invited** / **were inviting** all the neighbours to a house-warming party.
5 While we were in London, we **visited** / **were visiting** Buckingham Palace.
6 Dad **decorated** / **was decorating** when he accidentally kicked the paint can over.

2 Write sentences about what each person was doing when something else happened using the words and phrases given.

she / putting up a poster / the phone / ring

1 ________________________________
____

they / play a video game / the lights / suddenly / go off

2 ________________________________
____

he / do homework / the party upstairs / begin

3 ________________________________
____

we / walk home / it / start to rain

4 ________________________________
____

3 Complete the text using the verbs in brackets in the correct form.

A SEE-THROUGH HOUSE!

When one Japanese couple **(1)** ____________ **(plan)** their new home, they **(2)** ____________ **(have)** an incredible idea. Why not have glass walls and make a completely transparent building? It sounds crazy, but that's what Sou Fujimoto Architects **(3)** ____________ **(build)** for them in Tokyo. The architects say that their inspiration **(4)** ____________ **(come)** from trees. They **(5)** ____________ **(create)** a building on many floors, connected by stairs, ladders and wooden steps. While they **(6)** ____________ **(design)** the building, they soon **(7)** ____________ **(realise)** that the people in the building would need some privacy, so there are thick white curtains that can be pulled across the glass walls. Most of the time, though, anyone walking by can see exactly what the people inside are doing. No doubt the neighbours **(8)** ____________ **(find)** it a little strange at first, but everyone seems used to it now.

VOCABULARY | Topic vocabulary | Phrasal verbs | Word patterns

Words connected with *the house and home*

1 1.09 **Complete the picture with the words and phrases in the box. Listen and check.**

attic | balcony | basement | ceiling | chimney | dining room
fence | garage | hedge | living room | roof | study

Phrasal verbs

2 1.10 **Complete the sentences with the correct form of the phrasal verbs in the box. Listen and check.**

do up | move in | move out
pull down | put up | rent out
settle in | tidy up

1 I didn't like this house when we first ____________, but now I love it!

2 When we moved house, it took me a long time to make friends and ____________.

3 I ____________ my bedroom when I found some old comics I didn't know I had!

4 Come and stay for a few days! We can ____________ you ____________ in the spare room.

5 You could ____________ your flat ____________ while you're on holiday and make some money.

6 Jake couldn't afford the rent so he had to ____________.

7 I can't believe they're going to ____________ the house I was born in! It'll be gone forever!

8 My parents bought an old house so they can ____________ it ____________ and make it attractive again.

3 **Write the correct form of a phrasal verb from Exercise 2 in each gap to complete the diary entry.**

5TH OCTOBER

So, we're in our new house! It's fantastic! I was really sad to (1) ____________ of the old house, of course, but I really like where we are now. We (2) ____________ here two days ago and we met the neighbours yesterday. I feel at home already and I (3) ____________ very quickly. We still have to unpack and then (4) ____________ the mess, but I love it here!

Word patterns

4 1.11 **Choose the correct word or phrase. Use the words in italics to help you. Listen and check.**

1 It's *worth* **visiting** / **to visit** a new neighbourhood before you buy a house there.

2 I'm not *keen* **for** / **on** living on the 20th floor of a block of flats!

3 I think that your happiness *depends* **from** / **on** where you live.

4 I *told* you **tidying** / **to tidy** your room up and it's still a mess!

5 We had to *stop* the neighbours **from** / **with** playing loud music!

6 When we moved house, my parents *made* me **have** / **to have** the smallest bedroom!

SAY IT RIGHT

Resource centre: Unit 2
Stress in compound nouns

2 LISTENING | 3-option multiple choice (interview)

1 **Match the homes to the countries in the box. Say why you think houses in these countries might be like this.**

Mongolia	the Philippines	Tunisia

1 ____________________

2 ____________________

3 ____________________

EXAM SKILL

Predicting

- Predicting means asking yourself before you listen what you might hear.
- With multiple-choice questions, you should read the questions and options before you listen, and ask yourself what you might hear for each option to be correct.

2 **You are going to listen to an interview with an expert on houses around the world. Read the questions in Exercise 4 and decide if these predictions are T (True) or F (False).**

1 The interviewer is going to tell us the expert's name is Leyla. **T / F**
2 The expert is going to talk about the time she stayed in a yurt. **T / F**
3 The interview will mention stilt houses before houses in Tunisia. **T / F**
4 She is going to talk about weather or safety in Tunisia. **T / F**
5 The interviewer is going to ask her what her future plans are. **T / F**

3 1.12 **Listen to the interview and check your answers.**

OPTIMISE YOUR EXAM

3-option multiple choice (interview)

- Remember that the questions are in the same order as the answers that you will hear.
- If you miss an answer, don't get stuck on that question. Move quickly onto the next one, or you'll miss the answer to that one too. You'll hear the listening task again, so don't worry if you miss an answer the first time.

4 1.12 **Listen to the interview again and choose the correct answers.**

1 Why did Leyla first become interested in houses?
   A She moved to another country.
   B She trained as an architect.
   C She saw a programme on TV.
2 How did she feel when she stayed in a yurt?
   A surprisingly comfortable
   B a little afraid
   C excited
3 People sometimes build houses underground in Tunisia to keep
   A safe at night.
   B cool during the day.
   C warm during the winter.
4 Stilt houses are popular in areas where there is
   A a problem with animals.
   B a lack of space.
   C heavy rain.
5 In the future, Leyla would like to
   A visit houses in more countries.
   B build her own unusual home.
   C study other types of buildings.

▶ **Workbook Unit 2:** Listening, page 16, exercises 1, 2, 3, 4

GRAMMAR 2 | *used to* and *would*

Grammar in context

Read these sentences from the audio in the listening lesson on page 18 and then decide if the sentences are T (True) or F (False).

I ***used to want to be*** *an architect.*

1 This refers to a feeling in the past. **T / F**
2 She still wants to be an architect. **T / F**

I ***would often watch*** *programmes about unusual buildings on television.*

3 This refers to a habit in the past. **T / F**
4 She still often watches programmes like that. **T / F**

REMEMBER

- We can use *used to* and *would* to talk about past habits: *When I was young, I* ***used to / would*** *tidy my room up every day.*
- We can use *used to* (but not *would*) to talk about past states: *I* ***used to*** *like living here, but now I don't.*
- For negative statements with *used to*, we can use *never used to* or *didn't use to*: *There* ***never used to / didn't use to*** *be so many houses around here.*
- For questions with *used to*, we use *did … use to …?*: ***Did*** *they* ***use to*** *live next door to you?*

▶ **See Grammar reference, Unit 2,** page 149

1 Choose the correct word or phrase to complete each sentence. In some sentences, both answers are correct.

1 I remember that my father **would / used to** read to me every night.
2 Gemma **would often / often used to** cycle to school from her flat before she moved.
3 Where **would you / did you** use to live before you moved here?
4 I **would / used to** love playing in the park near our house.
5 There **wouldn't / didn't use to** be so many flats in this area when I was very young.
6 How **would you / did you** use to get to school when you were little?

2 Complete these sentences for yourself. Then compare with a partner and expand your answers. Use your imagination if necessary.

When I was younger …

1 my family and I used to ______________________ ______________________.
2 my grandparents would ______________________ ______________________.
3 I never used to ______________________ but I do now!
4 I used to ______________________ but now I don't!

3 Write the correct form of *would* or *used to* in each gap to complete the text. If there is more than one correct answer, write both answers.

Alice's Wonderland: My blog

Home | About me | Links

Posted at 8:34 pm by Alice

I was chatting to Mum earlier about when she was a teenager. She (**1**) ____________ share a bedroom with her sister and it sounds very different from my own room. They (**2**) ____________ have so much technology. They (**3**) ____________ listen to music in their room, but they (**4**) ____________ have a computer or TV. And they definitely (**5**) ____________ have a computer in their room! (**6**) ____________ get bored? Mum says 'no'. She (**7**) ____________ invite her friends round, and they (**8**) ____________ chat and have fun. That's just the same today!

+ Follow | Search | Comment | Archive

1980s

Today

323 likes | 45 comments | 19 shares

THINK | RESEARCH | CULTURE | LEARN | ME

What did houses and flats use to be like in your country? How were they different from houses and flats today?

SPEAKING | Extended turn (photos)

Talk2Me
In the background ...

Flipped classroom

1 Watch the *Talk2Me* video and answer the questions.

1 What is happening in the kitchen at the beginning of the video?
2 How old was Angus when he used to bake with his dad?
3 Describe the kitchen at the beginning, middle and end of the video.

2 Watch the video again. Underline the phrases in the *Phrase expert* box that you hear on the video.

PHRASE EXPERT

on the left | on the right | at the top | at the bottom | in the foreground | in the background | to the left/right of the … | above/below the … | near the … | behind/in front of the …

3 In pairs or as a group, answer the questions.

1 Describe what you can see in the photo.
2 What do you like or dislike about this bedroom?

EXAM SKILL

Saying where things are

- We often need to talk about where different objects are in a photo.
- Use expressions such as *on the left/right* and *at the top/bottom of the photo*. Be careful to use the correct prepositions.
- Objects near the camera are *in the foreground*. Objects far away from the camera are *in the background*.

4 1.13 Listen to a student describing a photo. As you listen, draw what you think the photo looks like. Don't worry if your drawing is very rough!

5 Compare your drawing with a partner's. Are the same things in the same places? Write where these things are in your pictures.

1 red lamps ____________
2 plant ____________
3 green cushions ____________
4 rug ____________

OPTIMISE YOUR EXAM

Extended turn (photos)

- Start by describing the most important details. What is it a photo of? Start by saying *This is a photo of (a girl in her bedroom / a boy playing tennis).*
- Say as much as you can about the main subject of the photo. Then describe other objects, such as what is in the foreground or background.

6 Look at the photo. It shows someone at home after school. Take turns to describe the photo.

1 **In pairs, ask and answer the questions.**

1 Describe what you can see in the picture.
2 What do you think life is like on a houseboat? Can you think of any positive or negative points?

REMEMBER

- We can use *so, such, such a, too* and *enough* to show the results of a situation or action.
- *So, such* and *such a* are often followed by a *that* clause which explains the result.
  *The weather is **so** bad that they closed the motorway. / It's **such** bad weather that we can't go out in the boat today. / Tom's got **such** a loud voice that I can hear him from across the street!*
- We use *too* when there is more than is necessary.
  *It's **too** dark to go in the attic. Take a torch!*
- We use *not* + adjective + *enough* to mean 'less (adjective) than is necessary'.
  *Jo isn't old **enough** to drive.*
- *Too* and *enough* are often followed by a full infinitive or *for* + *person/noun*.
  *Sunbathing on the balcony is **too** hot for me in the summer.*
- *Too* always refers to a negative result. To talk about a positive result, use a positive word such as *very, really, extremely*, etc.
  *It's **really** interesting to read about extraordinary houses around the world.*

2 **Choose the correct word.**

1 It's **so** / **such** a lovely day. Let's go for a picnic.
2 There are **so** / **such** many of us in my family that we need a large house.
3 Our house is **so** / **such** small that I have to share a room with my brother.
4 It's **so** / **such** an expensive house that I don't think we can afford it.
5 Our houseboat goes **so** / **such** slowly that you can chat to people walking on the path!
6 There's **so** / **such** a lot of rubbish in the canal these days that it's really unattractive.

3 **Choose the correct phrase to fill each gap. For each one, decide if you agree and give reasons using *so, such, too* or *enough* where you can.**

1 I think life on a houseboat would be ________ for me.
a) too boring **b)** boring enough
c) so boring

2 It wouldn't be ________ for me because I prefer to have more space.
a) so comfortable **b)** comfortable enough
c) too comfortable

3 You'd be ________ in the winter to enjoy it.
a) cold enough **b)** so cold
c) too cold

4 You wouldn't have ________ for all your things.
a) enough space **b)** such space
c) so space

5 You'd move around ________ to make friends.
a) such a lot **b)** so much
c) too much

OPTIMISE YOUR EXAM

Open cloze

- For each question, look at the words before and after the gap and think about the grammar used.
- For example, if there's the verb *be* before a gap, and an adjective + *that* after the gap, the answer might be *so*, e.g. *It's so great that you're here.* If there's *a/an* + adjective + noun + *that*, the gapped word might be *such*, e.g. *It's such a great surprise that you're here.*

4 **Write one word in each gap to complete the text.**

Life on a houseboat

Lucas is 13 and lives on a houseboat in Amsterdam with his mum and dad. He loves living there, although the boat is **(1)** ____ small that they don't have much space. In the summer, they sometimes take the boat for short trips along the canals. Lucas is still **(2)** ____ young to drive the houseboat on his own, so he is not allowed to do it. However, he is old **(3)** ____ to help with the steering. In the winter, they sometimes have **(4)** ____ bad weather that they can't leave home! Then, they stay on the boat and keep warm by the fire. Lucas has to make sure there is enough wood **(5)** ____ heat the boat.

Lucas and his parents have such **(6)** ____ great life on the houseboat that they would never want to live anywhere else!

▶ **Grammar reference,** page 150 ▶ **Workbook Unit 2:** Language in Use, page 17, exercises 1, 2, 3

1 **In pairs or as a group, answer the questions.**

1 Which of these kinds of article do you read?
- magazine articles
- online articles
- newspaper articles

2 What was the last article you read about?

EXAM SKILL

Using the right style

- In an article, use a style that's suitable for the reader and for the topic. Decide whether you need to be formal or informal. For informal articles, for example, you can use contractions, exclamation marks, personal examples and a more 'conversational' style.
- An article may have an interesting title that encourages a person to read it.
- Another way to get the reader's attention is to start with a question. For example, *What do you think makes a house a home?*

____

_________? Is it the people, the buildings, or something else? My neighbourhood is very friendly, and I think I know why.

First of all, you need to have good relationships with your neighbours. You can't do that if people move house a lot. Some families in my area have been there for 70 years!

I also think you need somewhere people can meet. This might be a square, a café or a local shop. In our local square, everyone shares their news. It's a great place to be on summer evenings.

So, if you want a friendly neighbourhood, make friends with your neighbours!

2 **Read the exam task and the article. Suggest a good title for the article.**

Articles wanted!

WHAT MAKES YOUR NEIGHBOURHOOD A GREAT PLACE TO LIVE?

Write an article telling us where you live and why you like living there.

Do you have a good relationship with your neighbours? Why / Why not?

Do you have a special place where you can meet?

The best articles will be published next month.

3 **Which of the questions below could you use at the start of the article to interest the readers?**

1 What makes a friendly neighbourhood?
2 Is your neighbourhood a friendly place?
3 Have you ever wondered what makes a friendly neighbourhood?
4 Do you make friends easily?
5 What's your favourite neighbourhood?

4 **Find and underline places in the article where the writer does these things.**

1 speaks directly to the reader
2 uses contractions
3 refers to his/her own experience
4 uses exclamation marks

OPTIMISE YOUR EXAM

An article

- An article task may ask you to write about something that you like or find interesting. Choose ideas that will give you enough material to write about on that subject.
- For each idea, make a note of the main reason for your choice. For example, one of the things you like best about your home might be your bedroom. The main reason might be that you enjoy listening to music there with your friends.

5 Look at this writing task and answer the questions.

You see this announcement in your school's English-language magazine.

Articles wanted!

WHAT DO YOU LIKE ABOUT YOUR HOME?

Write an article telling us what you like best about your home.

What do you think makes a house a home?

The best articles will be published next month.

Write your **article**.

1 Tick two things you like best about your home or add your own ideas.

- our neighbourhood ☐
- our garden ☐
- my bedroom ☐
- the things we have in the house ☐
- the people I live with ☐
- what I do at home ☐
- ____________________

2 For each idea you have ticked or added in question 1, write the main reason why you like it.

____

____

6 Plan Make a paragraph plan.

Part	Purpose	Useful phrases	My notes
Paragraph 1	introduce the subject in an interesting way	*What do you think …?* *Have you ever thought about/wondered /asked yourself …?*	
Paragraph 2	make your first main point and give a reason	*The first thing that I like best about my home is …*	
Paragraph 3	make your second main point and give a reason	*Another thing …* *As well as that, …* *You also need …*	
Paragraph 4	briefly conclude the article	*I believe that what makes a house a home is …*	

7 Write Write your article in an appropriate style. Write about 100 words.

8 Check Before you hand in your article, complete this checklist.

Checklist ✓

- ◯ I've started my article in an interesting way.
- ◯ I've used the appropriate style for the topic and the reader.
- ◯ I've written about 100 words.
- ◯ I've answered all parts of the exam question.
- ◯ I've given reasons to explain my main ideas.
- ◯ I've checked my spelling, grammar and punctuation.

▶ Writing reference, page 170 ▶ Workbook Unit 2: Writing, page 18, exercises 1, 2, 3, 4 and Progress check 2, page 19

PROGRESS CHECK UNITS 1–2

GRAMMAR AND VOCABULARY

1 Choose the correct word or phrase.

1 Every Saturday, my friends and I **meet** / **are meeting** at a pizzeria in the town centre.
2 Why **do you cry** / **are you crying**, Maria? What's wrong?
3 My sister **don't** / **doesn't** like onions, but I do.
4 How often **do you play** / **are you playing** video games?
5 **I'm not knowing** / **I don't know** where my red T-shirt is.

__/5

2 Put the verbs into the correct tense, past simple or past continuous.

1 I ______________ (**look**) for my sunglasses when I ______________(**find**) the book I lost last year.
2 Alfie ______________ (**not** / **go**) to the party because he ______________ (**feel**) ill.
3 What ______________ (**we** / **talk**) about when Jim ______________ (**come**) in and interrupted us?

__/6

3 Match to make sentences.

1 Every ____ **a)** magazines was too expensive.
2 Both of the ____ **b)** the boys in my class have short hair.
3 Each of the ____ **c)** girl in my class has long hair.
4 All of ____ **d)** are shy at first.
5 Lots of people ____ **e)** bikes were old.

__/5

4 If a word or phrase in bold is correct, put a tick. If it's incorrect, rewrite it correctly on the line.

1 I **use** to read comics, but I don't anymore. ______________
2 When I was young, we would **played** in the park for hours after school. ______________
3 Did you **use** to live in Germany? ______________
4 **Would** you have long hair when you were a teenager? ______________
5 I never **used** to like mushrooms but I do now. ______________

__/5

5 Write *so*, *such*, *too* or *enough* in each gap.

1 It was __________ hot that I couldn't sleep!
2 Are you old __________ to drive a car?
3 This is __________ a good book. You should read it!
4 I'm __________ tired to watch this film. I'm going to bed!
5 I haven't got __________ money to buy a new bike.

__/5

6 Choose the correct word.

1 I'm looking **forward** / **ahead** to your party on Friday.
2 Our new neighbours moved **in** / **up** next door yesterday.
3 Can you put me **up** / **in** for the night after the concert?
4 I didn't know that word so I looked it **over** / **up** in a dictionary.
5 She was a wild kitten, but she's turned **into** / **onto** a very friendly cat.

6 Mum, please stop Dylan **to make** / **from making** so much noise!
7 What I usually do at the weekend depends **from** / **on** the weather.
8 It's not worth **to see** / **seeing** that film – it's not very good!
9 My dad's really keen on **trying** / **try** new dishes. He's a great cook!
10 Mum makes us **tidy** / **to tidy** our bedrooms every evening.

__/10

7 Write a form of the word in capitals in each gap.

1 Linda's got a warm and kind ___________ . **PERSONAL**
2 My ___________ with Adam is very important to me. **FRIEND**
3 You need a lot of ___________ to design T-shirts. **CREATIVE**
4 I find it hard to meet people because of my ___________ . **SHY**
5 Thank you so much for your amazing ___________ ! **GENEROUS**
6 Dana's totally ___________ – you can't trust her to be there at the right time. **RELY**
7 Saying *please* and *thank you* is an example of ___________ . **POLITE**

__/7

8 Write a word from the box in each gap.

attic	balcony	big	deep	fast	hedge	wide

1 Maddie's ___________ asleep on the sofa. Don't wake her up!
2 Mr Baxter, our English teacher, has got a really ___________ voice.
3 I woke up tired, but had a shower and then felt ___________ awake.
4 The ___________ outside the front window has grown too high. You can't see out of the window now!
5 I'm in ___________ trouble because I forgot to do my homework.
6 My brother's room is in the ___________ at the top of the house.
7 Having a ___________ in our flat means we can sit outside in the summer.

__/7

Total score __/50

EXAM SKILLS

Tick the statements that are true for you. Review the skills in the unit if you need more help.

I can …	Unit/page
☐ skim an interview to get the general meaning	Unit 1 p4
☐ understand the general situation in a conversation	Unit 1 p8
☐ talk about myself	Unit 1 p10
☐ understand some phrasal verbs and use them in multiple-choice cloze activities	Unit 1 p11
☐ use the correct style to start and end an email	Unit 1 p12
☐ identify different text types	Unit 2 p14
☐ predict content in an interview	Unit 2 p18
☐ say where things are in a photo	Unit 2 p20
☐ understand result clauses and use them in open cloze activities	Unit 2 p21
☐ write an interesting article with a style that is suitable for the reader and topic	Unit 2 p22

3 On the road

READING | Gapped text | A project

1 **In pairs or as a group, make a list of as many different means of transport as you can.**

2 **Take turns to describe a means of transport without saying what it's called. The class have to guess what you're describing.**

Example: *It's like a bus but more comfortable. It's often used for long journeys. (coach)*

3 **Read the text quickly, ignoring the gaps. In pairs or as a group, answer the questions.**

1 What is the Hyperloop?
2 Have they started/finished building it yet?
3 Why will it be better than taking a train?

EXAM SKILL

Understanding tenses

- When you read a text, it's important to look at the verb tenses because they give information about time and the sequence of events. Look out for contractions with auxiliary verbs.
- With gapped text tasks, the verb tense in the removed sentence doesn't need to be in the same tense as the sentences before and after, but it does need to make logical sense. It might help you to draw a small timeline to order events.

4 **Read the sentences before and after gaps 1 and 2 in the text. Decide which sentences (a–c) *could* fill the gaps. Think about the tense and the information before and after the gap.**

gap 1

a) They travelled much faster than we did.
b) That's much faster than we can currently travel.
c) We'll be able to travel that fast very soon.

gap 2

a) His team opened the first Hyperloop last year.
b) His team has already finished the first Hyperloop.
c) His team is working on the first Hyperloop.

5 **Look at extracts 1–3 from the text and match each one to descriptions a–c.**

1 Although humans have flown in supersonic planes that go faster than the speed of sound, today most planes can't travel that fast … ____
2 There's still lots of work to do, but they have already started to build it. ____
3 Travelling by Hyperloop, it will only take about 30 minutes to go, for example, from Los Angeles to San Francisco in the USA. ____

a) This is talking about the past and the future.
b) This is only talking about the the future.
c) This is talking about the past and now.

THE HYPERLOOP

Turning sci-fi travel into reality!

by Ben Hudson, aged 13

Have you ever dreamt of travelling really fast, like people do in science-fiction films? In sci-fi, spaceships fly across the universe at the speed of light. **(1)** ____ Although humans have flown in supersonic planes that go faster than the speed of sound, today most planes can't travel that fast, and trains and cars are even slower.

As part of our class project on travel and transport, I've found out about a really exciting new means of transport called the Hyperloop. It's solar powered, environmentally friendly, safe, affordable – and fast! The inventor of the Hyperloop is Elon Musk. He thinks it will revolutionise travel for all of us. **(2)** ____ There's still lots of work to do, but they have already started to build it. The first Hyperloop may cost around €5 billion. That sounds like a lot, but Musk has been involved in other successful projects and he's already experienced in raising millions of dollars.

So how will the Hyperloop work? Imagine a long tube connecting two cities. The passengers will sit in a specially designed capsule, and there will be three capsules per train. Magnets will push the train down the tube at a speed of up to 1,200 kilometres per hour. That's almost the speed of sound! **(3)** ____

Travelling by Hyperloop, it will only take about 30 minutes to go, for example, from Los Angeles to San Francisco in the USA. That's half the time it currently takes by plane. **(4)** ____ It's only designed for journeys of 1,600 kilometres maximum. For longer journeys, taking a plane will still take less time.

I'm looking forward to hearing more about the Hyperloop. **(5)** ____ Who knows? Maybe we'll all travel by Hyperloop when we're older!

OPTIMISE YOUR EXAM

Gapped text

- Read the text quickly to get a general idea of what it's about. Ignore the gaps.
- Then carefully re-read the sentences in the text before and after each gap. Pay particular attention to the vocabulary, tenses and pronouns used.
- Look at the removed sentences and, for each one, ask if it logically fits in each gap.
- Decide whether the verb tenses and the pronouns in the sentences make sense in the context.

6 1.14 **Read the text again. Five sentences have been removed from the text. For each question, choose the correct answer. There are three extra sentences which you do not need to use.**

A Today, the fastest trains in the world only travel at about half that speed.
B I really hope it's a success!
C In real life, however, flying so quickly is impossible.
D He tried to persuade other people that it was safe.
E This is the fastest way to travel here on Earth at the moment.
F However, the Hyperloop won't take us to the other side of the world.
G Flying will still be more comfortable, however.
H Scientists have been working on the Hyperloop idea for several years.

7 Write a highlighted word or phrase from the text to match each definition.

1 not expensive ____________
2 a thousand million ____________
3 a shorter way of saying 'science fiction' ____________
4 people who travel on transport ____________
5 not bad for the environment ____________
6 at the moment ____________
7 faster than the speed of sound ____________
8 completely change ____________

THINK | RESEARCH | CULTURE | LEARN | ME

What do you think of the Hyperloop?
Which cities in your country would you connect with the Hyperloop?

3 GRAMMAR 1 | Present perfect simple and continuous

Grammar in context

Read the sentences below. Write a word or short phrase in each gap to complete the sentences and then find them in the project on page 27 to check your answers.

1 ______________ *you ever dreamt of travelling really fast?*

2 *As part of our class project on travel and transport,* ______________ *found out about a really exciting new means of transport.*

3 *Scientists have* ______________ *on the Hyperloop idea for several years.*

4 *Musk* ______________ *been involved in other successful projects.*

REMEMBER

- We use the present perfect simple for a situation that connects the past and the present – when the specific time it started in the past isn't mentioned. Compare: *I booked the tickets yesterday.* (specific time in the past – past simple), ***I've** already **booked** the tickets.* (*already* = before now – present perfect).
- Sometimes the situation began in the past and is still true (*She's been a tour guide for three years.*) and sometimes it's already finished (*She hasn't been to Spain before.*).
- We use the present perfect continuous to emphasise the continuing nature of situations (***Have** you **been thinking** about your next holiday?*).
- We often use the words *for, since, already, yet, ever, never* and *still* with the present perfect simple, and *for* and *since* with the present perfect continuous.

▶ **See Grammar reference, Unit 3,** pages 150–151

1 Choose the correct word or phrase.

1 They've **booked** / **been booking** a lovely resort by the sea.

2 I haven't **heard** / **been hearing** of the Hyperloop.

3 Have you **stayed** / **been staying** at that campsite before?

4 I've **written** / **been writing** this article about unusual holidays for hours and I still haven't **finished** / **been finishing**!

2 Write a word from the box in each gap.

already	ever	for	since	still	yet

1 I've had my bike ____________ three years.

2 Ellie has loved skateboarding ____________ she was little.

3 I don't need a new bike helmet – I've ____________ got one.

4 We ____________ haven't decided where we're going on holiday.

5 Has your Dad got his new car ____________ ?

6 Have you ____________ been to the USA before?

3 Complete the second sentence so it has a similar meaning to the first, using the word given in the correct form. Use the present perfect simple or continuous.

1 Dan got his motorbike four years ago. (**have**)
Dan ________________________________

2 Is this your first visit to Madrid? (**be**)
Have ________________________________

3 This will be my first time staying in a hostel. (**not / stay**)
I ________________________________

4 We started waiting for you at 1 o'clock! (**wait**)
We ________________________________

4 Put the verbs into the correct tense, past simple, present perfect simple or present perfect continuous.

(**1**) ______________ (**you / ever / be**) to London? If you have, (**2**) ______________ (**you / probably / travel**) on the London Underground, the third longest metro system in the world. Even if (**3**) ______________ (**you / not / be**) to London, (**4**) ______________ (**you / probably / hear**) of it. Read on for some fun facts!

- Did you know that the Underground, also known as the Tube, is the oldest metro in the world! It includes the tunnels of the Metropolitan Railway, which (**5**) ______________ (**open**) back in 1863. In other words, passengers (**6**) ______________ (**travel**) under London on the Tube for more than 150 years.
- The Tube (**7**) ______________ (**change**) a lot over the years. Lots of stations (**8**) ______________ (**open**) since 1863, and lots (**9**) ______________ (**close**), including the Tower of London (closed in 1884).
- In the past 24 hours, more than 3 million people (**10**) ______________ (**get on**) and off an Underground train.
- A final fun fact. No-one (**11**) ______________ (**actually / count**) them, but scientists (**12**) ______________ (**calculate**) that about half a million mice live in the tunnels of the Underground!

▶ **Workbook Unit 3:** Grammar 1, page 22, exercises 1, 2, 3

Words connected with *holidays*

1 1.15 **Choose the correct word to complete each definition. Listen and check.**

1 ***full*** / ***package*** *holiday*: a holiday where flights and accommodation are included in the price
2 ***cruise*** / ***voyage***: a holiday on board a big ship
3 ***camp*** / ***camping*** *trip*: a holiday where you sleep in a tent
4 *guided* ***tour*** / ***view***: when an expert shows you round a tourist attraction
5 ***job*** / ***business*** *trip*: when someone travels as part of their job
6 *school* ***trip*** / ***journey***: when students visit a place away from school

2 **Write a word or phrase from Exercise 1 in each gap.**

1 My mum went on a ___________ to Ireland for work.
2 Have you ever been on a ___________ ? It's exciting to wake up in a different port each day.
3 If you visit the Acropolis, take a ___________ to learn about its incredible history.
4 My grandparents have just booked a two-week ___________ to Portugal.
5 Our class is going on a ___________ to the National Museum next week.
6 We went on a ___________ last year but it rained every day and all my clothes in the tent got wet.

3 1.16 **Complete the table with the words and phrases in the box. Listen and check.**

backpacker | campsite | currency | guest
guidebook | hostel | luggage | passport
resort | sightseer | tour guide | tourist

places to stay	people	things to take on holiday

Adjectives with *un-* / *im-* / *il-* / *ir-* / *dis-*

4 1.17 **Write *un-*, *im-*, *il-*, *ir-* or *dis-* in each gap to make the words negative. Listen and check.**

1 ____certain
2 ____able
3 ____comfortable
4 ____helpful
5 ____honest
6 ____legal
7 ____happy
8 ____patient
9 ____popular
10 ____possible
11 ____abled
12 ____fair
13 ____responsible
14 ____tidy

5 **Write a negative adjective from Exercise 4 in each gap.**

1 It's ___________ to drive a car on a public road if you don't have a driving licence.
2 The bed in the hotel was so ___________ that I didn't sleep at all.
3 Wheelchairs and mobility scooters make life much easier for some ___________ people.
4 It's ___________ to describe how fantastic the cruise ship was!
5 The staff in the airport shop were really ___________ , so I didn't buy anything in the end.

Word patterns

6 1.18 **Choose the correct word or phrase. Listen and check.**

1 Will you *have time* **to look** / **looking** round the Colosseum while you're in Rome?
2 We *spent* a lot of *time* **to lie** / **lying** on the beach. It was so relaxing!
3 Are you *interested* **to come** / **in coming** on a camping trip in the summer?
4 I'm really *looking forward to* **go** / **going** on the sightseeing tour next week!
5 I'm not *keen* **on** / **in** having a job that involves lots of business trips.
6 I don't know why they *prevented* us **to go** / **from going** in that room in the castle.
7 Are you *ready* **for** / **with** your holiday next week? Have you packed yet?
8 Please don't *make* us **go** / **to go** on another guided tour tomorrow!

SAY IT RIGHT

Resource centre: Unit 3
/dʒ/, /ŋ/ and /g/

3 LISTENING | 3-option multiple choice (dialogues)

1 **In pairs or as a group, answer the questions.**

1 What problems can people experience when they travel or are on holiday?

2 Have you ever been on a journey or holiday where something has gone wrong? What happened? How did you feel?

EXAM SKILL

Listening for attitude and opinion

- The listening question may ask you how someone feels or what their opinion of something is.
- Remember that you're listening for ideas, not specific words. For example, someone who is 'disappointed' might say *I thought it would be a lot better than it was.*

2 **Read the statements and choose the correct word or phrase to complete each sentence.**

I really enjoyed our holiday together! It was really quiet so there was plenty of space in the pool.

1 This person **liked** / **didn't like** the fact that there weren't many other people.

Yes, I was surprised there weren't many people there. It's a shame we didn't have the chance to make many new friends.

2 This person **liked** / **didn't like** the fact that there weren't many other people.

I got a lot out of the tours. It was worth visiting the local area and finding out about it.

3 This person **enjoyed** / **didn't enjoy** the tours.

There wasn't much the guide didn't know, was there?

4 This person thinks the guide knew **a lot** / **very little**.

OPTIMISE YOUR EXAM

3-option multiple choice (dialogues)

- You will hear the context sentence and then there will be a pause of eight seconds.
- During the pause, read the question and the answer options. Think about what words you might hear for each answer option.

3 1.19 **For each question, choose the correct answer.**

1 You will hear two friends talking about a holiday they went on.
What did the girl think about it?
A The tour guide knew a lot.
B She met lots of other young people.
C People at the resort were very friendly.

2 You will hear two friends talking about a hotel they stayed at.
The man felt that the hotel
A was too big.
B was too far from the beach.
C was very expensive.

3 You will hear two friends talking about a TV programme they saw.
The girl says she would like to
A watch the next programme in the series.
B visit the place in the programme.
C learn more about the place in the programme.

4 You will hear two friends talking about going on a school trip.
The boy is looking forward to
A having a day away from school.
B finding out more about a topic.
C travelling there with his schoolmates.

5 You will hear a girl telling her friend about a camping trip.
What problem did she have on the trip?
A She took too many things with her.
B She couldn't find the campsite.
C She lost all her money.

6 You will hear two friends talking about their summer holidays.
The boy's family is planning to go
A to a place they have been to before.
B to a place that might be dangerous.
C somewhere close to home.

4 1.19 **Listen again and check your answers.**

THINK | RESEARCH | CULTURE | LEARN | ME

Do you prefer to go on holiday where there are lots of other people or somewhere quiet?

Have you ever been on a guided tour? What did you learn about? Did you enjoy it?

▶ **Workbook Unit 3:** Listening, page 24, exercises 1, 2, 3

Grammar in context

Read these sentences from the audio in the listening lesson on page 30 and then decide if each noun in bold is countable (C) or uncountable (U).

1 *It's a shame we didn't have the chance to make many new* ***friends****.* ____
2 *... so it was good to find out some* ***information****.* ____
3 *... I love visiting* ***places*** *and seeing how they really work.* ____
4 *I had lots of* ***luggage****.* ____
5 *And when I needed* ***clothes****, I couldn't find anything.* ____
6 *I'm glad I took plenty of* ***money****.* ____

REMEMBER

- Countable nouns can be counted and have a singular and plural form: *one suitcase, two suitcases.*
- Uncountable nouns only have a singular form. They are often abstract ideas (*truth, information,* etc.), materials *(iron, glass, water, wood,* etc.) and collections (*furniture, luggage, baggage, money,* etc.).
- To talk about one object in a collection, we can use *piece of, sheet of, item of,* etc., e.g. *a sheet of paper, two pieces of furniture.*
- Some nouns are both countable and uncountable. Often, this is because the word refers to a substance/material or a thing that's made of that substance: *That's made of glass.* (uncountable) and *There are three glasses on the table.* (countable).
- With countable nouns, we can use: *(a) few, fewer, many, a number of.*
- With uncountable nouns, we can use: *(a) little, less, much, an amount of.*
- We can use *a lot of* and *lots of* with both countable and uncountable nouns.

▶ **See Grammar reference, Unit 3,** page 151

1 **Write *was* or *were* in each gap to complete the sentences. Use the words in bold to help you.**

1 There __________ a lot of **luggage** in the car.
2 There __________ a lot of **guidebooks** in the library.
3 Some of the **ideas** about the Hyperloop __________ exciting!
4 Some of the **information** about the London Underground __________ very interesting.
5 Jan's **advice** __________ to read the online hotel reviews.
6 The **news** about the delay __________ annoying.

2 **Write a word from the box in each gap. Use six words. There are three extra words which you do not need to use.**

amount | few | fewer | less | little | lots | many | much | number

1 How __________ times did you change currency on your trip round Eastern Europe?
2 The guide didn't give us __________ information about how they built the castle.
3 You need a huge __________ of time to travel round the world!
4 We bought __________ of souvenirs and presents at the airport.
5 I've brought __________ luggage for the trip than I thought.
6 __________ people have ever stayed in an underwater hotel.

3 **If a word in bold is correct, put a tick. Add an *-s* onto each word which needs it.**

Strange hotels!

Every hotel provides (1) **accommodation** ____ for its guests. But some hotels are much stranger than others. Here are some of the weirdest (2) **place** ____ to stay in the world!

At the Palacio de Sal in Bolivia, the whole hotel is made of (3) **salt** ____ – even all the (4) **furniture** ____ !

If you like art, then Benesse House in Japan might be the perfect hotel for you. Guests sleep in a museum and gallery, surrounded by expensive (5) **work** ____ of (6) **art** ____ and sculptures.

If you're more interested in (7) **transport** ____ , then you would enjoy staying at Hotel Costa Verde in Costa Rica, where a full-size Boeing 727 aeroplane is part of the hotel.

Interestingly, there are several underwater hotels in the world. At Poseidon Undersea Resort in Fiji, the hotel is 12 (8) **metre** ____ below the surface of the (9) **water** ____ . It's like sleeping in an aquarium. Guests also have access to a small submarine – but of course you need lots of (10) **money** ____ to stay there!

3 SPEAKING | Discussion (pictures)

Talk2Me
What do you think about ...?

Flipped classroom

1 **Watch the *Talk2Me* video and answer the questions.**

1 What has Safi done in her first week in Portugal?
2 Who wants to go to: the zoo, the shopping centre, the museum?
3 Why can't Safi go to the museum?

2 **Watch the video again. Underline the phrases in the *Phrase expert* box that you hear on the video.**

PHRASE EXPERT

I think they should … | Maybe/Perhaps they should/could … | … might be a good idea | … would be (useful) | How about …? | What do you think about …?

3 **In pairs or as a group, look at these photos and answer the questions.**

1 What are the people in the pictures doing?
2 What equipment do you need to do these things?

EXAM SKILL

Making suggestions

- We often use modal verbs and conditional forms to make suggestions, e.g. *They could choose X. / X might be a good idea. / X would be useful.* We can add *perhaps* or *maybe* too, e.g. *Perhaps they could choose …*
- We can also make suggestions by asking questions, e.g. *What do you think about …? / How about …?*

4 1.20 **Read the task in Exercise 7. Then listen to students doing the task. Make notes to answer the questions.**

1 Which things do they say might be a good idea?

____

2 Which things do they say aren't a good idea?

____

5 1.20 **Listen again. Write down the phrases that the students use to make suggestions.**

____
____
____
____

6 **Look at the pictures in Exercise 7. In pairs or as a group, discuss what each object is called and used for.**

OPTIMISE YOUR EXAM

Discussion (pictures)

- If you don't understand what your partner says, don't panic! Ask *Do you mean …?* or ask them to repeat what they said.
- If you don't know the word for something in the pictures, use other words to describe it, e.g. *It protects your head when you're cycling.*
- You can also ask the examiner to repeat a question or instruction if you don't understand it.

7 **In pairs, do the task.**

A boy is leaving his school because his family is moving to another town. The students in his class want to buy him a present. They know he likes skateboarding, cycling and football. Talk together about the different presents they could give him and then decide which one is best.

1 In pairs or as a group, answer the questions.

1 How do you prefer to travel around where you live? What are your favourite and least favourite ways of travelling?
2 Which means of transport have you never been in/on?

REMEMBER

- If you aren't sure which particle to use in phrasal verbs, remember that particles aren't random. They contain meaning – usually a metaphorical meaning.
- For example, *up* sometimes means 'more' or 'increase' (e.g. *speed up, turn up the volume*) and sometimes means 'collect' (e.g. *pick up, pack up*).
- *Up* and *in* sometimes mean 'arrive' or 'appear' (e.g. *turn up, show up, check in, drop in*).
- *Off* is sometimes connected to the idea of 'departing' or 'leaving' (e.g. *set off, take off, drop off*).
- *Down* is sometimes connected to the idea of 'failing' and 'stopping' (e.g. *close down, break down*).
- *Out* is sometimes connected to the idea of something 'removed from where it was' or 'with nothing left' (e.g. *take out, go out*).

2 Choose the correct word. Use the words in italics to help you.

1 We were all late for school because the bus *broke* **down** / **out** / **up**.
2 Mr Jones asked the taxi driver to *speed* **off** / **down** / **up** because he was late for work.
3 If we *set* **up** / **off** / **away** at 7 am, we'll get there around lunchtime.
4 I love the feeling of a plane *taking* **up** / **off** / **down** / **out**.
5 My neighbours have just *turned* **in** / **up** / **off** in their new car.
6 When we get to the airport, we'll *check* **in** / **up** / **down** and then have lunch.
7 In the morning, Mum *drops* me **off** / **away** / **out** outside my school.
8 Dad usually *picks* me **out** / **up** / **off** from school in the afternoon.

3 Quickly read the text in Exercise 4 and answer these questions.

1 What kind of transport is the Transition? ______
2 How far can it fly? ______
3 At the moment, how many people can travel in the Transition? ______

OPTIMISE YOUR EXAM

Open cloze

- If there's a verb immediately before the gap, ask yourself if you need to write a particle to make a phrasal verb.
- If there's a particle (*off*, *up*, etc.) immediately after the gap, ask yourself if you need to write a verb to make a phrasal verb.

4 Write one word in each gap to complete the text.

The Transition

For years, people have dreamt of cars that can fly. With a flying car, you set off from home in your car, speed **(1)** ______ and then take **(2)** ______ into the sky.

Now, a company from the USA **(3)** ______ created the Transition, a two-seater plane that can also drive down a road.

With the Transition, you won't need to spend hours checking **(4)** ______ at a busy airport. Imagine leaving home and turning **(5)** ______ in a completely different city a couple of hours later.

The Transition will be able to fly a distance of about 800 kilometres. If you're interested **(6)** ______ finding out more about the Transition, have a look at their website.

▶ Vocabulary reference, page 163 ▶ Workbook Unit 3: Language in Use, page 25, exercises 1, 2, 3

The Big Lobster, Limestone Coast, Australia

1 In pairs or groups, answer these questions.

1. Look at the photo. Why would people visit this place? What can you do there?
2. What's the strangest or most interesting tourist attraction you've ever visited?

2 Read this review. In pairs or as a group, answer the questions.

Do something different at Athens Clue!

Are you on holiday in Athens? Are you keen on solving puzzles? If so, Athens Clue is the experience for you!

There are different 'scenarios', where you find and solve clues to escape from inside a mysterious room. It's a race against time and it's great fun!

The entry cost is €15 per player, which is expensive – but it's worth it. It's not easy, though. Some of the clues we had were hard. You need to speak English well, and you should go in a group of at least two people.

Athens Clue is perfect for teenagers and adults, but younger children might find it too difficult! If you like challenges, I'd recommend it.

1. What's the tourist attraction called? Where is it?
______
2. What can you choose from?
______
3. What do visitors do there?
______
4. How much does it cost?
______
5. Is the review generally positive or negative?
______
6. What positive points are mentioned?
______
7. What negative points are mentioned?
______

EXAM SKILL

Choosing positive and negative points

- In a review, you should describe the things you liked (positive points) and the things you didn't like (negative points).
- Before you start writing, make a list of the most important positive and negative points. It's fine to have more positive points than negative points, or more negatives than positives, or a balance. It's up to you!

3 In pairs or as a group, discuss whether these people would enjoy visiting Athens Clue. Give reasons for your opinions.

1. I'm on my own in Athens today.
2. I've got four teenage kids who are very competitive.
3. My cousins are four and eight years old.
4. There are five of us. We don't want to spend more than about €40 today.
5. My friends from Russia are visiting. They don't all speak English very well.

OPTIMISE YOUR EXAM

A review

- Reviews should be interesting to read, so use an appropriate style. Usually, this is the same style as an article in a magazine. It shouldn't be as serious as an essay, but it shouldn't be as informal as a letter to a friend.
- It's fine to use short forms (*you're, isn't,* etc.), and to address the reader directly (*Are you on holiday in Athens?*).

4 **Look at this writing task and answer the questions.**

You have seen this notice on a website for teenagers.

REVIEWS WANTED

We're looking for reviews of tourist attractions all round the world.
Could you write us a review of a tourist attraction where you live?
Include information about what and where it is, what you can do there,
and how much it costs. Explain why you would or wouldn't recommend it.

Write your **review**.

What is it?	
Where is it?	
What can you do there?	
How much does it cost?	
Positive points:	
Negative points:	

5 **Plan** **Make a paragraph plan.**

Part	Purpose	Useful phrases	My notes
Title	make the readers want to read your review by giving it an interesting title		
Paragraph 1	give basic information about the attraction (what/where it is)	*Are you on holiday in …?* *… you might want to …*	
Paragraph 2 **Paragraph 3**	give more detailed information about the attraction, include relevant positive and negative features	*There, you can …* *Visitors can also …* *One problem, however, is that …* *One excellent feature is …*	
Paragraph 4	say who, if anyone, you'd recommend it to	*It's (not) perfect/ideal for …* *I'd (definitely) recommend it to …*	

6 **Write** **Write your review in an appropriate style. Write about 100 words.**

7 **Check** **Before you hand in your review, complete this checklist.**

Checklist

- ◯ I've given my review an interesting title.
- ◯ I've tried to interest the readers and used the right style.
- ◯ I've included all the information from Exercise 4.
- ◯ I've followed my paragraph plan.
- ◯ I've checked my spelling, grammar and punctuation.

▶ **Writing reference,** page 171 ▶ **Workbook Unit 3:** Writing, page 26, exercises 1, 2, 3, 4 and Progress check 3, page 27

4 Give it a go

READING | Matching | An online guide

1 In pairs or as a group, answer the questions.

1 Look at the photo. What is the person doing?
2 Have you ever done something similar? If yes, what? If no, would you like to try it?

2 Match 1–5 to a–e to make collocations.

1 virtual ____	**a)** time
2 games ____	**b)** gadgets
3 free ____	**c)** event
4 sports ____	**d)** reality
5 high-tech ____	**e)** console

3 Scan the text and write the paragraph (A–H) which mentions these ideas.

1 watching films	____ , ____
2 playing video games	____ , ____ , ____
3 watching a sport	____
4 spending little money	____
5 listening to music	____ , ____
6 looking at paintings	____
7 travelling to space	____
8 downloading apps	____

EXAM SKILL

Scanning

- Scanning is a way of reading to find specific information.
- Don't read every word. Move your eyes quickly over the text and look for the information you need.
- Don't just look for a particular word or phrase. Look out for other ways that an idea might be expressed.

OPTIMISE YOUR EXAM

Matching

- When you have to match questions to paragraphs, words from the questions may appear in the text.
- Don't choose a paragraph just because it contains words from the questions as you may choose the wrong answer.
- When you find words from the questions, read that part of the text carefully. Check that it really does answer the question.

Maximum fun!

The web's best guide to fun, high-tech things to try in your free time!

A **Galactica**, a virtual reality rollercoaster in the UK, takes you on an amazing, some say 'frightening', journey! Riders actually travel on a real rollercoaster wearing a virtual reality headset. A computer calculates the exact position of your head and shows you stunning images. You will think you are flying beyond the stars, around black holes and through distant galaxies!

B Go along to the Science Museum's **Power UP** event and you'll be able to do much more than just look at the exhibits. Gamers of all ages can take on the challenge of classic games on games consoles from the last 40 years. While you are playing, you'll learn about the way gaming has developed into the multi-billion pound industry it is today.

C Judging by **HoloLens**, homes of the future are going to look very different. Go home, put the headset on and your video games seem to float in front of your eyes! As well as video games, you can watch movies on a giant virtual screen and surf the internet on a virtual computer.

D **SubPac** is a high-tech gadget you wear like a backpack. As you listen to your favourite music on your headphones, SubPac turns the low notes into powerful vibrations you can feel in your body. You'll really feel as if you're next to the speakers at a concert!

E When you enter **Virtually Live** through your headset, you can enjoy sports events and concerts from anywhere in the world. The system records a live event and then creates a virtual version online. It's just like really being there and taking part in the event with your friends from around the globe!

F Art lovers from all over the world can finally walk around the same gallery together with **Woofbert VR**. With special exhibitions and guided tours, it means that anyone from India to Indiana can enjoy and learn from the greatest art ever made. You'll even be able to virtually enter your favourite paintings!

G Download the **Google Cardboard** app on your phone, put your phone in the cardboard holder and suddenly you've got a genuine virtual reality system for your favourite games! Google Cardboard allows people to experience virtual reality for very little cost. Apart from games, other apps allow you to experience activities such as hang-gliding and deep-sea diving.

H Watching a film in a **D-BOX** seat will blow your mind! The film contains instructions that make the seat move to match what you can see on the screen. Both in the cinema with your friends or at home with your family, it puts you in the middle of the action with your favourite hero.

4 1.21 Decide which activity would be the most suitable for the teenagers below?

1 Grace enjoys finding out about the past and is interested in learning about how things work. She is also interested in business. ____

2 Joe loves going to the cinema and watches lots of films with friends. The next time he goes, he wants an unusual experience that makes the film even more exciting. ____

3 Ethan likes to visit exciting places with his friends. He likes to be active and doesn't spend much time online. He is also interested in astronomy. ____

4 Eva loves technology and she's looking for some exciting new experiences. She wants something cheap she can use at home to play video games. ____

5 Lily is a fan of a famous band, but she can't afford to go to their shows. She has friends in many countries and enjoys sharing music with them. ____

5 Find words in the text which match these definitions.

1 stay in the air without any support (*v*): ____________
2 accurate (*adj*): ____________
3 Something that blows your ____________ (*n*) is amazing.
4 a program that runs on your smartphone (*n*): ____________
5 people who love to play video games (*n*): ____________
6 very scary (*adj*): ____________

THINK | RESEARCH | CULTURE | LEARN | **ME**

Which of the activities interests you most? What do you think you would enjoy about it?

▶ **Workbook Unit 4:** Reading, pages 28–29, exercises 1, 2, 3

GRAMMAR 1 | *will* and *be going to*

Grammar in context

Look at these sentences from the online article on page 37 and match each sentence to a description.

1 *You will think you are flying beyond the stars …* ____

2 *Judging by Hololens, homes of the future are going to look very different.* ____

a) This is a prediction based on evidence we can see.

b) This is a general prediction.

REMEMBER

- For a general prediction, we often use *will*: *You **will** love Australia!*
- For a prediction based on evidence we can see, we often use *be going to*: *Look out! You**'re going to** fall!*
- Sometimes, *will* and *be going to* are both correct. *Be going to* is more informal.
- For intentions (things you want to do but have not yet arranged), we use *be going to*: *What **are** you **going to** do this weekend?*
- For decisions made at the moment of speaking, we use *will*: *Of course! I**'ll** ask Mum to help me.*
- For suggestions in the form of questions involving *I* and *we*, we use *shall*: ***Shall** we go bowling on Saturday?*

▶ **See Grammar reference, Unit 4,** page 151

1 **If the underlined word or phrase is correct, put a tick. If it's incorrect, rewrite it correctly on the line.**

1 'Have you ever tried hang-gliding?'
'No, but I<u>'m going to</u> have a go this weekend.'
____

2 'I've never been bowling, but I'd love to try it.'
'Me too. <u>Will</u> we give it a go this Saturday?'
____

3 'Look at those dark clouds.'
'Do you think it<u>'s going to</u> rain?'
____

4 'I'm going to go paintballing at the end of the month.'
'Oh, you<u>'ll</u> love it! It's a lot of fun.'
____

5 'Do you have any interesting hobbies?'
'I'm bored with my hobbies. I <u>will</u> see if I can find some exciting free-time activities to do.'
____

6 'Have you decided what you're having from the menu?'
'I think I<u>'ll</u> try the zebra burger. I've never had that before!'
____

2 **Choose the correct words or phrases to complete the advertisement. If both are correct, choose both.**

ALPHA ONE PAINTBALLING!

Have you ever been paintballing? No? You (**1**) **will / are going to** love it! Here at Alpha One Paintballing, we believe paintballing is for everyone. Book your party here and you (**2**) **will / are going to** have the time of your life! On the day, you (**3**) **will / are going to** receive all the safety training you need and we (**4**) **will / are going to** provide all the equipment. And if it looks like it (**5**) **will / is going to** rain … who cares? Paintballing is even more fun in the mud! So what (**6**) **will you / are you going to** do – spend another boring Saturday in front of the TV or try out ALPHA ONE PAINTBALLING? Call now to book your place.

3 **Write *will*, *shall* or an appropriate form of *be going to* to complete the messages. If more than one option is correct, write them both. Add any other words you need.**

Hey! I (**1**) ________ go paintballing this weekend. Do you want to come?

I would love to, but I think I (**2**) ________ be busy. (**3**) ________ I call you when I know more?

OK. I (**4**) ________ save a place for you. Let me know before Friday. It (**5**) ________ be awesome!

Sounds great! (**6**) ________ (you) invite Oscar?

Of course! In fact, I've already invited him. Oscar (**7**) ________ be there, and so is Matt.

OK – I (**8**) ________ let you know if I can make it. I hope I can! Speak to you later.

Words connected with *outdoor activities*

1 1.22 **Look at these pictures and complete the name of the activity. Work in pairs if necessary. Listen and check.**

1 h____________ing

2 h____________ing

3 i____________ing

4 r____________ing

5 s____________ing

6 s____________ing

7 s____________ing

8 s____________ing

2 **Choose two activities from Exercise 1 you have never done. Then talk about why you would like to try them with a partner. Say what you think they might be like.**

Phrasal verbs

3 1.23 **Read the sentences and choose the correct definition (a–h) for each phrasal verb in italics. Listen and check.**

1 I've got some free time so I'm going to *take up* sailing. ____
2 I've recently started to *work out* at the gym three times a week. ____
3 The bad weather means they are going to *call off* the tennis competition. ____
4 Are you going to *go out* this evening or help me clean the house? ____
5 At the weekend, my brother and I *stay up* and watch TV. ____
6 Let's *get together* on Sunday and I'll tell you all about my hiking trip. ____
7 My family and I try to *eat out* together at least once a month. ____
8 I'm really tired, so I'll probably *sleep in* tomorrow morning. ____

a) cancel
b) start doing (a new hobby)
c) don't go to bed until later than usual
d) go to a restaurant
e) stay in bed in the morning longer than usual
f) exercise
g) meet, spend time together
h) leave your house to meet friends, etc.

4 **Choose four phrasal verbs from Exercise 3 and write four sentences about yourself.**

1 ________________________
2 ________________________
3 ________________________
4 ________________________

Collocations connected with *free time*

5 1.24 **Choose the correct words to complete the collocations. Listen and check.**

1 I'd love to **have** / **make** *a go at* snowboarding because it looks like a lot of fun.
2 Do you like **doing** / **spending** *time with* friends at the weekend?
3 It's important to **do** / **make** *time for* your interests.
4 You should **do** / **take** *a break from* work and try to relax.
5 We **had** / **passed** *a good time* on the camping trip.
6 The next time we **have** / **go** *the day off* school, let's go ice skating.

THINK | **RESEARCH** | CULTURE | LEARN | ME

Find out where in your area or in your country you could do each of the activities in Exercise 1. Tell the class what you learn.

4 LISTENING | Multiple matching

1 **In pairs or as a group, answer the questions.**

1 How much time do you spend watching films, TV shows, online videos, etc. every week?
2 Do you prefer watching films at the cinema, on TV or online? Why?

EXAM SKILL

Listening for the main idea

- Each speaker will probably mention more than one idea. However, there is usually a main idea and one or two secondary ideas or supporting details.
- Concentrate on the gist of what the speaker is saying. Try to identify the most important idea by listening to what they talk about most.

2 1.25 **Read sentences 1–5 below then listen to the speaker. Tick the ideas she mentions. Then decide which idea is the main idea.**

1 She goes to the theatre regularly. ☐
2 Members of her family enjoy the theatre. ☐
3 The theatre can be expensive. ☐
4 She doesn't mind watching films with friends. ☐
5 At the theatre, you feel part of an audience. ☐

Main idea: ____

OPTIMISE YOUR EXAM

Multiple matching

- The first time you listen, you might not be sure of an answer. Put a question mark with the question number next to the possible answer so you know to pay particular attention to this detail when you listen for the second time.
- Remember that you should consider all the options for each speaker, even if you've already used that answer. Your first choice may not be correct.

3 1.26 **You will hear five short extracts in which teenagers are talking about things they like to watch.**

For questions 1–5, choose from the list (A–H) what each speaker likes most about it. Use the letters only once.

There are three extra letters which you do not need to use.

Speaker 1: ____
Speaker 2: ____
Speaker 3: ____
Speaker 4: ____
Speaker 5: ____

A showing friends new things
B seeing what different lives are like
C how it makes them feel
D being part of an audience
E how beautiful it is
F finding out about other places
G the chance to learn new skills
H meeting new people

4 1.26 **Listen again and check your answers.**

THINK | RESEARCH | CULTURE | LEARN | ME

Have you or anyone you know ever learnt a skill from watching an online video?

What skill did you learn?

Do you think watching an online video is a good way to learn something? Why / Why not?

What other ways can you learn new skills? Make a list.

▶ **Workbook Unit 4:** Listening, page 32, exercises 1, 2

Grammar in context

Look at these sentences from the audio in the listening lesson on page 40 and match each sentence to the explanation.

1 *Next Friday a new play **opens** at the theatre in town.* ____

2 ***I'm meeting** a friend this evening.* ____

a) This describes an arrangement, something we have agreed to do, often with other people.

b) This describes something that is scheduled to happen.

REMEMBER

- We use the present simple to talk about future scheduled events, timetables, etc.: *The next train **leaves** in half an hour.*
- We use the present continuous to talk about future arrangements: ***I'm meeting** Jamie at the bowling alley at 6 o'clock.*

▶ **See Grammar reference, Unit 4,** page 152

1 Put the verbs into the correct tense to complete the sentences.

1 The play ______________ (**start**) at 8 pm, so we should leave to go to the theatre at 7 pm.

2 What time __________ the film __________ (**start**)?

3 __________ you __________ (**see**) Olivia this weekend?

4 My dad ______________ (**drive**) me to the party, so we can pick you up on the way.

5 The new album by my favourite band __________ (**come**) out this week!

6 We've got plenty of time. The plane __________ (**not / leave**) for another hour.

7 Ben ______________ (**not / meet**) us tonight. He's too busy.

8 I ______________ (**go**) horse-riding for the first time next month for my birthday!

2 Write a verb from the box in the correct form to complete the blog post.

catch | go | have | leave | meet
play | record | start | take | write

Home | About me | Posts

My English blog
where I practise what I learn!

My weekend! posted at 8:54 pm

Hi, readers! What a weekend I've got planned! First of all, I (**1**) ______________ the train to visit my cousins! The train (**2**) ______________ at 6 am, so I've got to be up early. My mum (**3**) ______________ me to the station and my cousins (**4**) ______________ me at the other end.

My cousins live in a big city, so we have lots of plans! We (**5**) ______________ to a music festival on Saturday and my favourite band (**6**) ______________ . I can't wait! The festival (**7**) ______________ at 7 pm, so before that we (**8**) ______________ a Chinese meal. I love Chinese food!

Then, on Sunday, we (**9**) ______________ a podcast! My cousins make their own podcast about music, where they talk about what they like and what they've been listening to. I (**10**) ______________ a review of the music festival! Can you imagine – me, a music critic? When we've recorded it, I'll put a link here so you can download it. Wish me luck!

Post Reply

Page 1 of 4 ▶

3 In pairs, ask and answer these questions.

1 What are you doing this evening? Are you looking forward to it?

2 What are the different members of your family doing this weekend?

3 What are you doing next summer? Have you made any arrangements yet?

4 Are you doing anything for the first time soon? If not, use your imagination to talk about something exciting!

THINK | RESEARCH | CULTURE | **LEARN** | ME

Find blogs written by people learning English. Tell the class what you find. Why not start your own?

Talk2Me
I'm a big fan of ...

Flipped classroom

1 Watch the *Talk2Me* video and answer the questions.

1 What does Jamie complain about?
2 What does Maddy suggest they do?
3 What happens to their plans at the end of the episode?

2 Watch the video again. Write the names of the person who says the phrases in the *Phrase expert* box and what they like/dislike.

PHRASE EXPERT

I'm (not) keen on … | I (don't) really like … | I'm (not) a big fan of … | I prefer (… to …) | I don't mind | I (don't) feel strongly about … | I don't have a strong preference … | because/as/since/for the reason that … | That's because … | The reason is that …

3 In pairs or as a group, answer the questions.

1 What's happening in the photos?
2 Do you prefer doing indoor or outdoor activities in your free time? Why?

SAY IT RIGHT

Resource centre: Unit 4
/iː/, /uː/, /ɜː/, /ɔː/ and /ɑː/

EXAM SKILL

Expressing opinions

- Try to express your opinion in a variety of ways, such as *Personally, …, My opinion is that … is the best …, I (don't) really like …, I'm (not) a big fan of …, I really love it*, etc.
- Give reasons for your opinions. You can use linking words (*because, as, since*) or phrases such as *The reason is that …*

4 1.27 Listen to two students talking about what they like doing in their free time. Did they do well? Choose 1 (not good enough), 2 (good) or 3 (very good).

	Layla	Rory
A They express their likes and dislikes clearly.	1 2 3	1 2 3
B They give good reasons for their likes and dislikes.	1 2 3	1 2 3

5 1.27 Listen again and tick the expressions you hear.

1 I don't really like … ☐
2 Personally, I like … ☐
3 I'm not a big fan of … ☐
4 I'm not very keen on … ☐
5 I feel strongly about … ☐
6 That's because … ☐

OPTIMISE YOUR EXAM

General conversation

- To keep the conversation going, ask your partner about the reasons for their opinions, e.g. *Why do you think that?* or *Why do you feel that way?*
- You can also suggest a reason by asking a question. For example, if your partner says *I like playing football*, you might say *Is that because you can spend time with your friends?*

6 Work in pairs. Take turns to do the task below.

Talk about how you like spending your free time.
Talk about what you like doing now and what you would like to do in the future.

▶ **Workbook Unit 4:** Speaking, pages 32–33, exercises 1, 2, 3

LANGUAGE IN USE | Key word transformation

1 In pairs, ask and answer the questions.

1 Look at the photo. What is happening?
2 Have you ever done an extreme sport? Would you like to do one?

REMEMBER

- We use *although*, *even though*, *despite* and *in spite of* to contrast two ideas. They come at the start of a sentence or the start of a clause.
- *Although* and *even though* are followed by a **subject** plus a **verb**: *I enjoy snowboarding, although/even though* ***I'm not*** *very good at it. Although/Even though* ***I'm not*** *very good at snowboarding, I enjoy it.*
- *Despite* and *in spite of* are more formal than *although* and *even though*. They are followed by *-ing* or a noun, or the phrase *the fact that*: *Despite/In spite of* ***not being very good at snowboarding****, I enjoy it. I enjoy snowboarding,* ***despite / in spite*** *of* ***the fact that*** *I'm not very good at it.*

2 Write a word or phrase from the box in each gap to complete the sentences. There is more than one correct answer.

although | despite | even though | in spite of

1 She loved sailing, ____________ she wasn't a very good swimmer.
2 Lizzy's good at basketball, ____________ being quite short.
3 ____________ the fact that I live near a lake, I've never been sailing.
4 ____________ we go skiing every winter, I'm not very keen on it.
5 I would love to go sky-diving, ____________ I'm sure I'd be quite scared!
6 ____________ trying his best, my dad just can't stay upright on a skateboard!

3 Choose the sentence (a or b) that has a similar meaning to the first sentence.

1 I love skating, although I'm not very good at it.
a) Despite not being good at it, I love skating.
b) In spite of being good at it, I love skating.
2 Despite the fact that it's raining, I still want to go swimming in the sea.
a) It's raining, even though I still want to go swimming in the sea.
b) I still want to go swimming in the sea, even though it's raining.
3 In spite of not being very fit, my brother enjoys running.
a) My brother enjoys running even though he's not very fit.
b) Although he's very fit, my brother enjoys running.
4 We enjoyed the 4D cinema, although it was quite expensive.
a) Despite enjoying the 4D cinema, it was quite expensive.
b) Despite the fact that it was quite expensive, we enjoyed the 4D cinema.

OPTIMISE YOUR EXAM

Key word transformation

- Be careful when the word you are given is *despite* or *spite*.
- With *spite*, you need to add *in* and *of*. With *despite*, it's a common mistake to add *of*. You don't need it.

4 Complete the second sentence so it has a similar meaning to the first sentence, using the word given. Do not change the word given. Use two to five words, including the word given.

1 Despite being scared of heights, my sister wanted to go sky-diving! **EVEN**
My sister wanted to go sky-diving ____________ scared of heights.
2 Although bungee jumping looks dangerous, I'm keen to have a go. **DESPITE**
I'm keen to have a go at bungee jumping ____________ that it looks dangerous.
3 Alysha fell over in the snow but she still had a great time. **SPITE**
Alysha had a great time ____________ over in the snow.
4 I climbed to the top diving board despite feeling really nervous. **ALTHOUGH**
I climbed to the top diving board ____________ really nervous.
5 We knew the water was freezing but we still went in. **DESPITE**
We still went in ____________ the water was freezing.
6 Although it was windy, they landed the hang-glider safely. **OF**
They landed the hang-glider safely ____________ wind.

sailing

cycling

1 **In pairs or groups, answer the questions.**

1 Have you ever tried any of the activities in the photos?
2 Which activity would you like to try?

EXAM SKILL

Giving your opinion

- When giving your opinion, use a variety of phrases, such as *I think …*, *I believe …*, *In my opinion …*, *My view is that …*, etc.
- In addition to *I like/don't like …*, you can use *I'm (not) a big fan of …*, *I absolutely love …*, *I can't stand …*, *I hate …*, etc.

2 **Read the exam task and article. Underline ways the writer gives his/her opinion.**

Articles wanted!

WHAT NEW FREE-TIME ACTIVITY WOULD YOU LIKE TO TRY?

Write an article telling us about an interesting new activity and why you would enjoy it.

Do you think it's good for people to try new things? Why / Why not?

The best articles will be published next month.

A COOL NEW ACTIVITY

Do you enjoy learning new skills? I do! I'm a big fan of trying new things and there's one activity I think I would really enjoy: in-line skating.

In my opinion, it would be a lot of fun. I'm sure I'd absolutely love skating along the street with all my friends watching.

I believe that we should all try new things because it keeps life interesting and you can learn a lot about yourself. It's also a good way to meet new people.

If you ask me, everyone should try a new activity once a year. You're never too old to learn something new!

in-line skating

3 **Write one word in each gap to complete the sentences.**

1 Do you enjoy sailing? I ___________ !
2 I'm a big ___________ of spending time in a boat on a lake.
3 If you ___________ me, everyone should try sailing.
4 I absolutely ___________ being out on the lake in the sunshine – it's so nice!
5 I believe ___________ sailing teaches you how to work with other people.
6 In my ___________ , sailing is the best hobby!

4 **Choose one of the following questions and write two or three sentences giving your opinion. Share your opinion with a partner or with the class.**

1 Do you like camping? Why / Why not?
2 Do you like picnics in the park? Why / Why not?
3 What sport do you like playing or doing? Why do you like it?

OPTIMISE YOUR EXAM

An article

- When you are deciding what to write about, don't just choose your first idea. Think of a few ideas and then make notes about what you can say about each one.
- Choose the topic that you have most ideas about. For example, you might love football, but if you have more to say about camping, you should write about camping!

5 **Look at this writing task and answer the questions.**

You see this announcement in a magazine for teenagers.

Articles wanted!

WHAT OUTDOOR ACTIVITY DO YOU ENJOY MOST?

Write an article telling us about your favourite outdoor activity and why you enjoy doing it.

Do you think it's good for people to get outdoors? Why?

The best articles will be published next month.

Write your **article**.

1 Tick three of these outdoor activities that you know something about. You can add your own idea if you prefer.

camping	☐	hiking	☐
cycling	☐	playing football/tennis/etc.	☐
having a picnic	☐	sailing	☐
horse-riding	☐	skateboarding	☐
in-line skating	☐	______________	

2 For each activity you have chosen in question 1, quickly write down a few ideas you could write about. Decide which activity you have most ideas about.

1: ______________________________

2: ______________________________

3: ______________________________

3 Make a note of three reasons why people enjoy doing outdoor activities.

____

____

____

6 **Plan** **Make a paragraph plan.**

Part	Purpose	Useful phrases	My notes
Paragraph 1	introduce the subject in an interesting way	*Do you …?* *Have you ever …?*	
Paragraph 2	describe your favourite outdoor activity and say why you like it	*I absolutely love …* *I'm a big fan of …* *The reason for that is …*	
Paragraph 3	say if you think it's good for people to get outdoors	*My view is …* *In my opinion, …*	
Paragraph 4	briefly conclude the article	*We should all …* *Why don't you …?*	

7 **Write** **Write your article in an appropriate style. Write about 100 words.**

8 **Check** **Before you hand in your article, complete this checklist.**

Checklist

- ◯ I've started my article in an interesting way.
- ◯ I've used an appropriate style.
- ◯ I've given my opinion in different ways.
- ◯ I've written about 100 words.
- ◯ I've included all the necessary information.
- ◯ I've checked my spelling, grammar and punctuation.

▶ **Writing reference,** page 170 ▶ **Workbook Unit 4:** Writing, page 34, exercises 1, 2, 3, 4 and Progress check 4, page 35

PROGRESS CHECK UNITS 3–4

GRAMMAR AND VOCABULARY

1 If a word or phrase in bold is correct, put a tick. If it's incorrect, rewrite it correctly in each gap.

1 **Will** I help you mend your bike? ______________
2 When I grow up, I **will** be an astronaut! ______________
3 I **will have** a party on Friday. Would you like to come? ______________
4 Hurry up! We **will** miss the train! ______________
5 I know! **I'm getting** Dad a tie for his birthday! ______________

__/5

2 Put the verbs into the correct tense, present perfect simple or present perfect continuous.

1 Mum ______________ sandwiches for the picnic all afternoon. They're in the fridge. (**make**)
2 I ______________ in a helicopter before. It's exciting! (**never** / **be**)
3 Dan ______________ the tickets yet. (**not** / **buy**)
4 ______________ the new Matt Damon film yet? (**you** / **see**)
5 I ______________ for Susie since 1 o'clock. Where is she? (**wait**)

__/5

3 Match 1–6 to a–f to make collocations.

1 package ___ **a)** tour
2 virtual ___ **b)** console
3 guided ___ **c)** trip
4 games ___ **d)** holiday
5 school ___ **e)** off
6 have a day ___ **f)** reality

__/6

4 If a word or phrase in bold is correct, put a tick. If it's incorrect, rewrite it correctly in each gap.

1 I spend a lot of time **playing** my guitar. ____________
2 Are you interested **on** coming to the cinema with us tomorrow? ____________
3 Is that your new skateboard? Can I **make** a go? ____________
4 Are you looking forward to **go** to Spain? ____________
5 Let's **take** a break for five minutes. ____________
6 What prevented her **to take** part in the competition? ____________
7 I'm sure you'll all enjoy **you** on the cruise! ____________

__/7

5 Write one word in each gap.

1 I love staying ____________ late at the weekend and watching TV.
2 Could you drop me ____________ outside the park, please?
3 Do you want to go ____________ this evening, or shall we stay in?
4 Our car broke ____________, so we had to wait by the side of the road for an hour.
5 I'm thinking of taking ____________ a sport like judo or taekwondo.
6 We'll have to set ____________ early if we're going to be at the airport for 11 am.
7 Mum can't pick me ____________ from school today, so I'll get the bus home.

__/7

6 Choose the correct word or phrase.

1 **Although** / **Despite** she wasn't feeling well, Karen still took part in the race.
2 We ordered a big pizza **even though** / **in spite of** we weren't very hungry.
3 I passed the test **in spite** / **despite** of the fact that it was really hard.
4 **Although** / **Despite** looking everywhere, Paul didn't find his watch.

__/4

7 Write a form of the word in capitals in each gap.

1	It's ___________ to drive at 200 km per hour!	**LEGAL**
2	It's ___________ to lie to your parents.	**HONEST**
3	This chair's really ___________ . I think I'll move!	**COMFORTABLE**
4	Jim, your bedroom's really ___________ . Can you go and tidy it, please?	**TIDY**
5	Don't be so ___________ ! The bus will be here soon.	**PATIENT**
6	My best friend's allowed to go to the concert but I'm not. It's so ___________ !	**FAIR**

__/6

8 Write a word from the box in each gap.

few | little | many | much | piece

1 I haven't got ___________ cousins – just two, in fact.
2 How ___________ money have you got on you?
3 A ___________ people have bought tickets for the show, but not many so far.
4 There wasn't one ___________ of furniture in the room! It was totally empty!
5 We've got a ___________ time until the train leaves – about ten minutes.

__/5

9 Choose the correct word.

1 You need to show your **resort** / **passport** when you enter a different country.
2 The word **luggage** / **backpacking** means suitcases and bags.
3 Someone who travels on trains, planes, etc. but is not the driver is a **passenger** / **tourist**.
4 The science show was amazing. It blew my **brain** / **mind**!
5 If a number or price is **affordable** / **exact**, it's accurate.

__/5

Total score __/50

EXAM SKILLS

Tick the statements that are true for you. Review the skills in the unit if you need more help.

I can ...	**Unit/page**
☐ understand tenses and the information they give about time and the sequence of events	Unit 3 p26
☐ listen for attitude and opinion in a conversation	Unit 3 p30
☐ make suggestions in a discussion	Unit 3 p32
☐ use particles to make phrasal verbs in open cloze activities	Unit 3 p33
☐ choose the positive and negative points in a review	Unit 3 p34
☐ scan an online guide to find specific information	Unit 4 p36
☐ identify the main idea of what a speaker is saying	Unit 4 p40
☐ express my opinion in a general conversation	Unit 4 p42
☐ recognise connectors of contrast and use them in key word transformations	Unit 4 p43
☐ give my opinion in an article	Unit 4 p44

5 In good health

READING | Matching | An online article

1 **Look at the photo above. Discuss in pairs if you think this person has a healthy lifestyle.**

2 **Read the article quickly and decide if the statements are T (True) or F (False).**

1 All four people help animals in their spare time. T / F
2 All four places help the same kind of animals. T / F
3 Dom usually helps pets. T / F
4 Jen pays money to stay at the rescue centre. T / F
5 Fiona says she often takes animals to her house. T / F
6 Alex is 16 years old. T / F

EXAM SKILL

Paraphrasing

- Paraphrasing is taking an idea that's expressed one way and expressing it a different way.
- Sometimes you have to find information in a text that matches a question. Often, the question uses paraphrasing. Don't only look for words and phrases that mean the same thing, e.g. *too young* / *not old enough*. Also look for ideas expressed in a very different way, e.g. *I'm not old enough.* / *You have to be 18, but I'm 16.*

3 **Look at each paragraph A–D and find ideas with the same meaning as sentences 1–4. There is one idea in each paragraph.**

1 Injured animals are treated at one of our centres.
2 They don't have to pay for living expenses separately.
3 I was keen to begin.
4 They get in touch and we go quickly to assist.

OPTIMISE YOUR EXAM

Matching

- Read the texts quickly to get a general idea of what they're about.
- For each question, underline the key idea(s). Then scan the texts again looking for a similar idea.
- When you think you've found a corresponding idea, read that part of the text very carefully to check you're right.

TeenLife > Animal lives

Helping sick and injured animals!

In their free time, four volunteers take care of animals in need.

A

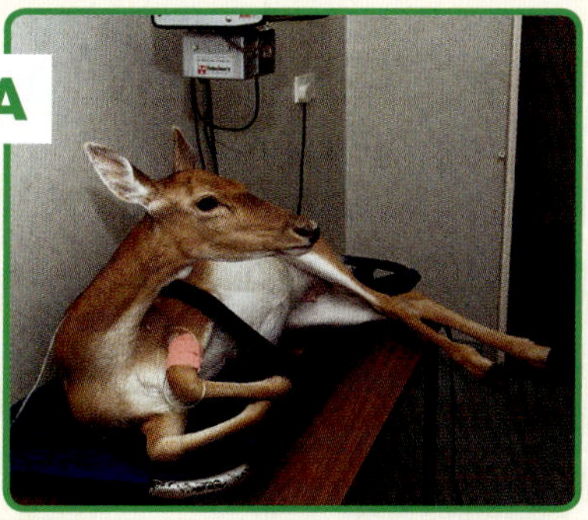

Dom – Wildlife A&E

I live in the south-east of England and help with the rescue, treatment and release of injured wild animals – mainly deer, foxes, badgers and squirrels. Often, someone walking or riding sees an animal in trouble. They contact us and we hurry to help. If you're in the area and see an animal that needs help, you should call our emergency phone number immediately. And if you see people carrying a deer on a stretcher, they're probably from Wildlife A&E* – so you'll know the deer is in good hands!

Jen – Costa Rica Animal Rescue Centre

B

We look after ill or hurt wild animals and birds such as monkeys, tortoises, and parrots. We treat them, then release them when they're healthy again. Volunteers must be at least 14 years old, and have to pay for the organised programme (from 1 to 12 weeks). When they get here, though, they don't have to find somewhere to stay, as food and accommodation are part of the package. If you can afford it, and your parents say you can go, it's an amazing experience!

Fiona – Wellington SPCA Animal Rescue Unit

C

Here in New Zealand, our Animal Rescue Unit rescues trapped animals, often pets. If you join the team, you'll be able to help with an animal that needs rescuing from a cliff, tree or hole in the ground. Rescued animals sometimes return to their owners, if we know who they are. If the animals are badly hurt, they receive medical care at an SPCA** Centre, but many go to volunteer foster parents. These people take an animal into their home for a while until it's well enough to find a permanent home.

D

Alex – Sea Turtle Rescue Centre, Greece

You have to be over 18 to be a volunteer here. I've always loved turtles, so I applied as soon as I was old enough. I couldn't wait to start! Since then, I've needed to have lots of training so I know what to do. Each year, around 50 injured turtles from all over the country arrive at our centre. Many of them have had accidents with fishing boats or speedboats. Members of the public can come and see the turtles, and learn about them and how to help protect them.

** Accident and Emergency*
*** Society for the Prevention of Cruelty to Animals*

4 2.01 **For questions 1–10, choose from the teenagers A–D. The teenagers may be chosen more than once.**

Which teenager

1 says they were very excited to become a volunteer? ____
2 talks about getting permission from an adult to be a volunteer? ____
3 describes an animal staying in someone's house for a short time? ____
4 mentions members of the public finding injured animals? ____
5 is most likely to help a cat or dog in trouble? ____
6 mentions different types of transport hurting animals? ____
7 advises people to ring the organisation? ____
8 says that anyone can visit the animals? ____
9 definitely doesn't work as a volunteer there all year round. ____
10 talks about their organisation giving them meals? ____

5 **Write a word or phrase from the text in each gap to complete the sentences.**

1 If you ____________ an animal or bird, you let it go.
2 'Temporary' means *for a short time* and '____________' means *forever*.
3 If paramedics need to carry someone, they use a ____________ .
4 If you ____________ of an animal by helping and feeding it, you ____________ it.
5 If an animal is ____________ , it can't escape or get out.

THINK | RESEARCH | **CULTURE** | LEARN | ME

What animal rescue organisations are there in your area or country? What do they do? Would you like to help them in the future?

▶ **Workbook Unit 5:** Reading, pages 36–37, exercises 1, 2, 3, 4

Grammar in context

Read these extracts from the article on page 49 and then decide if each word or phrase in bold describes A (Ability), O (Obligation), L (lack of obligation), AD (advice) or P (permission).

1 *If you* ***can*** *afford it ...* ____
2 *... and your parents say you* ***can*** *go ...* ____
3 *Volunteers* ***must*** *be at least 14 years old ...* ____
4 *... and* ***have to*** *pay for the organised programme ...* ____
5 *... they* ***don't have to*** *find somewhere to stay ...* ____
6 *... you* ***should*** *call our emergency phone number ...* ____
7 *... you'****ll be able to*** *help with an animal that needs rescuing ...* ____

REMEMBER

- Modals include *can, could, may, might, must* and *should*. Semi-modals include *have to, ought to* and *need to*.
- To express ability, we can use *can, could* (past ability) and *be able to*.
- To express permission, we can use *can* and *may*, and the verbs *let* and *allow*.
- To express advice and criticism, we can use *should* and *ought to*.
- To express obligation, we can use *must* and *have to*. Be careful with *mustn't* and *don't have to*: *mustn't* expresses obligation, but *don't / doesn't have to* expresses lack of obligation.
- Modals are followed by the bare infinitive.

▶ **See Grammar reference, Unit 5,** pages 152–153

1 Choose the correct word or phrase.

1 Veronica **couldn't** / **mustn't** go to school yesterday because she was ill.
2 I'm allergic to milk so I **mustn't** / **don't have to** eat any cheese or yoghurt.
3 My grandma's eyesight isn't great, so she **has to** / **will be able to** wear glasses when she reads.
4 After I injured my shoulder, my doctor said I **shouldn't** / **ought to** play football until I recovered.
5 When Tim is better, he **could** / **will be able to** do a first-aid course.

2 Look at Exercise 1 again. What other words and phrases could replace the words in bold?

3 Write a modal or semi-modal in each gap to complete the text. Sometimes more than one answer is correct.

my life
my work
my interests

Gemma's blog

24th April

Hey everyone! I've been working as a student paramedic for a month now, so here's a typical day in my new life.

I have to get up early because I (**1**) ____________ be at the ambulance station at 6:15 am. Luckily, I (**2**) ____________ think about what to wear – it's the same uniform every day! I know I (**3**) ____________ have breakfast before I leave, but I usually have something on the way. I work until 7 pm, so it's a really long day, but I (**4**) ____________ usually take a 30-minute lunch break around 2 o'clock.

Every day is different, so if you don't like surprises, you (**5**) ____________ become a paramedic! Sometimes we pick up a patient from home and take them to hospital. We provide basic medical care when they're with us, but obviously we (**6**) ____________ do anything major like an operation.

Other times we take patients home. This is satisfying, because you know they'll (**7**) ____________ be with their families there and be more comfortable. A difficult part of the job is when someone's had an accident and needs urgent medical attention. You (**8**) ____________ panic – you (**9**) ____________ stay calm and help them the best way you can.

The ambulance (**10**) ____________ get untidy during the day, and it (**11**) ____________ be clean and neat before we (**12**) ____________ go home. When I get home at about 7:30 pm, I'm usually exhausted – but glad I have a job where I help people in need.

THINK | RESEARCH | CULTURE | LEARN | ME

What are the best/worst parts of a paramedic's job?

Words connected with *health and illness*

1 2.02 **Complete the table with the words in the box. Listen and check.**

ache | ankle | bandage | blood | bone | chin
cold | cough | cut | flu | hurt | infection
injure | knee | medicine | operation | pain
prescription | shoulder | skin

the body	problems and illness	treatments and help

2 **Write the correct form of a word from Exercise 1 in each gap to complete the text.**

I fell over playing football yesterday and (**1**) ____________ my knee. I didn't cut it – I just banged the (**2**) ____________ . It still (**3**) ____________ quite badly, but the doctor says it's not broken. She wrapped a (**4**) ____________ round it. She told me to take paracetamol and said she might need to give me a (**5**) ____________ for some medicine if the (**6**) ____________ gets worse.

Phrasal verbs

3 2.03 **Look at the phrasal verbs in italics. Match each sentence to a definition below. Listen and check.**

1 ____ : It took me a week to *get over* my cold.
2 ____ : Janie's *come down with* flu, so she won't be coming to school this week.
3 ____ : My dad's on a diet because he *put on weight* over the summer.
4 ____ : I know you've got a bad stomach ache, but do you *feel up to* having some lunch?
5 ____ : Our 22-year-old cat's very ill, so the vet might have to *put her down*. It's very sad.
6 ____ : I felt really lightheaded at school this morning and nearly *passed out*.
7 ____ : *Cheer up*! Don't look so sad.
8 ____ : It really *gets* me *down* when people don't look after animals properly.

a) become happier
b) become ill with
c) faint, become unconscious
d) feel well enough for
e) gain, add extra
f) kill (a very sick animal)
g) make sad or miserable
h) recover from

Collocations with *have, take, make* and *do*

4 2.04 **Write *have, take, make* or *do* in each gap to complete the phrase. Listen and check.**

1 ____________ or ____________ a bath or shower
2 ____________ or ____________ a decision
3 ____________ a headache
4 ____________ a mistake
5 ____________ an effort
6 ____________ care of someone
7 ____________ flu, a cold or a cough
8 ____________ fun of someone
9 ____________ or ____________ medicine
10 ____________ or ____________ some exercise
11 ____________ surgery or an operation
12 ____________ up your mind
13 ____________ your bed
14 ____________ homework or housework
15 ____________ your teeth or hair

5 **Rewrite the sentences using phrases from Exercise 4.**

Example: Tim laughed when his sister fell over.
Tim made fun of her.

1 Karen's decided to foster a sick animal.
____
2 Aidan's doing the washing-up, then he's going to vacuum the living room.
____
3 Toby wasn't thinking and gave cat food to the rabbit, and rabbit food to the cat!
____
4 Helen's in hospital. The doctors are going to try to treat her knee tomorrow.
____
5 My sister runs round the park every morning before work.
____
6 Greg's really tried hard to lose weight.
____

5 LISTENING | 3-option multiple choice (interview)

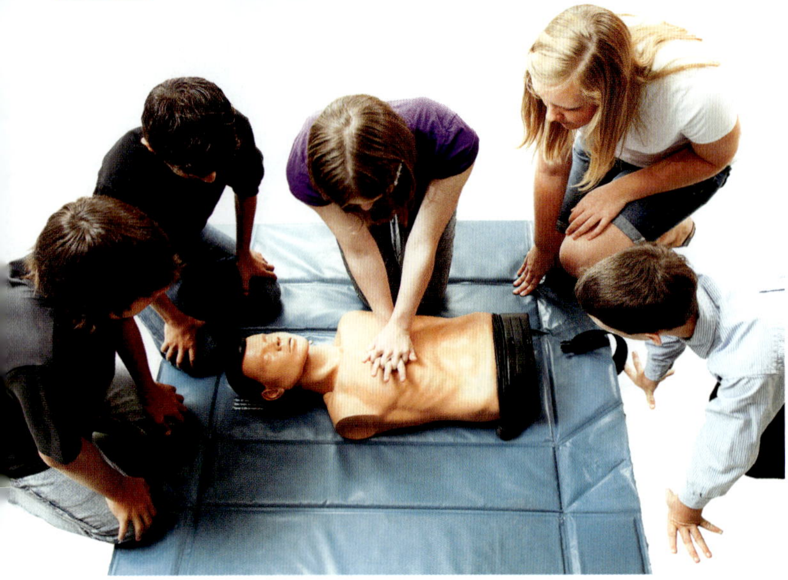

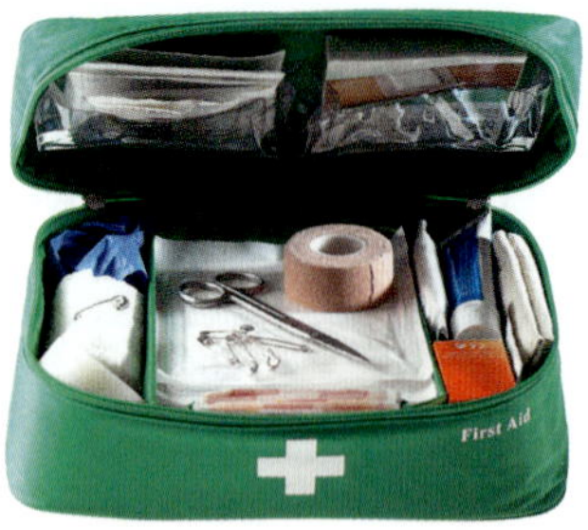

1 **In pairs or as a group, answer the questions. Use the words in the box and a dictionary to help you.**

1 What skills do you learn on a first-aid course?

2 How much first aid do you know?

allergic reaction | bleeding | broken arm/leg | CPR | first-aid kit | head injury | nose bleed | recovery position | unconscious

EXAM SKILL

Recognising synonyms

- The questions in this type of exam task often paraphrase ideas from the recording using different words and phrases.
- When listening, you need to check for synonyms of the words you hear in the question and answer options. For example, you may hear the words *scared* or *frightened* and the question may include the word *afraid.*

2 2.05 **You will hear a woman, Kate, talking about a first-aid course she attended. Answer the questions.**

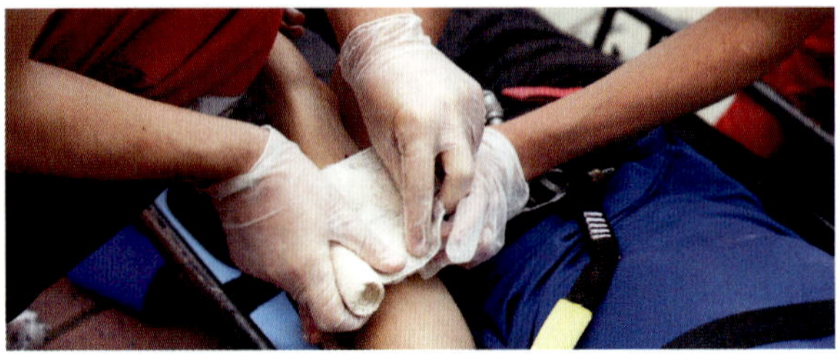

1 What was the first thing the course covered?

____

2 Look at question 3 in Exercise 3. Which word is a synonym for your answer to question 1?

____

OPTIMISE YOUR EXAM

3-option multiple choice (interview)

- Sometimes, you may be uncertain of the correct answer but feel more confident that one of the answers is definitely incorrect.
- Cross off the incorrect choice so you only have two possible answers to choose from instead of three. Then when you listen again, make your final choice.

3 2.06 **For each question, choose the correct answer.**

1 What does Kate say about the other people on the course?
A They knew more than her.
B She made friends with some of them.
C She already knew some of them.

2 Kate felt that the course
A should have been longer.
B was too long.
C was the right length.

3 What was the most useful thing that was covered?
A helping people who are bleeding
B the equipment you need
C removing small things from eyes and ears

4 Kate says people are sometimes afraid to help because they
A don't like the sight of blood.
B don't know what to do.
C are afraid of getting hurt themselves.

5 Kate thinks knowing CPR is useful because
A it helps you understand medical shows on TV.
B emergencies can happen anywhere.
C you only need a short time to do it.

6 Why does Kate recommend the course to the interviewer?
A It would help with his future career.
B He often gets injured.
C He might find it useful if someone is hurt.

4 2.06 **Listen again and check your answers.**

THINK | RESEARCH | **CULTURE** | LEARN | ME

How common is it for people in your country to go on a first-aid course? Where can you do a first-aid course in your country?

▶ **Workbook Unit 5:** Listening, page 40, exercises 1, 2

GRAMMAR 2 | Modals (2): possibility, probability, certainty

Grammar in context

Read these extracts from the audio in the listening lesson on page 52 and then decide if the speaker is expressing P (possibility), PR (probability) or C (certainty). Use the words in bold to help you decide.

1 *… it **must** be scary with all that blood.* ____
2 *That **can't** be very easy …* ____
3 *You never know when you **might** need to use it …* ____
4 *I **may** do it too.* ____
5 *I **should** get it in a couple of weeks.* ____

REMEMBER

- We can use *may, might* and *could* to express possibility, e.g. *Dad **might** be at the doctor's now.* = It's possible he's there.
- We can use *should* and *ought to* to express probability, e.g. *Gabi **should** be at the rescue centre now.* = She's probably there.
- We can use *must* and *can't* to express certainty, e.g. *Ruth **must** be at the first-aid course now.* = I'm sure she's there. *Mum **can't** be at the dentist's surgery now.* = I'm sure she's not there.
- We can also use a continuous infinitive to show that a situation is in progress, e.g. *John **must** be **ringing** the emergency services right now.*

▶ **See Grammar reference, Unit 5,** page 153

1 **Choose the correct word or phrase.**

HAY FEVER by Jason Morgan

Scientific research shows that in some countries, 60% of students taking exams are suffering from hay fever. It (1) must / can't be awful!

What's more, the research indicates that they (2) might / have to perform worse in their exams because of it. It also shows that students who take medicine as a treatment for their hay fever do even worse. This (3) may / must be because the medicine makes you tired, or it (4) can't / could be because their hay fever is very bad. Either way, it (5) mustn't / can't be easy for them.

On the day of an exam, they should wear clean clothes because clothes they've worn before (6) could / are allowed to contain pollen, which causes hay fever. Wearing sunglasses to protect eyes and drinking lots of water (7) should / can't help too.

2 **Look at the photos. Complete the sentences using the words in brackets to describe possibility, probability and certainty.**

1 The injured girl ______________________. **(must)**
2 The operator ______________________. **(may)**
3 The boy on the phone ______________________. **(might)**
4 The friends ______________________. **(ought to)**
5 The injured girl ______________________. **(might not)**
6 The injury ______________________. **(could)**

THINK | **RESEARCH** | CULTURE | LEARN | ME

Think of some family members and friends who are not in the room with you now. Write sentences about where they *must/can't/should be*, and what they *must/can't/might be doing.*

5 SPEAKING | Questions

Flipped classroom

1 ▶ **Watch the *Talk2Me* video and answer the questions.**

1 How does Angus feel in this video?
2 When does Angus' throat hurt?
3 Who is Louise and what treatment does she suggest?

2 ▶ **Watch the video again. Underline the phrases in the *Phrase expert* box that you hear on the video.**

PHRASE EXPERT

On (schooldays) / At (the weekend), I … | In the (morning/afternoon/evening), I … | I always/usually/often/sometimes/rarely/never … | I … all the time | I … quite/fairly often | It/That depends (on …) | I don't … very often because … | I'd like to … more often, but …

3 **In pairs or groups, answer the questions.**

1 What's your morning routine before going to school?
2 What's your afternoon/evening routine after school?

EXAM SKILL

Talking about habits

- Make sure you can say how often you do something. You can use words and phrases such as *all the time, usually, quite/fairly often, not very often, rarely* and *never*.
- If you want to be more exact, you can use phrases such as *once a week, twice a month, three times a year*, etc.
- Remember to explain why you do (or don't do) an activity frequently.

4 🔊 2.07 **Listen to four students answering personal questions. Match them with the questions they are asked.**

Student 1: ____
Student 2: ____
Student 3: ____
Student 4: ____

a) How often do you see a dentist?
b) Are you good at getting out of bed early?
c) Which do you have more often, a shower or a bath?
d) What kind of exercise do you do? How often do you do it?

5 🔊 2.07 **Listen again and write the frequency expressions (*often, three times a week*, etc.) that the students use in their answers.**

Student 1: ____________
Student 2: ____________
Student 3: ____________
Student 4: ____________

OPTIMISE YOUR EXAM

Questions

- Use the present simple to talk about general situations and things that you do regularly, for example, *We usually have PE on Thursdays*.
- Use the present continuous for temporary situations happening now or around now, for example, *This week we're not having PE because Mrs Thomas is away.*

6 **In pairs, ask and answer the questions in Exercise 4.**

1 **In pairs or as a group, answer the questions.**

1 What are common treatments for illnesses like colds, stomach aches, etc.?
2 What are less common treatments?

REMEMBER

- Some nouns end in *-ity* (e.g. *popularity*), some end in *-ness* (e.g. *illness*). Others end in *-ment*, *-ation* or *-ion*.
- Sometimes the final *-e* stays (e.g. *improve – improvement*), and sometimes it doesn't (e.g. *organise – organisation*).
- Sometimes you have to change other letters too (e.g. *decide – decision*).

2 **Complete the table with the words in the box.**

accommodate | agree | amaze | communicate | decide | enjoy | entertain | equip | excite | improve | infect | operate | organise | prescribe | protect | treat

-ment	-ion
agreement	*accommodation*

3 **Quickly read the text in Exercise 4 and answer the questions.**

1 What examples of music therapy does the text mention?
2 In what ways can music therapy help?
3 Which of the words in capitals on the right is not a verb?
4 Which gap needs a plural noun?

OPTIMISE YOUR EXAM

Word formation

- Always read the text all the way through before filling the gaps.
- Then, for each gap, ask yourself what kind of word you need (noun, adjective, etc.).
- If you need a noun, is it singular or plural? Is it positive or negative?

4 **Write a form of the word in capitals in each gap to complete the text.**

Music therapy: music as medicine!

If you're sick, the doctor might give you a **(1)** ___________ for some medicine. **PRESCRIBE** If you're very ill, you might need an **(2)** ___________ to get better. But these **OPERATE** aren't the only **(3)** ___________ . Sometimes, **TREAT** music can help us to recover. Doctors now know that music isn't just about **(4)** ___________ . **ENTERTAIN**

Millie, 15, is recovering from a very serious **(5)** ___________ . She's receiving music **ILL** therapy, which involves writing lyrics, making recordings and watching music videos. Her music therapist says it helps reduce stress, which helps her body heal faster.

Some children and teenagers have problems with **(6)** ___________ . **COMMUNICATE** They find it difficult to express themselves. Music can really help them too. Even if they don't want to speak, they often get great **(7)** ___________ from singing. **ENJOY** Because of music, there's often an **(8)** ___________ in other parts of their **IMPROVE** lives too.

SAY IT RIGHT

Resource centre: Unit 5
Changing stress

1 In pairs or as a group, answer the questions.

1. What types of injuries can happen if you fall off a bike or skateboard?
2. Have you ever hurt yourself while doing sport or playing?

2 Read this story and answer the questions.

The Jump

Danny knew it was dangerous. But he was good at skateboarding and liked taking risks. Alex was standing at the bottom of the steps. Mel was filming on her phone.

'It's seven steps,' Danny thought. 'I can do this.' He set off. Suddenly, he was flying through the air.

Danny shouted, 'I've done it!' when he hit the ground. But then things went wrong. The skateboard went left, and he fell to the right.

Danny wasn't moving and his eyes were shut. Alex was very worried. 'Danny, are you OK?' he asked. 'Call an ambulance!' shouted Mel.
'No,' said Danny, opening his eyes. 'I'm fine. Just tell me you filmed it!'

1. Underline all the verbs in the past simple.
2. How many verbs are in the past continuous? For each one, discuss why it's past continuous and not past simple.
3. Find examples of the present simple. How many of them are in direct speech?
4. Find an example of the present perfect. Is it in direct speech?
5. Find two examples of the imperative. Are they in direct speech?

EXAM SKILL

Using narrative tenses

- The main narrative tense in a story is the past simple.
- You can also use the past continuous for background information, or an action taking place when another action happened.
- Be very careful with tenses in direct and reported speech.

3 This is the start of a story. Put each verb into the correct tense.

The Human Pyramid

Toby (1) ________________ (not / want) to do it, but he (2) ________________ (have) no choice. Four of his classmates (3) ________________ (kneel) on the ground. Three others (4) ________________ (be) on top of them. Two more then (5) ________________ (climb) on them. Toby (6) ________________ (have) to be at the top of the human pyramid.

'I really (7) ________________ (not / like) this,' he (8) ________________ (think). He (9) ________________ (not / want) to break his arm. He (10) ________________ (start) to climb.

OPTIMISE YOUR EXAM

A story

- Always plan your ideas before you start writing.
- Remember to use the first sentence to start your story.
- You should also use the first sentence to help you plan your story. For example, if the first sentence is *Danny knew it was dangerous*, ask yourself: Who is Danny? Where is he? What's he about to do? Why is it dangerous? Does he do it? Does he have an accident? What happens at the end?

4 **Look at this writing task and answer the questions.**

Your English teacher has asked you to write a story.
Your story must begin with this sentence:

Rebecca knew it was difficult, but she wanted to try.

Write your **story**.

Who is Rebecca? (a teenage girl? an adult?)	
Where is she?	
What does she want to try? Why is it difficult?	
Who is with her? What are they doing?	
Does she try to do it? What happens?	

5 **Plan** **Make a paragraph plan.**

Part	Possible plan	My plan	My notes
Paragraph 1	start with the exact sentence they've given you, set the scene: who else is there? what are they doing?		
Paragraph 2	describe the beginning of the attempt: how is Rebecca feeling?		
Paragraph 3	describe the end of the attempt: was it successful?		
Paragraph 4	describe what happened at the end: what was the final outcome? who was there?		

6 **Write** **Write your story in an appropriate style. Write about 100 words.**

7 **Check** **Before you hand in your story, complete this checklist.**

Checklist

- ◯ I've started with the sentence I was given.
- ◯ I've written at least four paragraphs.
- ◯ I've used a variety of tenses.
- ◯ I've included some direct speech.
- ◯ I've checked my spelling, grammar and punctuation.

▶ **Writing reference,** page 172 ▶ **Workbook Unit 5:** Writing, page 42, exercises 1, 2, 3, 4 and Progress check 5, page 43

6 A piece of cake!

READING | 4-option multiple choice | An article

1 **Look at the healthy-eating plate. In pairs, make a list of different types of food you know in English in each category.**

> **EXAM SKILL**
>
> **Identifying synonyms**
>
> - The text might use different words and phrases to express the idea in the question.
> - Underline key words and phrases in the question and look for synonyms (words and phrases that mean the same) in the text. For example, Exercise 3, question 5, option D says *Once a month*. The text might say *monthly* or *every four weeks*.

2 **Read these words and phrases from Exercise 3. Write a word or phrase from the text that means the same in each gap.**

1 famous ____________
2 getting things ready ____________
3 instructions for dishes ____________
4 family dinners ____________
5 filmed ____________
6 cook for themselves ____________

> **OPTIMISE YOUR EXAM**
>
> **4-option multiple choice**
>
> - Remember that the order of the questions follows the order of the information in the text.
> - This means that if you find the answer to question 1 and the answer to question 3, you know that the answer to question 2 comes somewhere in between.
> - Underline the answers to the questions in the text and number them to help you find any you aren't sure about.

A young star of the kitchen

Remember the anchovy and tomato pizza that you created? For most of us, it takes a long time to learn how to make something tasty, but not for Remmi Smith. Still a teenager, she's already creating fantastic dishes. She's also becoming well known for her Italian salad dressing, which is delicious. And with her knowledge of social media, she's making sure that everyone knows she's here!

Remmi, who lives in the USA, is just 16. She has already starred in two **cookery** shows and has published a book of healthy recipes. From the age of four, Remmi helped in the kitchen by preparing vegetables. By the age of seven, Remmi was a real **foodie** who could cook complete meals for her family.

Remmi, who was born in China, began making videos for fun. Her mother took videos of her while she was cooking and put them online. A local **cable channel** broadcast them. They then asked Remmi to create another show for them.

That show focused on Remmi's main interest, which is getting teenagers to take healthy eating seriously. She believes that when young people make their own food, they care more about what they eat. Remmi works with a company in the USA which shows her videos in school cafeterias. About 3.5 million students watch her every day!

Remmi believes that young people can create a healthy meal for their family which isn't expensive. Her **delicious** recipes include vegetable paella and strawberry kebabs. In fact, strawberries, which are Remmi's favourite food, appear in other recipes, including strawberry sandwich!

Her latest idea is a healthy-snack service. For a monthly **subscription** you receive snacks, which include fruit bars and popcorn, and fun cooking activities that help you develop a healthy **lifestyle**.

3 2.08 **Read the text again. For each question, choose the correct answer.**

1 Why is Remmi different from most of us?
  A She likes unusual pizza toppings.
  B She is famous in Italy.
  C She has learnt an important skill at a young age.
  D She knows about social media.

2 How did Remmi start cooking?
  A by getting things ready for cooking
  B by writing down instructions for dishes
  C by making family dinners
  D by starring in shows about food

3 What happened that introduced Remmi to a wider audience?
  A Her videos appeared on local TV.
  B Her mum filmed Remmi and showed the videos to family members.
  C She was asked to appear on a TV show.
  D She moved from China to America.

4 What does Remmi think about other young people?
  A They aren't interested in healthy eating.
  B They already love cooking and eat well.
  C They eat healthily when they cook for themselves.
  D They eat in cafeterias too often.

5 What might Remmi write on her blog about her new service?

  A Snacks aren't a part of healthy eating so I show people how to stop eating so many of them and eat more fruit instead.

  B People who eat too much popcorn can find out how to eat better from my cookery shows and my book.

  C I regularly put new videos online that show you how to make your own fruit bars and have fun at the same time.

  D Once a month, I send tasty food and interesting healthy-eating ideas to the people who pay for the service.

4 **Complete the sentences with highlighted words or phrases from the text.**

1 I'm a real ____________ . I love food and I'll try anything!
2 This cake is absolutely ____________ ! Could I have another slice?
3 I'm going to change my ____________ and start exercising regularly.
4 I pay a ____________ every month to get healthy snacks in the post.
5 I got the recipe from a ____________ book that I got from the library.
6 The ____________ has some really good programmes on this week.

THINK | RESEARCH | CULTURE | LEARN | **ME**

What are some of your favourite dishes? What dishes do you like cooking?

Grammar in context

Read these sentences from the article on page 59 and match each sentence to a description. Then underline other examples of relative clauses in the article.

1 *Remember the anchovy and tomato pizza **that you created**?* ____

2 *Remmi, **who lives in the USA**, is just 16.* ____

a) This relative clause identifies exactly which thing or person we are talking about.

b) This relative clause just gives us extra information about the thing or person we are talking about.

REMEMBER

- A relative clause tells us more about something. It starts with *which* (for things), *who* (for people), *that* (for people and things), *whose* (for possession), *where* (for places) or *when* (for time).
- A **defining relative clause** identifies which thing or person we are talking about. Without the relative clause, we don't know who we are referring to and the sentence may not make complete sense: *The pizza **that I made** was delicious!*
- In a defining relative clause, we don't use a comma and we can use *that* instead of *who* or *which*. We can also leave out the relative pronoun when it is the object of the clause: *The pizza I made was delicious!*
- In a **non-defining relative clause**, we already know which thing or person we are talking about and the relative clause just gives us extra information: *Pizza, **which is originally from Italy**, is one of my favourite dishes.*
- In a non-defining relative clause, we use a comma and we can't use *that* instead of *who* or *which*. We can't leave out the relative pronoun.

▶ **See Grammar reference, Unit 6,** page 153

1 Choose the correct relative clause.

1 **a)** My dad who does most of the cooking makes great curries.
  b) My dad, who does most of the cooking, makes great curries.

2 **a)** The French dish that I absolutely love is *crème brûlée*.
  b) The French dish, that I absolutely love, is *crème brûlée*.

3 **a)** I've been finding out about Remmi Smith, who is a young Chinese-American chef.
  b) I've been finding out about Remmi Smith who is a young Chinese-American chef.

4 **a)** This is the restaurant where we ate last week.
  b) This is the restaurant, where we ate last week.

2 Write a word from the box in each gap to complete the sentences. There may be more than one correct answer.

that	when	where	which	who	whose

1 The meal ____________ you made for us last night was delicious!

2 Do you remember the time ____________ you put sugar in the soup instead of salt?

3 Remmi Smith, ____________ show is called *Cook Time with Remmi*, loves cooking.

4 This is the restaurant ____________ we celebrated my mum's birthday.

5 Anchovies, ____________ I love, go really well on pizza.

6 Are there any celebrity chefs ____________ you admire?

3 Rewrite the sentences using the information given. Use a relative clause in each sentence.

1 Jamie Oliver was born in Essex. Essex is a county in England.
____

2 He first worked in the kitchens of a restaurant. His parents owned the restaurant.
____

3 His many cookery shows have appeared on TV around the world. They include *Jamie's School Dinners* and *Jamie at Home*.
____

4 *Jamie's School Dinners* tried to improve the quality of food. The food is served in schools.
____

5 It was hard to get pupils to eat well. The pupils didn't like eating vegetables.
____

6 In the end, he was successful and the government agreed to spend more on school meals. The government pays for school meals.
____

▶ **Workbook Unit 6:** Grammar 1, page 46, exercises 1, 2, 3

Words connected with *food*

1 2.09 **Write a word from the box in each gap. Listen and check.**

cake | chillies | coffee | crisps | curry | dark chocolate | lemon | lime | milk chocolate | orange | popcorn | strawberries

1 bitter: ___________
2 juicy: ___________
3 salty: ___________
4 sour: ___________
5 spicy: ___________
6 sweet: ___________

2 **Match the pictures to the verbs. Then use the words to describe how to make your favourite food.**

bake | barbecue | boil | fry | grill | microwave | roast

Phrasal verbs

3 2.10 **Match 1–8 to a–h to make sentences. Use the phrasal verbs in italics to help you. Listen and check.**

1 Next, you need to *chop* the tomatoes ____
2 Wait for your soup to *cool* ____
3 Recently, I've *cut* ____
4 Make sure you *eat* ____
5 I think I should probably *give* ____
6 Fruit juice starts to *go* ____
7 If it was up to him, my brother would *live* ____
8 There's no time to cook, so I'll *warm* ____

a) *up* sweets and crisps, at least for a while.
b) *up* all your vegetables, or there's no dessert!
c) *down* or you'll burn your mouth!
d) *up* the leftovers from last night's dinner.
e) *up* into very small pieces.
f) *down* on the amount of sugar I eat.
g) *on* takeaways and junk food!
h) *off* after being open in the fridge for a few days.

Adjectives/nouns/verbs

4 2.11 **Work out the anagrams and write forms of the word given. Listen and check.**

1 **fry**: a (**gfnyir**) ___________ pan, a (**iedfr**) ___________ egg
2 **mix**: a cake (**remtuix**) ___________ , (**idxme**) ___________ flavours, a (**gimnxi**) ___________ bowl
3 **spice**: a (**ysicp**) ___________ curry
4 **cream**: a (**ceyamr**) ___________ sauce, (**aedmcre**) ___________ corn
5 **blend**: a food (**erbndel**) ___________
6 **boil**: (**ibilgno**) ___________ hot, (**dobeil**) ___________ potatoes
7 **satisfy**: feel completely (**sfiiesatd**) ___________ , a (**tynissifag**) ___________ meal
8 **taste**: a (**aytst**) ___________ dish, ___________ (**ssteleats**) vegetables

5 **Write a form of the word in capitals in each gap.**

You might think the national dish of Great Britain is fish and chips, the famous combination of battered fish and (**1**) ___________ potatoes. Some people, though, say that chicken tikka masala is the true national dish! It's a combination of Indian food and British preferences. It's a popular, (**2**) ___________ dish, consisting of pieces of chicken that are served in a (**3**) ___________ tomato sauce. **FRY** **SPICE** **CREAM**

It contains a (**4**) ___________ of spices such as ginger, coriander and cumin, which are cooked and then mixed with tomatoes, yoghurt and cream, often in a (**5**) ___________ . The chicken is grilled and added to the sauce. The dish is then usually served with (**6**) ___________ rice. **MIX** **BLEND** **BOIL**

Nobody knows who first created this (**7**) ___________ curry, but some people think it first appeared in Scotland, in the 1970s. Others say that it has its origins in the (**8**) ___________ Indian dish, butter chicken. **SATISFY** **TASTE**

SAY IT RIGHT
Resource centre: Unit 6
/aʊə/, /əʊə/

1 **In pairs or as a group, answer the questions.**

1 Describe what is happening in the photo.
2 Would you like to take part in a competition like this?

EXAM SKILL

Recognising similar meaning

- With sentence completion listening tasks, you might not hear many of the words in the questions. What you'll hear is the same idea expressed in a different way.
- For example, in Exercise 3, number 1, it says *contained over …* in the question, but you won't hear this phrase in the recording. Instead, you'll hear *had more than … in it*.

2 **Find words or phrases in Exercise 3 which match these definitions.**

1 had more than ____________
2 a type of bread ____________
3 less difficult to get down ____________
4 grilling or frying ____________
5 preparation ____________

OPTIMISE YOUR EXAM

Gap fill

- You will hear the exact words you need to fill the gaps.
- Don't change the form of the words you hear into a different form. Use the word or phrase exactly as you hear it.

3 2.12 **You are going to listen to someone talking about food world records. For each question, write the correct answer in the gap. Write one or two words or a number or a date or a time.**

FOOD WORLD RECORDS

The largest cheeseburger weighed 913.54 kg and contained over 18 kg of **(1)** ____________ .

The burger took four hours to cook and the bun took **(2)** ____________ .

The record for burger eating is 12 burgers in **(3)** ____________ .

Making the burger **(4)** ____________ makes it easier to eat.

Before grilling, **(5)** ____________ is 110 g.

Training for a competition involves eating and **(6)** ____________ .

4 2.12 **Listen again and check your answers.**

THINK | **RESEARCH** | CULTURE | LEARN | ME

Find out about some more amazing food world records. Tell the class what you discover.

Grammar in context

Look at this sentence from the audio in the listening lesson on page 62. Explain why each underlined phrase uses *a*, *the* or no article.

Many of us love to eat a hamburger once in a while, but the world's biggest cheeseburger was enough to feed hundreds of people!

REMEMBER

- We use *a* with singular countable nouns (when we are not being specific or when we mention something for the first time): *Do you have **a** good cookery book?*
- Before a vowel sound, we use *an*: *Do you have **an** Indian cookery book?*
- When we want to be specific, we use *the* with singular countable nouns (*Where's **the** cookery book I gave you?*), with plural countable nouns (*Where are **the** cookery books I gave you?*) and with uncountable nouns (*Did you follow **the** advice in the cookery book?*).
- We can also use *the* with singular uncountable nouns when we are talking generally: ***The** information in the recipe was wrong.*
- We usually use *the* when there is only one of something: ***the** world, **the** Earth, **the** Queen of England*, etc.
- When we are talking generally, we use no article with plural countable nouns (*I love peaches!*) or with uncountable nouns (*Rice is an important part of many people's diet.*).

▶ **See Grammar reference, Unit 6,** page 154

1 Choose the correct article. If no article is necessary, choose the dash (–).

There's (1) **an / the** unusual fruit from (2) **the / –** south-east Asia called (3) **a / the** durian fruit. It has such (4) **a / the** bad smell that it is banned from (5) **the / –** public transport in many places. Some people say it smells like (6) **the / –** rotten onions, but (7) **a / the** taste is completely different. When they try it, (8) **the / –** people often say it tastes of (9) **the / –** sweet custard with (10) **an / –** almonds.

2 Find and underline the mistake in each sentence. Explain why they are incorrect.

1 When we went to the Thailand, my brother tried durian fruit, but I thought the smell was awful!
2 Did you know carrot was originally purple or white and people first grew them in the area around Afghanistan?
3 Some people eat insects, such as grasshoppers, but the only time I've eaten the insect is when I accidentally swallowed a fly!
4 Honey is almost the only food that will never go bad, and the jar of it with the lid on can last forever.

3 Write the correct article in each gap. If no article is necessary, put a dash (–).

Amazing food facts!

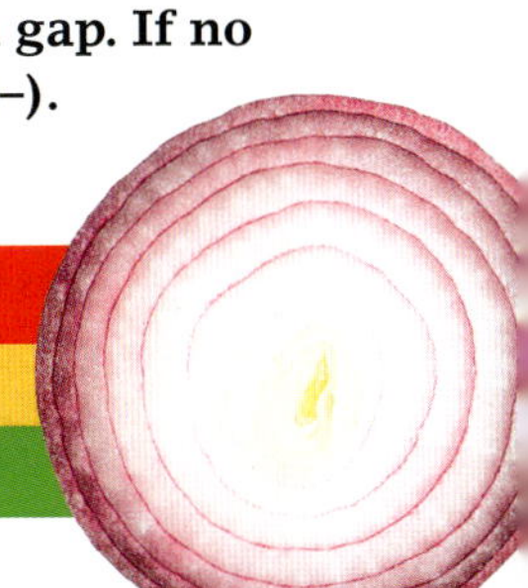

- Apples, onions and potatoes all taste (**1**) ___________ same! It's (**2**) ___________ smell that makes them different. Try biting into (**3**) ___________ apple, (**4**) ___________ onion and (**5**) ___________ potato while holding your nose. You won't be able to tell (**6**) ___________ difference!

- Sweets are often covered in (**7**) ___________ same material that people use to wax their cars! Carnauba wax comes from (**8**) ___________ leaves of (**9**) ___________ carnauba palm tree from (**10**) ___________ Brazil. You can find it in (**11**) ___________ floor polish and in (**12**) ___________ chewy, fruit-flavoured sweets!

- A lot of (**13**) ___________ fruit juice, (**14**) ___________ yoghurt and (**15**) ___________ ice cream has (**16**) ___________ red food colouring added to give it (**17**) ___________ bright red colour. One common red food colouring is carmine, which is made from (**18**) ___________ bodies of (**19**) ___________ insects from (**20**) ___________ South America!

THINK | RESEARCH | CULTURE | LEARN | ME

Why do you think honey never goes off? Have a guess, then check with your teacher.

▶ **Workbook Unit 6:** Grammar 2, page 47, exercises 1, 2

Talk2Me
The photo shows a ...

Flipped classroom

1 **Watch the *Talk2Me* video and answer the questions.**

1 Does Jamie's dad plan to cook a meal or buy a takeaway?
2 Why is Maddy taking photos of her school lunch?
3 Why is pizza good 'movie food'?

2 **Watch the video again. Number the phrases in the *Phrase expert* box in the order that you hear them on the video.**

PHRASE EXPERT

The photo shows (a ...) | It looks like (a ... / it's ...) | I think (they're in a ...) | The photo was (probably/possibly) taken in (a ...) | The people are/seem to be (+ *-ing*) | It looks like they're (+ *-ing*) | They're probably (+ *-ing*)

3 **In pairs or as a group, brainstorm as many words and phrases as possible related to the photo.**

EXAM SKILL

Describing situations and actions

- Be careful with tenses. Use the present simple to describe the general situation and the people and places that you can see in the photo, e.g. *The restaurant has a lot of tables.*
- Use the present continuous to say what's happening in the photo, e.g. *They're eating in a restaurant. Everyone is laughing and talking.*
- Try to use one or two adverbs to describe how people are doing things, e.g. *The waiter is serving the food carefully.*

4 2.13 **Complete the sentences to describe the photo in Exercise 3 using the present continuous or simple. Then listen and check your answers.**

1 The family ____________________ (**have**) dinner at home together.
2 It looks like it ____________________ (**be**) somebody's birthday. There are balloons and a cake.
3 The cake ____________________ (**look**) delicious.
4 I think the girl ____________________ (**open**) a present.
5 Everyone seems to ____________________ (**have**) a good time.

OPTIMISE YOUR EXAM

Extended turn (photos)

- Ask yourself questions to help you focus on the photo, for example, *Who/What is it a photo of? Where was it taken? What's happening in the photo?*
- Answer these questions when you describe the photo.

5 **Describe this photo. Talk on your own for about a minute.**

LANGUAGE IN USE | 4-option multiple-choice cloze

1 **In pairs, ask and answer the questions.**

1 Have you eaten food from other countries? Which countries?

2 What cuisine is your favourite? What do you like about it?

EXAM SKILL

Collocations

- Some words often appear together to make phrases. These are called **collocations**.
- A collocation might be noun + noun (e.g. *cookery book*), verb + noun (e.g. *make a meal*), adjective + noun (e.g. *fried egg*), or other combinations of words.
- Try to learn some common collocations.

2 **Read the underlined phrases in each sentence (1–6). For each one, choose the word or phrase (a–f) that means the same.**

1 We tried a wide variety of amazing food when we were on holiday. ____

2 My brother fell ill after eating some fish that wasn't fresh. ____

3 I'm really looking forward to trying the food when we're in Brazil! ____

4 How can I make a meal when we don't have any food in the house? ____

5 Isn't the Chinese restaurant in the opposite direction? ____

6 What do you think Greek food and Turkish food have in common? ____

a) the other way
b) share
c) a lot of different types
d) became sick
e) cook
f) excited to think about

3 **Quickly read the text in Exercise 4 and answer the questions.**

1 Why did Europeans not eat potatoes before 1492?

2 What food and animals went from the New World to the Old World?

3 What food and animals went from the Old World to the New World?

4 Apart from food and animals, what else did Europeans bring to the New World?

OPTIMISE YOUR EXAM

4-option multiple-choice cloze

- Sometimes the missing word is part of a collocation. Look at the words on both sides of the gap to work out what phrase is missing.
- Say the phrase using each of the four possible answers. Perhaps you have heard the collocation before. Which word sounds the best? Choose that word as your answer.

4 **Choose the correct word to fill each gap.**

THE COLUMBIAN EXCHANGE

Italian food is famous and the **(1)** ____ world enjoys pasta with tomato sauce. Many people who visit the UK **(2)** ____ forward to trying fish and chips. And Belgium makes great chocolate. But what do tomatoes, potatoes and chocolate **(3)** ____ in common? None of them existed in Europe until Christopher Columbus went to the Americas!

In 1492, Columbus arrived in the Americas. Over the years, a **(4)** ____ variety of food and animals were exchanged between the New World (the Americas) and the Old World (Europe, Africa and Asia). Europeans learnt how to **(5)** ____ meals with corn, beans, turkey and chilli peppers. In return, they sent coffee, onions, bananas and other fruit in the **(6)** ____ direction. They also introduced horses, cattle and sheep to the Americas.

Unfortunately, Europeans also brought diseases with them to the Americas, and many Americans fell ill. After the Columbian Exchange, the world would never be the same again.

	A	B	C	D
1	**A** whole	**B** complete	**C** total	**D** final
2	**A** come	**B** go	**C** look	**D** run
3	**A** do	**B** get	**C** have	**D** take
4	**A** big	**B** long	**C** high	**D** wide
5	**A** build	**B** make	**C** join	**D** put
6	**A** opposite	**B** back	**C** behind	**D** backward

THINK | **RESEARCH** | CULTURE | LEARN | ME

Find out if there are any types of food, plants or animals you have in your country as a result of the Columbian Exchange. Tell the class what you learnt.

▶ **Vocabulary reference,** page 165 ▶ **Workbook Unit 6:** Language in Use, page 49, exercises 1, 2

1 **In pairs or groups, answer the questions.**

1 Describe the photos. What occasion do you think it might be?

2 What was the last family party you went to? Describe it.

EXAM SKILL

Making suggestions

- When you write an email, you sometimes need to make suggestions to the person you're writing to if they have asked for your ideas or advice.
- Use words and phrases such as *Maybe/Perhaps you should/could …, How/What about -ing …?, If I were you, I'd …, One thing you could do is …, Don't forget to …*

2 **Read Grace's email and Nick's notes. Decide if the statements are T (True) or F (False).**

From: Grace
To: Nick
Subject: Family dinner

Hi Nick!

We're having a family dinner for my mum's birthday next week. — *Fun!*

My brothers and I are each going to cook a course. Do you think I should make the starter, the main course or the dessert? — *Suggest …*

Where can I find some good recipes? — *Tell Grace*

Have you ever made anything for your family? What did you make? Was it a success? — *Describe*

Love,

Grace

In his reply, Nick should …

1 say that the dinner sounds like fun. **T / F**

2 say what course Grace should make. **T / F**

3 tell Grace how to cook a dish. **T / F**

4 describe something he once cooked. **T / F**

3 **Read Nick's reply. Find four places where he makes suggestions and write the phrases he uses.**

From: Nick
To: Grace
Subject: RE: Family dinner

Hi Grace,

Thanks for your email. The family dinner for your mum's birthday sounds like a lot of fun!

If I were you, I'd make a dessert. Desserts are easier than main courses, and tastier than starters! What about making a cheesecake?

It's easy to find recipes on the internet. Why not go online and type the name of the dish you want to make and see what comes up?

I don't cook much, but I once made a pizza. I used tomato sauce, cheese and olives, and it was a great success! You could make that for your family another time.

Good luck!

Love,
Nick

1 ______________________

2 ______________________

3 ______________________

4 ______________________

OPTIMISE YOUR EXAM

An email

- If you have to make suggestions in your email, make notes about the things you are going to suggest before you start writing.
- Then think of reasons for each suggestion. For example, if you are going to suggest someone makes a dish from your country, the reasons might be because it's spicy/unusual/traditional, etc.

4 Look at this writing task and complete the sentences with your own ideas.

Read this email from your friend Freya and the notes you have made.

From: Freya
Subject: Class party

Hi

Our class is having a party next weekend and I have to make some food for it! — *Great!*

I could make something simple or try to do something more adventurous!
What do you think? — *Give opinion*

Do you think people would prefer something sweet or something healthy? — *Tell Freya*

Can you suggest something from your country I could make? — *Suggest …*

Love,
Freya

Write your **email** to Freya using **all the notes**.

1 Freya should make something **simple / more adventurous** because ______________________ .
2 People would prefer something **sweet / healthy** because ______________________ .
3 I suggest Freya makes ______________ , because ______________ and ______________ .

5 Plan Make a paragraph plan.

Part	Purpose	Useful phrases	My notes
First line	greet the person you are writing to	*Dear …, Hi …*	
Paragraph 1	write about the first note on the email	*… sounds great!* *… sounds like a lot of fun!*	
Paragraph 2	write about the second note on the email	*I think you should …* *I suggest you …*	
Paragraph 3	write about the third note on the email	*I think that …* *You should …*	
Paragraph 4	write about the fourth note on the email	*What about -ing …?* *Why don't you …?*	
Closing expressions 1	wish them luck, ask them to reply, say goodbye	*Good luck! Write soon! Bye for now!*	
Closing expressions 2	express friendship	*Love, Lots of love, Best wishes,*	
Your name	first name		

6 Write Write your email to Freya in an appropriate style. Use all the notes. Write about 100 words.

7 Check Before you hand in your email, complete this checklist.

Checklist

- ◯ I've written an informal email.
- ◯ I've followed my paragraph plan.
- ◯ I've started and ended my email the right way.
- ◯ I've written about all four notes in the exam task and developed them further.
- ◯ I've checked my spelling, grammar and punctuation.

▶ **Writing reference,** page 173 ▶ **Workbook Unit 6:** Writing, page 50, exercises 1, 2, 3, 4 and Progress check 6, page 51

PROGRESS CHECK UNITS 5–6

GRAMMAR AND VOCABULARY

1 Choose the correct word or phrase.

1 I **can** / **could** read when I was three years old.
2 I don't think you **should** / **might** watch this film. It's scary!
3 You **don't have to** / **mustn't** come shopping with me, but you can if you want to.
4 I hope we'll **can** / **be able to** visit you again soon.
5 I **can** / **could** get a new phone for my birthday – if I'm lucky!
6 My mum's gone shopping, but she **should** / **can** be back soon.
7 Fran **mustn't** / **can't** be away on holiday. I saw her this morning!

__/7

2 Write a relative pronoun or adverb in each gap. Use each one only once.

1 That's the restaurant ___________ they make great salads.
2 Do you remember the time ___________ Liam fell in the lake?
3 My best friend, ___________ mum is a food journalist, is excellent at cooking.
4 I can't find the recipe ___________ you gave me.
5 My best friend, ___________ is a top chef, is going to be on a cookery show.
6 Pasta, ___________ is my favourite food, is easy to prepare.

__/6

3 Match to make collocations.

1 set ____ a) world
2 fall ____ b) variety
3 look ____ c) foot in
4 a wide ____ d) direction
5 the whole ____ e) forward to
6 the opposite ____ f) ill

__/6

4 If a word or phrase in bold is correct, put a tick. If it's incorrect, rewrite it correctly in each gap.

1 It took me about two weeks to completely **make** over that cold. ___________
2 It was so hot in the school assembly, I nearly **passed** out. ___________
3 I've got a terrible headache. I hope I'm not **arriving** down with flu. ___________
4 You can't **live** on junk food! You have to eat fruit and vegetables regularly. ___________
5 The cakes are still hot. Wait for them to **cold** down first. ___________
6 **Happy** up! It's not the end of the world. It's just an English test. ___________
7 Don't go to school if you don't **feel** up to it. ___________
8 We should all **reduce** down on how much sugar we consume. ___________

__/8

5 Write *do, have, make* or *take* in each gap.

1 __________ care of
2 __________ an effort
3 __________ fun of
4 __________ homework/housework
5 __________ flu
6 __________ up your mind
7 __________ your teeth/hair
8 __________ a mistake

__/8

6 Write a form of the word in capitals in each gap.

1	Have you made a __________ yet?	**DECIDE**
2	This soup is __________ hot. I can't eat it yet!	**BOIL**
3	That cake was really __________ ! Can I have some more, please?	**TASTE**
4	The doctor gave me a __________ for antibiotics.	**PRESCRIBE**
5	Pour the oil into a __________ pan.	**FRY**
6	I'm not very keen on __________ food.	**SPICE**
7	The __________ at the event was fantastic!	**ENTERTAIN**
8	What __________ do we need to go camping?	**EQUIP**

__/8

7 Write the correct article in each gap. If no article is necessary, put a dash (–).

1 The hotel provides __________ accommodation for up to 300 people.
2 Do you need __________ orange to make that dessert?
3 __________ bandages are what you use to wrap around an injury.
4 We went to __________ best Japanese restaurant in town last night.
5 __________ honey is 80% sugars and 20% water.
6 I can't find __________ blender. I used it last night!
7 Do you have __________ food delivery subscription? You receive food and recipes every week.

__/7

Total score __/50

EXAM SKILLS

Tick the statements that are true for you. Review the skills in the unit if you need more help.

I can …	Unit/page
☐ find information that is paraphrased in an online article	Unit 5 p48
☐ recognise synonyms in a formal conversation	Unit 5 p52
☐ talk about habits in an interview	Unit 5 p54
☐ understand how nouns are formed and use them in word formation exercises	Unit 5 p55
☐ use narrative tenses in a story	Unit 5 p56
☐ identify synonyms in an article	Unit 6 p58
☐ recognise similar meaning in a short talk	Unit 6 p62
☐ describe situations and actions in a photo	Unit 6 p64
☐ form collocations and use them in a multiple-choice cloze activity	Unit 6 p65
☐ make suggestions in an email	Unit 6 p66

7 Shop till you drop!

READING | Gapped text | A magazine article

1 In pairs or as a group, answer the questions.

1 How many different types of shop can you think of? Make a list.

2 What are your favourite types of shop? What can you buy there?

2 Read the article quickly, ignoring the gaps and the removed sentences. Make notes to answer the questions.

1 Who sells things at these markets?

2 What does Adam Enan sell?

3 Who is Aidan McCallum?

EXAM SKILL

Understanding time words and phrases

- Time words and phrases help us understand when things happen. For example, the sentence before gap 5 in the article starts with *Before*. This sentence tells us that something happened in the past that doesn't happen today.
- With gapped text tasks, look for time words and phrases in the sentences before or after the gap or in the removed sentences. These words/phrases can help you choose the right sentence to complete the gap.

3 Decide which four sentences *could* fill the gap. Use the words in bold to help you.

At first, she only sold jewellery. ____ **Today**, she sells a wide variety of clothing, jewellery and other accessories.

a) **Since then**, she's started selling other things too.

b) She'll probably start selling other things **in the future**.

c) **Then**, she started selling other things as well.

d) She **soon** started selling other things too.

e) But she **immediately** realised she could sell other things too.

f) **Before**, she had also started selling other things.

OPTIMISE YOUR EXAM

Gapped text

- When you've chosen a removed sentence to fill a gap, put a tick next to it. This will help you make sure you don't use it again by mistake.
- Do the easiest gaps first. If you're not sure which sentence fills a gap, go on to the next one. Come back to the most difficult ones at the end.

TEENAGERS TAKE OVER THE MARKET

by Jess Owen

'Teenagers today are lazy and just play video games.' 'People only shop online these days.' Teenage Markets show us that neither of these statements is true. (**1**) ____ There, they browse and buy from market stalls – all run by teenagers.

Adam Enan, 16, runs Yummy Candles, a stall which sells luxury soaps and candles. Abigail Howard, 13, sells accessories for the house and garden. (**2**) ____ From clothing to comics, there's a wide variety of products on offer. Several teenage artists exhibit and sell at the markets, including Aidan McCallum, who's 13. (**3**) ____ 'I've taken part in many exhibitions and craft fairs, and I also sell my work in a shop,' he said. 'By doing this, even more people will see my pictures.'

The Teenage Market was the idea of two teenage brothers, Joe and Tom Barratt. They had heard about a successful event called the Vintage Village, where people sell vintage items. They wondered if a similar event run by teenagers could work. They posted a video on social media, asking for interested teenagers to apply. 'For our first event, we had 70 applications!' said Joe. '(**4**) ____'

Their first market was a success, leading to more appearing around Britain. They give teenagers experience running businesses and also help local areas. Before, some town centres had been empty on Sundays. (**5**) ____ And having more people spending money there helps the local economy too.

If you're a teenage entrepreneur, the Teenage Market can help you find customers, promote your products and make sales. To get involved, just create a profile on the Teenage Market website and then apply to take part in upcoming events.

4 2.14 **Read the text again. Five sentences have been removed from the text. For each question, choose the correct answer. There are three extra sentences which you do not need to use.**

A We immediately realised there were young people out there with the right skills and creative talent.
B Since then, they've learnt what shoppers want to buy.
C Of course, these teenagers will be adult shoppers in the future.
D They're just two of many teenagers who sell their products at a Teenage Market.
E Not many people were interested at first.
F Now, they're fun and lively places to visit.
G At weekends in the UK, shoppers are visiting their local Teenage Market.
H He had been selling his work for several years before he joined the Teenage Market.

5 **Write a highlighted word from the text to match each definition.**

1 something from the past which is old but interesting and attractive ____________
2 future ____________
3 tables used for selling things ____________
4 look at things which are on sale ____________
5 advertise ____________
6 businessperson ____________

THINK | RESEARCH | CULTURE | LEARN | ME

Imagine you are going to have a stall at a Teenage Market. Create your own profile. What would you sell?

7 GRAMMAR 1 | Past perfect simple and continuous

Grammar in context

Read these extracts from the article on page 71 and then put the verbs into the correct tense.

1 *The Teenage Market was the idea of two teenage brothers, Joe and Tom Barratt. They ___________ **(hear)** about a successful event called the Vintage Village …*

2 *Before, some town centres ___________ **(be)** empty on Sundays.*

3 *He ___________ **(sell)** his work for several years before he joined the Teenage Market.*

Look at the sentences. In pairs, ask and answer these questions.

Sentence 1: *heard* isn't wrong here, but *had heard* makes something clearer. What?

Sentence 2: Could we say *were* instead of *had been* here?

Sentence 3: Could we say *had sold* instead of *had been selling* here? What about *sold*?

REMEMBER

- We use the past perfect simple for actions and situations that started or happened before another moment in the past: *I **had visited** three shops before I found a watch I liked.*

visited 1st shop ↑ visited 2nd shop ↑ visited 3rd shop ↑ found a watch ↑

- We use the past perfect continuous to emphasise the continuing progress of actions and situations that started or happened before another moment in the past: *I **had been looking** for hours before I found a present for Mum.*

started looking ↑ still looking ↑ found a present ↑

- Sometimes we can choose whether to use past perfect or past simple: *I (**had**) **visited** four stalls before I found a bag I liked.*

▶ **See Grammar reference, Unit 7,** page 154

1 Read the sentences and decide which action happened first. Choose the correct option.

1 I'd bought the shoes before I went on holiday.
   a) I bought the shoes.
   b) I went on holiday.

2 When I went on holiday, I bought the shoes.
   a) I bought the shoes.
   b) I went on holiday.

3 When I went to Tunisia, I'd already bought a great T-shirt.
   a) I bought the T-shirt.
   b) I went to Tunisia.

4 I bought a great T-shirt after I came back from Tunisia.
   a) I bought it.
   b) I came back.

5 I broke my glasses just after I'd cleaned them.
   a) I broke them.
   b) I cleaned them.

6 She'd been thinking about buying a bike before she saw Jenny's.
   a) She saw Jenny's bike.
   b) She was thinking about buying a bike.

2 Put the verbs into the correct tense, past simple, past perfect simple or past perfect continuous. Sometimes more than one answer is correct.

My trip to Istanbul

by Ben Tyler, Year 9

Last summer, my family and I (**1**) ___________ (**go**) to Istanbul for a week. I (**2**) ___________ (**never** / **visit**) Turkey before, so I was very excited. It was a fantastic trip!

We stayed in a hotel in Sultanhamet. The first evening, we went to a restaurant nearby. The food was even more delicious than I (**3**) ___________ (**expect**)! The next morning, we went to Topkapi Palace and the Blue Mosque. They were both amazing!

We (**4**) ___________ (**walk**) for several hours by the time we got to the Grand Bazaar, so we were a little tired, but it was definitely worth visiting. It's an incredible place, with over 5,000 shops. My mum (**5**) ___________ (**say**) for months that she wanted to find some jewellery there. I (**6**) ___________ (**hope**) to find a vintage watch. We (**7**) ___________ (**look**) around for about half an hour when we (**8**) ___________ (**find**) a jewellery shop. My mum (**9**) ___________ (**buy**) a lovely necklace, and I got a watch that's more than 100 years old. Luckily, I had enough money because I (**10**) ___________ (**save up**) my pocket money for several months.

 ▶ **Workbook Unit 7:** Grammar 1, page 54, exercises 1, 2, 3

Words connected with *shopping*

1 2.15 **Write a word or phrase from the box in each gap. Listen and check.**

cash card | change | voucher

1 ___________ : coins, or the money you get back when you buy something
2 ___________ : an official piece of paper that you can use instead of money
3 ___________ : people use this to take money out of a bank machine

bargain | brand-new | half price second-hand | special offer

4 If it's ___________ , it's usually 50% cheaper.
5 If it's a ___________ , it's very cheap.
6 If it's on ___________ , it's cheaper than usual.
7 If it's ___________ , someone has owned it before.
8 If it's ___________ , it hasn't been used before.

cost | exchange | order | rent | return

9 The bike isn't in stock, but we can ___________ it for you.
10 This jumper's too small. Can I ___________ it for a bigger one, please?
11 I got two of these for my birthday, so can I ___________ one of them?
12 Are you going to buy the film or just ___________ it?
13 How much does this phone ___________ ?

Phrasal verbs

2 2.16 **Each of the words in bold is in the wrong sentence. Write the correct word in each gap and then listen and check.**

1 I'm going to **get** ___________ *up* my pocket money and buy a new comic.
2 If you **pay** ___________ *around*, I'm sure you'll find a bargain somewhere else.
3 These shoes are really uncomfortable so I'm going to **run** ___________ them *back*.
4 If you lend me the money for the ticket, I'll **add** ___________ you *back* tomorrow.
5 My uncle doesn't earn much money, and he finds it difficult to **give** ___________ *by* on his salary.
6 We don't want to **shop** ___________ *out of* snacks during the picnic, so let's get some more now.
7 With all the desserts, the bill will **save** ___________ *up to* at least €50.
8 I've got too many clothes so I'm going to **take** ___________ some *away* to charity.

Idioms for *shopping and spending*

3 2.17 **For each idiom, choose the best meaning. Listen and check.**

1 We're going to *shop till we drop* tomorrow!
a) try not to drop bags
b) go shopping for a long time

2 The cheapest kind of shopping is *window shopping*!
a) looking but not buying
b) buying windows

3 Dana won the lottery so *she went on a spending spree.*
a) bought lots of things
b) stopped buying things

4 Their youngest kid was rushing around *like a bull in a china shop*!
a) likely to cause damage
b) very carefully

5 I'm celebrating, so the pizza *is on me* tonight!
a) I'm paying
b) I'm holding it

SAY IT RIGHT

Resource centre: Unit 7
Short vowels

7 LISTENING | 3-option multiple choice (pictures)

1 **In pairs or as a group, answer the questions.**

1 When you go shopping, what kind of shops do you spend most time in?
2 Do you like window shopping, or do you prefer buying things?

2 2.18 **You will hear four short extracts. Match each speaker to a situation.**

1 ____ a) shopping at a Teenage Market
2 ____ b) shopping in the sales
3 ____ c) window shopping
4 ____ d) online shopping

EXAM SKILL

Understanding relevant information

- Pay attention to who's speaking, who they're talking to, and what their relationship is.
- It's also important to understand when the speakers are talking about other people rather than themselves.

3 2.19 **Listen to the complete extracts and make notes to answer the questions.**

Situation 1:
1 Who is the woman? ______________
2 Who is Tim? ______________
3 Who's older, Dan or Tim? ______________

Situation 2:
4 Who is going to order something online? ______________

Situation 3:
5 Who is 13? ______________

Situation 4:
6 Who is Jack with? ______________
7 Who do they look for at the end? ______________

OPTIMISE YOUR EXAM

3-option multiple choice (pictures)

- You'll hear information about all three pictures.
- Only one picture is the correct answer, so ask yourself why that picture is right and why the other two are wrong.

4 **Can you remember what the speakers said? For each question, choose the correct answer. Make a guess if you aren't sure.**

1 What do they decide to get Tim?

A

B

C

2 What does Aisha decide to try on?

A

B

C

3 What did Karen like the most?

A

B

C

4 How does Jack's mum pay for his shoes?

A

B

C

5 2.19 **Listen again and check your answers.**

Grammar in context

Read these extracts from the audio in the listening lesson on page 74 and then complete the words in the sentences. The first letter is there to help you.

1 *He's two years y__________ than you.*
2 *I knew you'd be better at this t__________ me!*
3 *It was one of the b__________ paintings I've ever seen.*
4 *They're m__________ comfortable than the shoes I'm wearing now.*

REMEMBER

- We use comparative adjectives and adverbs to show that things or people are different or separate from each other: *This phone's **better than** that one. / This guitar's **more expensive than** that one. / Those trainers are **less expensive than** these.*
- We use superlative adjectives and adverbs to show that one member of a group is at the top or bottom of the group: *This is **the best** camera in the shop. / This is **the most attractive** painting in the gallery. / This is **the least colourful** lamp on the stall.*
- We can also use (***not***) ***as*** … ***as*** to make comparisons: *This MP3 player isn't **as heavy as** that one. / This watch is **as cheap as** that one.*

▶ **See Grammar reference, Unit 7,** page 155

1 Choose the correct word.

1 These trainers are much nicer **from** / **than** those.
2 This is **the** / **a** best restaurant I've ever been to.
3 In fact, the tickets cost **less** / **little** than I'd expected.
4 Staying in a hotel will be a lot **much** / **more** comfortable than sleeping in a tent!
5 I'm not as good **is** / **as** my sister at saving money.
6 That was the **worst** / **worse** pizza I've ever eaten!

2 Complete each sentence using the word in brackets so that it has a similar meaning to the first sentence.

The supermarket is far away but our local shop is close.

1 Our local shop is ______________ the supermarket. (**than**)
2 Our local shop is ______________ the supermarket. (**not**)
3 The supermarket is ______________ our local shop. (**than**)
4 The supermarket is ______________ our local shop. (**not**)
5 Our local shop is ______________ to home. (**the**)
6 Of the two, the supermarket is ______________ away. (**the**)

3 Write the comparative or superlative form of the word given. Add any words you need, such as *the* and *than*.

West Edmonton Mall

- West Edmonton Mall, in Edmonton, Canada, is (**1**) ______________ (**large**) shopping centre in North America and one of (**2**) ______________ (**big**) in the whole world. Only ten or so other shopping centres are (**3**) ______________ (**large**).
- With more than 800 shops, it would take even (**4**) ______________ (**dedicate**) shopper more than three full days to visit each one.
- If you think amusement parks are a lot (**5**) ______________ (**enjoyable**) shopping, there's still plenty for you to do at West Edmonton Mall. It's got Galaxyland, the world's (**6**) ______________ (**large**) indoor amusement park. There you can ride on the Mindbender, one of (**7**) ______________ (**long**) and (**8**) ______________ (**high**) indoor rollercoasters in the world. The Mindbender is (**9**) ______________ (**long**) 48 blue whales lying end to end!
- If you're (**10**) ______________ (**interested**) in waterparks than rollercoasters you can visit World Waterpark. There are 17 water slides and one of (**11**) ______________ (**good**) and (**12**) ______________ (**powerful**) wave pools in the world!

THINK | RESEARCH | CULTURE | LEARN | ME

Have you ever been to a very large shopping centre? If yes, tell the class what you did and saw there. If no, would you like to? What do you think it would be like?

7 SPEAKING | General conversation

Flipped classroom

1 **Watch the *Talk2Me* video and answer the questions.**

1 Why doesn't Jamie like shopping?
2 What do the friends want to buy from the shopping centre?
3 What does Jamie like best about his old trainers?
4 What do Angus and Maddy do when they finish shopping?

2 **Watch the video again. Who uses which of the phrases in the *Phrase expert* box?**

> **PHRASE EXPERT**
> What do you think? | Why do you think that? | What's your opinion? | How about you? | Do you think/agree that …? | Personally, I … | I'm not sure … | That's a good question! | I agree with you.

3 **In pairs or groups, answer the questions.**

1 Do you get pocket money each week/month?
2 If you do, what do you spend it on? If you don't, when do you get money?
3 Do you prefer to spend or save the money you are given? Why?

> **EXAM SKILL**
> ## Asking questions
> - In a discussion, listen carefully to your partner and ask them questions about what they say.
> - *Wh-* questions (*who*, *what*, *where*, *why*, *when* or *how*) keep the conversation going better than questions where the answer is just *yes* or *no*.

4 2.20 **Complete the questions. Then listen to two students having a discussion and check your answers.**

1 __________ did you get her?
2 __________ you saved up for anything?
3 __________ much did it cost?
4 __________ you saving up for anything at the moment?
5 __________ do you think will give it to you?

5 **Which of the questions can you answer with *yes* or *no*? Can you think of *wh-* questions that you could ask instead?**

6 **In pairs or groups, do this task.**

> I'd like you to talk together about things that you have saved up to buy in the past, and things you're saving up to buy at the moment.

> **OPTIMISE YOUR EXAM**
> ## General conversation
> - Try giving your opinion in the form of a question. For example, instead of *I think …*, say *Do you think/agree that …?*

7 **In pairs, ask and answer these questions.**

1 Do you get enough pocket money each week? What's the right amount of money for someone your age?
2 Do you prefer going to shops or buying things online? Why?
3 What would you like to buy right now if you could afford it?
4 Do you like going shopping with your family? What about with your friends?
5 Do you like buying presents for other people? Do you find it easy to decide what to get them?
6 Have you ever bought something and then regretted buying it?

▶ **Workbook Unit 7:** Speaking, pages 56–57, exercises 1, 2, 3

LANGUAGE IN USE | Word formation

1 **In pairs, ask and answer the questions.**

1 What types of part-time jobs do teenagers do in your country?
2 How common is it for teenagers to have part-time jobs in your country?

REMEMBER

- Many job nouns are the same for men and women, e.g. *writer*, *doctor*, *teacher*.
- Some job nouns are only for men, e.g. *policeman*, *fireman*, *waiter* and some are only for women, e.g. *policewoman*, *actress*, *waitress*.
- However, we use *actor* for both men and women, and we often use *police officer* instead of *policeman* or *policewoman*, and *firefighter* instead of *fireman*, because it includes women.

2 **Complete the people nouns.**

1 assist____	**6** hairdress____	**11** mechan____	**16** sell____
2 buy____	**7** law____	**12** optic____	**17** shop____
3 cash____	**8** librar____	**13** own____	**18** supervis____
4 custom____	**9** manag____	**14** reception____	**19** visit____
5 electric____	**10** managing direct____	**15** salesman/sales____/ salesperson	**20** wait____/wait____

OPTIMISE YOUR EXAM

Word formation

- Remember that people nouns often end in *-er*, *-or* and *-ist*, but there are other endings too.
- These include *-ier*, *-yer*, *-ian* and *-ic*.

3 **Write a form of the word in capitals in each gap to complete the text.**

Part-time jobs for teenagers

In some countries, it's very common for teenagers to have a part-time job, often at the weekend.

Many teenagers work as shop (**1**) ____________ on Saturdays – usually the busiest shopping day. Whether it's in a shoe shop, bookshop or pet shop, they help the regular staff, and (**2**) ____________ too. **ASSIST** **CUSTOM**

In the UK, teens often work in cafés and restaurants as waiters and (**3**) ____________ . Others sometimes get a job at a hairdresser's, where they help keep the place clean and tidy, or help the (**4**) ____________ deal with appointments. **WAIT** **RECEPTION**

In tourist areas, it's possible to find a job at a tourist attraction. This might involve showing (**5**) ____________ round, or selling tickets. Of course, if you want to work as a (**6**) ____________ , you have to be good at maths, and very responsible with money. **VISIT** **CASH**

Many of these jobs involve dealing with the public, so good social skills are important. You have to be friendly and polite. You also have to be hardworking, and must be able to follow the instructions your (**7**) ____________ or manager gives you. **SUPERVISE**

Working part-time gives teenagers experience in the world of work, and they earn money too. Even if you want to be a doctor, teacher or (**8**) ____________ when you're older, working in a café or shop as a teenager can teach you a lot. **LAW**

1 In pairs or as a group, answer the questions.

1 What are the advantages/benefits of online shopping?
2 What are the disadvantages?

EXAM SKILL

Using direct speech

- In a story, we sometimes want to write the exact words someone says. This is called 'direct speech'.
- You need to know some rules for direct speech. The main ones appear in Exercise 4.

2 Put the paragraphs of this story in the correct order.

Paragraph 1: ____
Paragraph 2: ____
Paragraph 3: ____
Paragraph 4: ____

A *'Don't worry. We can buy the watch online,' said Aidan.*
'No, we can't! It's vintage and we have to buy it here!' she said.
'I think we'll be too late,' said Tom.

B *Jo looked at her brothers.*
'What shall we do now?' she asked.

C *It was a race against time for Jo, Aidan and Tom. They had missed the bus and the shop was going to close in five minutes. 'Hurry up!' shouted Jo at her brothers as they ran along the street.*

D *'Then Mum's birthday will be ruined and it will be our fault!' said Jo. And she started running faster. They got to the shop but it wasn't good news. The sign in the window said 'Closed'.*

3 Can you think of a good title for the story in Exercise 2?

4 Look at these examples and choose the correct word to complete the rules.

1 ✔ *'Hurry up!' shouted Jo at her brothers …*
✔ *'Hurry up!' Jo shouted at her brothers …*
When it's someone's name, or there's a noun (e.g. *her mum*), we **can** / **can't** choose which way round to write it: *asked Aidan* or *Aidan asked*, *said her mum* or *her mum said*.

2 ✔ *' … we have to buy it here!'* she said.
✘ *' … we have to buy it here!'* said she.
When it's a pronoun (e.g. *she*), we **can** / **can't** choose which way round to write it.

3 ✔ *' … we have to buy it here!'* she said.
'I think we'll be too late,' said Tom.
When a new person speaks, we **start** / **don't start** their speech on a new line.

4 ✔ *' … we can buy the watch online,'* said Aidan.
When there's no exclamation mark or question mark at the end of the direct speech, we put a **comma** / **full stop**.

5 ✔ *"What shall we do now?"* she asked.
✔ *'What shall we do now?'* she asked.
✘ *'What shall we do now?"* she asked.
We can use double inverted commas or single inverted commas for speech. We **don't have to** / **must** use the same ones all the way through the story.

6 ✔ The sign in the window said 'Closed'.
✘ The sign in the window said "Closed".
For quotes that aren't direct speech, we **can** / **can't** use double inverted commas.

OPTIMISE YOUR EXAM

A story

- You can give your story a title that will interest the reader and make them want to read it.
- Try to have four main paragraphs. The first paragraph sets the scene. The middle paragraphs are the main events, and the final paragraph tells us what happened at the end.

5 **Look at this writing task and answer the questions.**

> Your English teacher has asked you to write a story.
> Your story must begin with this sentence:
>
> *As soon as Paul saw it, he knew he wanted to buy it.*

Write your **story**.

Who is Paul? (a teenage boy? an adult?)

What does he see? ______

Why does he want it? ______

Who is with him? What are they doing? ______

What happens next? ______

6 **Plan** **Make a paragraph plan.**

Part	Possible plan	My plan	My notes
Title	give your story an interesting title		
Paragraph 1	start with the exact sentence you are given, and set the scene: what does he see? why does he want it?		
Paragraph 2	describe the main events		
Paragraph 3	describe the main events		
Paragraph 4	describe what happened at the end		

7 **Write** **Write your story in an appropriate style. Write about 100 words.**

8 **Check** **Before you hand in your story, complete this checklist.**

Checklist ✓

- ◯ I've given my story an interesting title.
- ◯ I've started with the sentence I was given.
- ◯ I've written at least four paragraphs.
- ◯ I've included some direct speech.
- ◯ I've followed the rules for direct speech.
- ◯ I've checked my spelling, grammar and punctuation.

▶ **Writing reference,** page 172 ▶ **Workbook Unit 7:** Writing, page 58, exercises 1, 2, 3, 4, 5 and Progress check 7, page 59

8 A sense of style

READING | Matching | A project report

1 In pairs or as a group, answer the questions.

Do you have any clothes made out of the materials in the box? When do you wear them?

cotton	denim	fur	leather	silk	wool

2 Read the text quickly and match each person (1–4) to an idea (a–d).

1 Robert ____
2 Jen ____
3 Lewis ____
4 Grace ____

a) be careful which companies you buy from
b) use clothes in a different way
c) how they make jeans
d) let someone else have your old clothes

EXAM SKILL

Understanding attitude and opinion

- Writers and speakers often use phrases such as *in my opinion*, *if you ask me*, *personally*, *to my mind*, *in my view* to introduce their own thoughts.
- In multiple-matching tasks, look out for opinion/attitude words and phrases as they can help you choose the correct answer.

3 Look at the text again. Find these phrases in the text and then answer the questions.

1 'In my opinion, …'

What is important?

____

2 'In my view, …'

Why is it great?

____

3 'If you ask me, …'

What should we do?

____

OPTIMISE YOUR EXAM

Matching

- When you find the answer to a question in the text, underline the relevant section and write the question number next to it. This will help you check your answers at the end.
- Do the easiest questions first. If you have one or two questions left at the end, try to find the answers in the parts of the text that you haven't underlined.

PROJECT FASHION! BY YEAR 8 STUDENTS

Our class has been doing a project on the fashion industry. Read on to find out what some of us discovered!

A Robert

Does your typical **outfit** have an effect on the environment? I wear jeans almost every day. Jeans are made of denim, which is a form of cotton. It takes a lot of water and chemicals to produce the cotton, which is then dyed (usually blue) and the **dye** often ends up in rivers. When making 'stonewashed' or faded jeans, volcanic stones are used to 'hit' the denim. Those stones are shipped around the world, using a lot of fossil fuel. Even a simple pair of jeans causes environmental problems!

C Jen

The fashion industry causes some environmental problems. The idea that we can do something about the problems the fashion industry causes is called 'ethical fashion'. In my opinion, supporting ethical fashion is extremely important! We can do this by checking how the clothes we want were made. Some companies try to protect the environment and only use green chemicals. We can support ethical fashion by only buying from these companies, and we can put pressure on other companies by writing to them or organising a social media campaign. I've already started a Facebook page on ethical fashion!

B Lewis

My friends and I often organise a clothes-swapping party. It's great fun! You get together and take along all the clothes you're bored with or that don't fit you anymore and then swap them. I swapped two old tops I never wear for two T-shirts that really **suit** me! In my view, it's great because you avoid buying new clothes and that helps the environment. It's easy to organise. You don't even have to be the same size because you can **alter** the clothes to **fit** you!

D Grace

Often, clothes are thrown away after being worn only a few times. If you ask me, we should make our clothes last longer by taking better care of them. And when we've finished with an **item of clothing**, why not **recycle** it? That might mean taking it to a recycling point, or even finding a way to **reuse** it yourself! With a bit of imagination, that old T-shirt with a hole in it could become a **trendy** scarf or a headband! I rarely throw clothes away now!

4 2.21 **For questions 1–10, choose from the teenagers A–D. The teenagers may be chosen more than once.**

Which teenager

1 believes we can do things online to help? ____
2 regularly takes part in an event? ____
3 talks about moving a product long distances? ____
4 says people should choose carefully before they buy? ____
5 says that arranging something is not difficult? ____
6 encourages being creative to think of different uses? ____
7 describes what they often wear? ____
8 recommends that people look after their clothes more? ____
9 says they really enjoy doing something? ____
10 says that some businesses do less harm than others to the environment? ____

5 **Answer the questions with a highlighted word or phrase from the report.**

1 What is a word for a set of clothes which are worn together? ______________
2 *Clothes* is a plural noun. What phrase do we use to talk about one thing we wear? ______________
3 What do we call the chemical we add to clothes to give them colour? ______________
4 What words mean *use again*? ______________ and ______________
5 What is another word for *fashionable*? ______________
6 What word do we use when clothes are exactly the right size for your body? ______________
7 What word do we use when clothes look good on you? ______________
8 What word do we use when we cut or sew clothes so that they are the right size for us? ______________

Grammar in context

Read these sentences from the report on page 81 and underline the verbs in the passive form. Then underline all the other verbs in the passive in the report.

Jeans are made of denim, which is a form of cotton.

It takes a lot of water and chemicals to produce the cotton, which is then dyed …

REMEMBER

- We form the passive with *be* (in different tenses/ forms) + past participle.
- We use the passive when we don't know who does an action or when it's unimportant or obvious: *These jeans **were made** in China.*
- We also use the passive for emphasis, to focus on a particular subject or to be more formal: *This dress **was designed** by Stella McCartney.* (The topic is the dress, not Stella McCartney.)
- To put the verb *be* in the right tense in the passive form, it helps to think of an active sentence with the same meaning: *Someone **stole** my jacket!* (*stole* = past simple) = *My jacket **was stolen**!* (*was* = past simple).
- We normally use *by* if we want to say who or what does the action of the main verb, but sometimes we use other prepositions with the passive form, such as *with*, *for*, *of* and *as*, depending on the meaning: *Many clothes are designed **with** the help of computers. / This coat was made **for** me personally. / Is this made **of** silk? / She is known **as** a very creative designer.*

▶ **See Grammar reference, Unit 8,** page 155

1 Find and underline one mistake in each sentence. Write the correct form in each gap.

1 I was gave a great new outfit for my birthday! ________________

2 My mum has some shoes that were design by a famous designer! ________________

3 Did you know that lots of chemicals used in making a pair of jeans? ________________

4 My white shirt was been dyed pink when I washed it with a red jumper! ________________

5 My purse was stole, but it was returned later when the police found it. ________________

6 Your new coat is so soft – I wonder what it's made with. ________________

7 Have you got any clothes that were designed with a famous designer? ________________

8 When my clothes no longer fit me, they have given to my younger sister. ________________

2 Write sentences in the passive using the words given.

1 many years ago / jeans / wear / factory workers

____

2 many items of clothing / sell / cheaply these days

____

3 where / your new trainers / make

____

4 these shoes / buy / my birthday money

____

5 jeans material / know / 'denim', from the name of the French town Nîmes

____

6 a special dye / use / to make the clothes bright pink

____

3 Read the text and write words in each gap to complete the sentences. Use the passive.

ISABELLA ROSE TAYLOR

Isabella Rose Taylor designs some of the most exciting clothes for teenagers. And that's amazing because she is still a teenager herself! Many teens around the world wear her cool designs. They include T-shirts, jumpers and caps from her seasonal collections. She bases her style on her love of painting and creating new things.

She set up her company in 2010 and a major retailer gave her the chance to sell her clothes in 2014. The fashion media has given her latest collection great reviews! Isabella continues to design trendy clothes for young people, which include examples of her own art. Recently, a magazine named her one of the 'Most Creative People in Business'. She is definitely a name to look out for in the fashion industry!

1 Some of the most exciting clothes for teenagers ________________ Isabella Rose Taylor.

2 Her cool designs ________________ many teens around the world.

3 Her style ________________ her love of painting and creating new things.

4 Her company ________________ in 2010 and she ________________ the chance to sell her clothes by a major retailer in 2014.

5 Her latest collection ________________ great reviews.

6 Recently, she ________________ one of the 'Most Creative People in Business'.

 ▶ **Workbook Unit 8:** Grammar 1, page 62, exercises 1, 2

Words connected with *clothes and accessories*

1 2.22 **Write each word from the box in the correct category. Listen and check.**

belt | bracelet | button | cap | collar | earring | glove | handbag | jewellery | jumper | necklace | pocket | sandals | shorts | sleeve | socks | suit | sweatshirt | trainers | wristband

parts of clothes	accessories	other items of clothing

Phrasal verbs

2 2.23 **Look at the phrasal verb in italics in each sentence. If it is correct, put a tick. If it is incorrect, rewrite it correctly in each gap. Listen and check.**

1 I went to a fashion show and all the models *had* really strange clothes *on*. ______
2 Why don't you *hang* your clothes *off* instead of leaving them on the floor? ______
3 I was in a hurry, but I couldn't *do* the zip *up* on my coat! ______
4 Do we need to *dress up* for the party or is it just an informal event? ______
5 I was glad to get home and be able to *take* my shoes *on* after a long day! ______
6 If you're going out, make sure you *put* a coat *off* because it's going to rain. ______
7 Kieran *tried* about a dozen tops *in* but he didn't like any of them. ______
8 My trainers are starting to *wear out* so I'll need some new ones soon. ______

3 **Choose four phrasal verbs from Exercise 2 and write example sentences of your own. Compare sentences with a partner.**

1 ______
2 ______
3 ______
4 ______

Adjectives/nouns/verbs

4 2.24 **Work out the anagrams and write the words. Listen and check.**

1 **cloth**: new (**tloehcs**) ______, the (**glotnhic**) ______ industry
2 **design**: celebrity (**eregsidn**) ______, badly (**gniedesd**) ______
3 **trend**: a (**enrdty**) ______ outfit, a real (**nserrtttede**) ______
4 **amaze**: to my (**mmtazaeen**) ______, feel (**mzedaa**) ______, an (**azgmina**) ______ experience
5 **create**: express your (**raticviyet**) ______, feel (**irevcate**) ______, the (**erratoc**) ______ of a design
6 **fashion**: a (**safaileonbh**) ______ pair of jeans, an (**dlo-hedisnfao**) ______ shirt
7 **appear**: improve your (**peaancarpe**) ______, become ______ (**tprapaen**)
8 **beauty**: a (**tiubuleaf**) ______ face

5 **Write a form of the word in capitals in each gap to complete the text.**

What are they wearing?

You often see some strange items of (**1**) ______ at fashion shows! **CLOTH** For fashion (**2**) ______, **DESIGN** the fashion show allows people to see their ideas. However, many of those ideas can seem a little crazy. Even (**3**) ______ people find some **TREND** of the outfits crazy! So, why do they have these shows? First of all, it's a bit like art. The (**4**) ______ designs show how **AMAZE** (**5**) ______ the fashion company is. **CREATE** The clothes aren't meant to be sold. Secondly, the fashion company may sell (**6**) ______ **FASHION** clothes that include ideas from the fashion show. If they have a model dressed as a giant button, they might produce clothes with large buttons on them. The (**7**) ______ **APPEAR** of clothes in the shops is influenced by the clothes on the catwalk. So, next time you see models in (**8**) ______ **BEAUTY** but strange clothes, look out for the colours and shapes in your local clothes shops!

▶ Vocabulary reference, page 166 ▶ Workbook Unit 8: Vocabulary, pages 62–63, exercises 1, 2, 3

8 LISTENING | Gap fill

1 **In pairs or as a group, answer the questions.**

1 Do you wear trainers? When do you wear them? How many pairs do you have?

2 When do you think trainers became popular with young people?

EXAM SKILL

Knowing what type of information to listen for

- When you listen for different kinds of information, such as numbers, dates, short phrases, etc., it helps to know what details you are listening for.
- Read the whole sentence that includes the gap. Try to predict what type of information the answer could be before you listen.

2 **Look at Exercise 3 and then answer the questions below.**

1 Which of these could fill gap 1?
a place / a year / a person

2 Which of these could **not** fill gap 2?
a place / a year / a person

3 Gap 3 could be a sport. Name a sport where players wear trainers. ___________

4 Which of these could not fill gap 4?
players / actors / sports

5 Guess a word that could fill gap 5. ___________

6 What kind of word could fill gap 6?
a noun / an adjective / a verb

OPTIMISE YOUR EXAM

Gap fill

- Before you listen, you have 20 seconds to look at the sentences. Read them carefully.
- Try to predict words and phrases that might fill each gap. Think about what details you might hear.

3 2.25 **You are going to listen to someone talking about trainers. For each question, write the correct answer in the gap. Write one or two words or a number or a date or a time.**

THE HISTORY OF TRAINERS

Shoes with rubber soles were first made in
(1) _______________ .

Simple trainers called Keds appeared in
(2) _______________ in 1916.

In the 1920s, 'Converse All-Stars' were used in
(3) _______________ .

In the 1950s, trainers were worn by
(4) _______________ , including James Dean.

In the 1980s, the 'Air Jordan' became
(5) _______________ .

Today, trainers are designed using
(6) _______________ .

4 2.25 **Listen again and check your answers.**

THINK | RESEARCH | CULTURE | LEARN | ME

Why do some people spend a lot of money on trainers?

▶ **Workbook Unit 8:** Listening, page 64, exercises 1, 2

Grammar in context

Look at this sentence from the audio in the listening lesson on page 84 and answer the questions.

Trainers are everywhere, aren't they?

1 Is the speaker asking for information or asking us to agree?

2 What's the difference between this question and the question: *Are trainers everywhere?*

REMEMBER

- We form question tags using **auxiliary verb + pronoun + ?**
- If the main part of the sentence has an auxiliary verb, the question tag uses the same auxiliary. If there is no auxiliary verb, the question tag uses *do* (or *be* if the main verb is *be*): *You **haven't** seen my new trainers, **have** you? / You **left** them upstairs, **didn't** you? / You **aren't** tired, **are** you?*
- If the verb or auxiliary verb in the rest of the sentence is positive, the question tag is negative and vice versa.
- We use question tags to get people to agree with us and to check information: *It's cold today, **isn't it?** / You're from Russia, **aren't you?***
- For imperatives, we use ***will you?*** and for phrases that begin with *Let's*, we use the question tag *shall we?*: *Make dinner, **will you?** / Let's go to the park, **shall we?***
- When the main part of the sentence expresses a negative idea using a word such as *never, nobody, very few*, etc., the question tag is positive: *Nobody wears those shoes anymore, **do they?***

▶ **See Grammar reference, Unit 8,** page 156

1 Choose the correct word to complete each sentence.

1 Jasmine always dresses really well, ____ she?
a) doesn't **b)** isn't **c)** won't

2 This is the best clothes shop in town, ____ it?
a) wasn't **b)** doesn't **c)** isn't

3 You haven't got a shirt this colour already, ____ you?
a) haven't **b)** are **c)** have

4 I should buy this top for the party, ____ I?
a) shall **b)** shouldn't **c)** won't

5 You've never worn a pirate costume before, ____ you?
a) have **b)** aren't **c)** haven't

6 Let's see if these trainers are available, ____ we?
a) do **b)** will **c)** shall

2 Write a question tag in each gap to complete the dialogue.

Sam: Those hats look great – they're new designs, **(1)** ______________ ? Pass me that one, **(2)** ______________ ?

Luke: Here you go.

Sam: Yeah. It's cool, **(3)** ______________ ? Nobody at school has one like it, **(4)** ______________ ?

Luke: That's right, you'd be the first, **(5)** ______________ ? Try it on.

Sam: It fits perfectly! It's quite brightly coloured, **(6)** ______________ ?

Luke: Yeah. It will match lots of your clothes, though, **(7)** ______________ ?

Sam: Let's see if we can find different colours online, **(8)** ______________ ? Prices are often lower online too, **(9)** ______________ ?

Luke: Good idea. They'll have them on *hatshop.com*, **(10)** ______________ ? Let's check on my phone.

3 Write questions with the words given. Include a question tag in each one.

1 **you / from / Germany** ______________
Yes, I am. Actually, I'm from a small town near Berlin.

2 **you / not / bring / a coat** ______________
No, I haven't. And it looks like it's going to rain!

3 **let's / try on / those expensive trainers** ______________
Good idea!

4 **Mo / not / be going to / wear / his cowboy hat / tonight** ______________
You never know with Mo! He might do!

SAY IT RIGHT

Resource centre: Unit 8
Intonation in question tags

8 SPEAKING | Discussion (pictures)

Talk 2 Me

On the one hand ...

Flipped classroom

1 **Watch the *Talk2Me* video and answer the questions.**

1 How does Jamie feel about Angus' birthday?
2 What does Angus' granny send him?
3 How many presents does Angus open before tea?

2 **Watch the video again. Underline the phrases in the *Phrase expert* box that you hear on the video.**

> **PHRASE EXPERT**
> … would be too (formal), wouldn't it? | … is very (warm in winter), isn't it? | A and B are both/equally … | A is … However, B is also … | A is (more …) than B | A isn't as … as B | A is …, whereas B is … | on the one hand, … / on the other hand, …

3 **In pairs or as a group, answer the questions.**

1 What are the people in the photos wearing?
2 Does your school have a uniform? If it does, describe it. If it doesn't, say what you are/aren't allowed to wear at school.

> **EXAM SKILL**
> ## Discussing alternatives
> - It's important to talk about all the pictures in the task, saying what's good and bad about them, e.g. *A tie is very smart, isn't it?*
> - A way to make sure you mention all the options is to compare and contrast them. You can do this using comparatives (e.g. *better than*) or words and phrases like *both*, *whereas*, *however*, *on the one hand/on the other hand*, e.g. *On the one hand, trainers are more comfortable than formal shoes. On the other hand, they're not as smart.*

4 **Look at the items of clothing in Exercise 7. Write down one advantage and one disadvantage of having each of these items as part of a school uniform.**

____

____

____

5 2.26 **Listen to two students doing the task in Exercise 7. Tick the points from your answers in Exercise 4 that the students also mention.**

6 2.26 **Listen again. What words or phrases do the students use to compare and contrast the items of clothing?**

____

____

> **OPTIMISE YOUR EXAM**
> ## Discussion (pictures)
> - Sometimes, the conversation might stop. Don't panic! You can start the conversation again by asking your partner a question, e.g. *What do you think of …? / Do you think …?*

7 **In pairs, do the task.**

> Your school is going to have a new school uniform and the headteacher is thinking about including some of the items of clothing in the pictures below. In pairs, talk together for two minutes about which items the new uniform should include.

1 In pairs, ask and answer the questions.

1 Describe the photo. When might people wear these things?
2 Are there any special occasions in your country when people wear fancy-dress costumes? What costumes are popular?

REMEMBER

- Some verbs (or phrases) are usually followed by either the *-ing* form or the **full infinitive**. Learning this type of verb pattern in English is very important.
- Some verbs can be followed by either. This often doesn't change the meaning, but with some verbs (*stop, try,* etc.) it does.

2 Choose the correct word or phrase.

1 I really enjoy **to shop** / **shopping** for new clothes!
2 Did you manage **to find** / **finding** a pair of sandals that fit you?
3 Have you ever considered **to get** / **getting** really fashionable trainers?
4 My parents have promised **to buy** / **buying** me a new necklace this weekend.
5 Which jacket have you decided **to get** / **getting**?
6 My sister denied **to take** / **taking** my favourite bracelet but I knew she had!
7 Many clothing designers refuse **to use** / **using** animal fur.
8 Can you imagine **to wear** / **wearing** a woollen jumper on the beach in summer?

3 Write the correct form of the word in bold to complete each sentence.

wear

1 Do you remember ___________ that superhero outfit at Amelia's party?
2 Did you remember ___________ something warm when you went camping?

buy

3 On our way to the fashion show, we stopped ___________ new wristbands!
4 I've stopped ___________ new clothes and I've started swapping with friends instead.

ask

5 If you want to organise a fashion event, try ___________ your friends to help you.
6 I tried ___________ the assistant for help, but he was busy with other customers.

OPTIMISE YOUR EXAM

Key word transformation

- Look at each sentence and the key word given and ask yourself: what is being tested?
- Is it a grammatical structure, a phrasal verb, a passive, a collocation, etc.? When you know what is being tested, you can think about the answer more clearly.

4 Complete the second sentence so it has a similar meaning to the first sentence, using the word given. Do not change the word given. Use two to five words, including the word given.

1 Anna was surprised when she got an invitation to the fancy-dress party. **EXPECTED**
Anna ______________ an invitation to a fancy-dress party.

2 They did a lot of sewing to make the clothes for the fashion show. **INVOLVED**
Making the clothes for the fashion show ______________ a lot of sewing.

3 'I'll go clothes shopping with you, Tonya,' said Sam. **OFFERED**
Sam ______________ clothes shopping with Tonya.

4 Buying a suit for the wedding is too expensive for Dan. **AFFORD**
Dan ______________ buy a suit for the wedding.

5 I finally managed to find some shoes I liked! **SUCCEEDED**
I finally ______________ some shoes I liked!

6 Tim was happy that he went to the concert. **ENJOYED**
Tim ______________ to the concert.

8 WRITING | A story

1 In pairs or groups, answer the questions.

1 What do you think the life of a model is like?
2 Would you like to be a model?

EXAM SKILL

Writing descriptions

- In a story, you may have to describe people, actions or feelings. A good description helps the reader imagine the situation.
- Adjectives and adverbs help bring a description to life. Compare these two sentences: *Dan ran into the room. / Dan ran quickly into the dark room*. The adverb and adjective make the description much more interesting.

2 Read the story and answer the questions.

Models for a day!

I was really looking forward to the school fashion show. All the students were excited about the show and we were waiting for it to start. Suddenly, I heard my teacher's voice.

'Come with me,' she whispered. I nervously followed her into a classroom. 'One of the models is ill. I need you to be in the show!' she announced.

I was shocked! I was given some amazing clothes to put on. I got changed quickly and joined the other students who were models.

We walked out onto the catwalk in our fantastic outfits. All the students clapped and cheered and we felt so pleased!

1 What does the writer expect to happen that day?
____
2 What actually happens?
____
3 What adjectives does the writer use?
____
4 What descriptive adverbs does the writer use?
____
5 What descriptive verbs does the writer use to report direct speech?
____

OPTIMISE YOUR EXAM

A story

- You can make your story more interesting by thinking carefully about your choice of vocabulary.
- Instead of always using simple words like *say* or *tell*, try to use other words that are more descriptive, for example, *whisper*, *shout*, *cry*, etc.
- Think about how people felt in the situation and make notes of adjectives that could describe their feelings, for example, *ashamed*, *cheerful*, *frightened*, *impressed*, etc.

3 **Look at this writing task and make notes to answer the questions. Use your imagination!**

> Your English teacher has asked you to write a story.
> Your story must begin with this sentence:
> *Inside the envelope, there was an invitation to a fancy-dress party!*

Write your **story**.

1 Who was the invitation from?

____

2 How did you feel when you got the invitation?

____

3 What costume did you decide to wear to the party?

____

4 Why did you choose that one?

____

5 Did you make it yourself or hire it?

____

6 How did you feel when you got to the party?

____

7 What happened at the party? (e.g. someone else was wearing the same costume, etc.)

____

8 What happened in the end?

____

9 How did you feel in the end?

____

4 **Plan** **Make a paragraph plan.**

Part	Purpose	Useful phrases	My notes
Title	make the reader want to read your story		
Paragraph 1	use the exact sentence you are given, and describe the situation and your first thoughts/ feelings	*I felt excited/nervous/worried …* *I was/wasn't looking forward to …*	
Paragraph 2	Describe what happened	*I decided to …* *I thought it would be a good idea to …* *Suddenly, …* *… she shouted/whispered/suggested, etc.*	
Paragraph 3	Explain how you felt	*I was happy because …* *I felt …*	
Paragraph 4	describe what happened and how you felt in the end	*In the end, …* *It had been an amazing party.* *I'll never forget that party.*	

5 **Write** **Write your story in an appropriate style. Write about 100 words.**

6 **Check** **Before you hand in your story, complete this checklist.**

Checklist

- ◯ I've given my story a title.
- ◯ I've started with the sentence I was given.
- ◯ I've written at least four paragraphs.
- ◯ I've used some good adjectives and adverbs.
- ◯ I've included some direct speech.
- ◯ I've checked my spelling, grammar and punctuation.

▶ **Writing reference,** page 172 ▶ **Workbook Unit 8:** Writing, page 66, exercises 1, 2, 3, 4 and Progress check 8, page 67

PROGRESS CHECK UNITS 7–8

GRAMMAR AND VOCABULARY

1 Write one word in each gap to complete the text.

You might think that before the internet (**1**) ___________ created, people always went to a shop to buy clothes. However, there was another option: mail order. With mail order, you choose clothes from a catalogue. The prices are often lower (**2**) ___________ the prices in the shops, so you can find something that costs much less than normal and get a real (**3**) ___________ ! Like shopping online, you can't try the clothes (**4**) ___________ before you buy them, but anything that doesn't fit can (**5**) ___________ returned. With mail order, you can often pay for things over time, so you don't have to save (**6**) ___________ before buying. These days, more clothes (**7**) ___________ bought online than from catalogues, but some people still prefer (**8**) ___________ buy their clothes by mail order.

__/8

2 Choose the correct word.

1 My ice skates are beginning to wear **out** / **over** / **up** and I'll soon have to get new ones.
2 For the lowest prices, you need to shop **around** / **back** / **through** before you buy.
3 The wind was very cold so I did **down** / **on** / **up** my jacket to keep warm.
4 I think you should take that ridiculous hat **away** / **off** / **over** your head!
5 When do you think you'll be able to pay **away** / **back** / **over** the money I lent you?
6 These days, many families find it hard to get **by** / **in** / **off** on the money they have.
7 I was too tired to hang my clothes **in** / **on** / **up** so I just threw them on a chair.
8 The cost of the meal added **out** / **up** / **through** to much more than we expected.

__/8

3 Write the comparative or superlative form of the words in brackets. Add any other words you need.

1 Your shoes are much _____________ mine! (**big**)
2 Mum says I spend a lot because I always choose _____________ clothes! (**expensive**)
3 I don't like clothes shops and find going to them _____________ buying things online. (**enjoyable**)
4 Buying this dress was _____________ decision I've ever made! (**bad**)
5 Don't you think this hat is _____________ the other one? (**pretty**)
6 Dad's _____________ person I know! He never buys new clothes. (**fashionable**)

__/6

4 Write a question tag in each gap.

1 You don't like going to football practice, _____________ ?
2 It's really hot today, _____________ ?
3 You had a different top on earlier, _____________ ?
4 Your dad won't let you go the party, _____________ ?
5 Let's go shopping in town later this afternoon, _____________ ?
6 No-one at school has these trainers, _____________ ?

__/6

5 Write a form of the word in capitals in each gap.

1	When I arrived at school in a helicopter, everyone looked at me in ___________ .	AMAZE
2	I'd like to be a ___________ in a large business when I'm older.	DIRECT
3	Jenny's so ___________ that I'm sure she'll be an artist one day.	CREATE
4	Followers of fashion will love this ___________ outfit!	TREND
5	When my phone rang, the ___________ told me to be quiet.	LIBRARY
6	The flowers you got me are really ___________ !	BEAUTY
7	I refuse to say anything else until I speak to my ___________ .	LAW
8	The shop ___________ asked me if I needed any help.	ASSIST

__/8

6 Choose the correct word or phrase.

1 George denied **to take / taking** my notebook, but I didn't believe him.
2 The night before the exam, I decided **to do / doing** some last-minute revision.
3 When Sasha looked in her bag, she realised she **had lost / had been losing** her phone!
4 Did you remember **to buy / buying** milk from the supermarket?
5 This dress is made **for / of** silk, it's so soft!
6 All my new designs **sold / are sold** online.
7 Oh, no! My bag has **stolen / been stolen**!
8 The participants for the school fashion show haven't **been chosen / chosen** yet.

__/8

7 Read the definitions and write the correct words. The first letters have been given.

1	swap, give something and get something else back	e_ _ _ _ _ _ _
2	a chemical used to change the colour of clothes	d_ _
3	an official piece of paper that can be used instead of money	v_ _ _ _ _ _
4	look at things for sale in a shop	b_ _ _ _ _
5	the part of a shirt that covers your arms	s_ _ _ _ _
6	the money you get back when you buy something	c_ _ _ _ _

__/6

Total score __/50

EXAM SKILLS

Tick the statements that are true for you. Review the skills in the unit if you need more help.

I can …	Unit/page
☐ understand time words and phrases in a magazine article	Unit 7 p70
☐ understand relevant information in short extracts of speech	Unit 7 p74
☐ ask questions to keep a conversation going	Unit 7 p76
☐ understand how nouns are formed and use them in word formation exercises	Unit 7 p77
☐ use direct speech in a story	Unit 7 p78
☐ understand attitude and opinion in a project report	Unit 8 p80
☐ think about what type of information to listen for to complete gaps in sentences	Unit 8 p84
☐ discuss alternatives in a discussion	Unit 8 p86
☐ understand the form and function of different verbs and use them in key word transformations	Unit 8 p87
☐ use the correct language to describe people, actions and feelings in a story	Unit 8 p88

9 Playing to win!

READING | 4-option multiple choice | An online article

1 In pairs or as a group, answer the questions.

1 Which sports do you do at school and in your free time?
2 What was the last new sport you tried?

2 Read the article and find words 1–7. Then match each word to its definition.

1 chaser ____	a) a ball which the beaters throw
2 quaffle ____	b) tries to catch the snitch
3 beater ____	c) the main goal-scorer
4 bludger ____	d) a volleyball they use to score goals
5 keeper ____	e) a person, but not a team member
6 seeker ____	f) throws balls at the chasers
7 snitch ____	g) guards their team's hoops

EXAM SKILL

Understanding implication

- Writers and speakers don't always tell you everything explicitly (in a direct way). Sometimes you have to work out what the person is saying.
- For example, if someone says *We have to throw or kick the ball into one of the opposing team's three hoops*, you can understand the implication that both teams have three hoops.

3 Find these sentences in the article. Then choose the option that explains the implication.

1 *I wouldn't want to be a chaser – we throw quite hard!*
a) It's difficult to hit a chaser.
b) If the ball hits you, it might hurt.

2 *Catching the snitch gets you 30 points – but the snitch is usually a very fast runner!*
a) It's difficult to get 30 points.
b) It's not difficult to get 30 points.

OPTIMISE YOUR EXAM

4-option multiple choice

- Some multiple-choice questions test your understanding of implication. In other words, you have to think about what else you can learn/understand from what the text says.
- For example, in Exercise 4, question 3, you won't find the answer stated explicitly in the text. Find the part connected to the question and think about what it says.

Want to play Quidditch?

If you're a fan of Harry Potter, you'll know what quidditch is. It's the game where they fly around on broomsticks. But did you know that we Muggles (or non-wizards) can also play quidditch?

Comments (41)
Like this
Share

Real-life quidditch isn't exactly the same as the sport in the novels and movies. If flying broomsticks existed, perhaps it would be. But sadly, they don't exist, so real-life quidditch is played on the ground. But it's similar in other ways. I asked a team from Poland to tell me about it.

Jarek 'It's fun! Each team consists of a seeker, three chasers, two beaters and a keeper. There are boys and girls in each team – a maximum of four boys or four girls. All the players play with broomsticks between their legs. I'm the team captain and the position I play is chaser.'

Marta 'I'm also a chaser. We try to score goals using a volleyball, called a quaffle. We have to throw or kick the ball into one of the opposing team's three hoops. If we score a goal, we get 10 points.'

Wojtek 'I'm a beater. There are three other balls on the pitch during a match, called bludgers. Beaters throw these at the other team's players. If a bludger hits a chaser, the chaser has to drop the quaffle (if they're holding it), go back to their side of the pitch and touch one of the goalposts. I wouldn't want to be a chaser – we throw quite hard!'

Ewa 'I'm the keeper. I defend our team's hoops, but I can also try to score goals.'

Tomek 'I'm our team's seeker. At the 17th minute of the game, the snitch comes onto the pitch. This is a person wearing a yellow sports kit with a 'tail' attached to their shorts. The seekers come on a minute later. If a seeker catches the snitch and pulls the tail, the game stops. Catching the snitch gets you 30 points – but the snitch is usually a very fast runner!'

Would you like to play real-life quidditch? If so, which position would you choose?

4 3.01 **Read the text again. For each question, choose the correct answer.**

1 The writer believes that
  A it is a good thing flying broomsticks don't exist.
  B it is a shame flying broomsticks don't exist.
  C flying broomsticks will exist one day.
  D real-life quidditch is completely different from the sport in the books and films.

2 What does Wojtek suggest about chasers?
  A They are very difficult to hit.
  B They sometimes drop the quaffle by mistake.
  C What happens to them might be painful.
  D When they touch a goalpost, they score a point.

3 What does Tomek say about the snitch?
  A He or she joins the game before the seekers.
  B He or she wears the same sports kit as one of the teams.
  C He or she never stops running when on the pitch.
  D He or she is trying to get 30 points.

4 Which comment best answers Amy's second question at the end of the article?
  A **LucyP – 11:32 am:** Jarek is a great team captain. I hope your team wins its next match, Jarek!
  B **Matt3000 – 11:33 am:** I had no idea real-life quidditch existed! I'd love to try it one day!
  C **JohnClark – 11:34 am:** Being a beater sounds like a lot of fun. I can't think of many games where you can throw balls at the other players!
  D **HelenTime – 11:35 am:** Hi, Amy! Are the hoops like basketball hoops, or are they different?

5 **Find these words and phrases in the article. In pairs or as a group, discuss what they mean.**

defend | fan | goalposts | match
opposing team | pitch | position | sports kit

THINK | RESEARCH | CULTURE | LEARN | ME

Can you think of other sports from books or films? Which would you like to play in real life?

▶ **Workbook Unit 9:** Reading, pages 68–69, exercises 1, 2, 3

9 GRAMMAR 1 | Conditionals (1): zero, first and second conditionals

Grammar in context

Read these sentences from the article on page 93. Match each sentence to a description a–d.

1 *If you're a fan of Harry Potter, you'll know what quidditch is.* ____
2 *If flying broomsticks existed, perhaps it would be.* ____
3 *If a seeker catches the snitch and pulls the tail, the game stops.* ____
4 *If you had the chance to play real-life quidditch, which position would you choose?* ____

a) This is a rule of the game.
b) This is a real, likely situation for some people.
c) This is an unlikely situation, but it is possible.
d) This is an impossible, hypothetical situation.

REMEMBER

- The zero conditional is ***if*** + **present simple**, **present simple**. We use it for general truths, including game rules, and scientific facts: *In rugby, if you score a try, you **get** five points.*
- The first conditional is ***if*** + **present simple**, ***will***. We use it for real, likely and possible situations now, generally or in the future: *If we **lose** the match, **I'll be** really upset.*
- The second conditional is ***if*** + **past simple**, ***would***. We use it for unlikely or impossible situations now, generally or in the future. Unlikely (but possible): *If I **won** the whole competition, **I'd be** so happy!* Impossible (hypothetical): *If people **were** five metres tall, basketball hoops **would be** much higher!*
- **Unless** = *if not*, or *except if*: *We'll go swimming in the sea tomorrow **unless** the weather's really bad.*

▶ **See Grammar reference, Unit 9,** page 157

2 Choose the correct word or phrase.

From: Max To: Jan

Hi Jan,

Great to hear from you! I'm sorry you're still feeling a bit unfit after your accident.

Here's a suggestion from my cousin Vicky in the UK: parkrun. Have you heard of it? If you (**1**) **want** / **will want** to get fit and have some fun, you (**2**) **'ll love** / **love** it! I've checked and there are regular events near you in Copenhagen. If I lived in a country with parkrun, I (**3**) **will** / **would** definitely do it.

One of the great things about it is that it's totally free. If I (**4**) **have** / **had** to pay to do a run each week, I probably wouldn't try it, and I expect you wouldn't either! If a runner (**5**) **does** / **will do** well, the results (**6**) **go** / **will go** up on the parkrun website. But it's not really about racing – it's about getting and staying fit and having fun.

If you (**7**) **go** / **went** online, you'll find loads of information about it. If I (**8**) **am** / **were** you, I (**9**) **'d** / **'ll** think about volunteering as an organiser too – (**10**) **if** / **unless** you're too busy with your schoolwork, of course.

Let me know what you think!

Bye for now,

Love,

Max

1 Complete the rules using the zero conditional.

1 **Pool:** If a player ______________ (**hit**) the black ball into one of the pockets by mistake, he or she ______________ (**lose**) the game.

2 **Darts:** If a dart ______________ (**go**) into the central circle, the player ______________ (**get**) 50 points.

3 **Table tennis**: If a player ______________ (**not return**) the ball, the other player ______________ (**win**) a point.

4 **Bowling:** If you ______________ (**not knock down**) any of the pins, you ______________ (**not get**) any points.

3 Complete these sentences for you.

1 If I have some free time after school today, ______________
2 If the weather's good on Saturday, ______________
3 If I wanted to take up a new sport, ______________
4 If I had the chance to go to a parkrun event, ______________
5 I wouldn't ______________ unless ______________

THINK | RESEARCH | CULTURE | LEARN | **ME**

What would you prefer to play right now if you could: pool, darts or table tennis?

Words connected with *people in sport*

1 3.02 **Write a word from the box in each gap. Listen and check.**

acrobat | athlete | captain | climber | cyclist | gamer | gymnast | player | referee | rider

Someone …

1 … in a football/basketball team: ___________
2 … who plays computer games: ___________
3 … who leads a sports team: ___________
4 … who judges a football/basketball match: ______
5 … on a horse or sometimes a bike: ___________
6 … on a bike but not a horse: ___________
7 … who does athletics, or who is good at sport: ___________
8 … who does gymnastics: ___________
9 … who can balance and jump well, often in a circus: ___________
10 … who goes up mountains, walls or rocks: ______

Phrasal verbs

2 3.03 **Choose the correct word. Use the words in italics to help you. Listen and check.**

1 Mum, they won't let me *join* **up** / **in** with the game!
2 The team with the lowest points at the end of the round *is knocked* **down** / **out**.
3 The referee held up a red card and *sent* Garcia **off** / **away**.
4 She's had to *pull* **out** / **off** of the competition because of a knee injury.
5 The weather's so bad, I think we'll have to *put* the match **over** / **off** until next week.
6 Can you help me *set* **up** / **in** the table tennis net?
7 *Put* **away** / **down** all the equipment when you've finished using it, please.
8 I'm surprised that real-life quidditch *caught* **on** / **up** so quickly!

3 **Match each phrasal verb from Exercise 2 to its definition.**

1 leave a game/competition because of a problem or accident ___________
2 prepare the equipment ___________
3 take part ___________
4 become popular ___________
5 store something in its usual place ___________
6 make someone leave a game because they break the rules ___________
7 delay, postpone ___________
8 eliminate from a competition because they lose ___________

Collocations with *do*, *play* and *go*

4 3.04 **Write the correct form of *do*, *play* or *go* in each gap. Listen and check.**

1 How often do you ___________ tennis/football/basketball?
2 Have you ever ___________ golf?
3 Do you ___________ athletics at school in the summer?
4 How often do you ___________ swimming in the winter?
5 Have you ever ___________ ice-skating?
6 Do you ___________ gymnastics sometimes in PE?
7 Have you ever ___________ windsurfing?
8 Do you know anyone who ___________ horse-riding regularly?
9 When was the last time you ___________ for a bike ride?
10 Have you ever ___________ water-skiing?
11 Do you know anyone who ___________ surfing regularly?
12 Do you know anyone who ___________ yoga?

REMEMBER

- The verb *go* has two past participles, *gone* and *been*:
She's ***gone*** *sky-diving.* = she's sky-diving now, or is on her way
She's ***been*** *sky-diving.* = sometime in the past, and she's returned

SAY IT RIGHT

Resource centre: Unit 9
Silent letters

9 LISTENING | 3-option multiple choice (dialogues)

1 **In pairs or as a group, answer the questions.**

1 Do you like doing watersports? Which ones have you tried?
2 Do you prefer individual sports or team sports?

EXAM SKILL

Identifying why answers are incorrect

- Sometimes the speaker says something linked to one of the possible answers. However, an answer is incorrect unless it has exactly the same meaning as what you hear.
- An answer may sound correct but it may not contain all the relevant information, or it may be a different person speaking.
- Listen to the grammar used. There may be negative words or different tenses that mean what you hear is different from what is in the questions.

2 3.05 **Listen to the dialogue and explain why none of the answers is correct.**

The girl is happy because
a) the lesson went well.
b) she was very good at standing up.
c) she learnt how to ride a wave.

OPTIMISE YOUR EXAM

3-option multiple choice (dialogues)

- Before you listen, underline key words in the question to help you focus on the relevant information.
- Key words are the most important nouns, verbs and adjectives. For example, in Exercise 3, question 6, you might underline *surfing*, *lesson*, *feel*, *surprised*, *difficult*, *happy*, *managed*, *ride*, *worried* and *successful*.

3 3.06 **For each question, choose the correct answer.**

1 You will hear two friends talking about a competition they entered.
What was the result of the competition?
A The boy won the competition.
B The girl was last in the competition.
C The winner was a beginner.

2 You will hear two friends talking about a football match they saw.
The boy thinks that
A the match wasn't very exciting.
B their school's team is improving.
C the match produced the wrong result.

3 You will hear a boy telling a friend about an athletic event.
The boy was surprised at
A how long the event took.
B how much he enjoyed the event.
C the number of people at the event.

4 You will hear two friends talking about rock-climbing.
They agree that
A they need to find out more about it.
B they're going to try it.
C it's probably too dangerous for them.

5 You will hear two friends talking about how they organise their time.
The boy advises the girl to
A give up another activity.
B get up earlier to practise.
C plan her time better.

6 You will hear a girl telling her friend about a surfing lesson.
How did she feel about it?
A surprised it was so difficult
B happy that she managed to ride a wave
C worried that the lesson wasn't successful

4 3.06 **Listen again and check your answers.**

THINK | RESEARCH | CULTURE | LEARN | ME

What does it take to be the best at sport?

▶ **Workbook Unit 9:** Listening, page 72, exercises 1, 2, 3

GRAMMAR 2 | Time clauses

Grammar in context

Read these extracts from the audio in the listening lesson on page 96 and choose the correct word or phrase.

1 *When you **get** / **will get** there, you'll soon relax and enjoy it.*

2 ***Until** / **As soon as** you do that, you'll find that you've got a lot more time.*

REMEMBER

- Some time words and phrases are immediately followed by a present tense (present simple, present continuous, present perfect) when they refer to the future and NOT by *will*. These include: *when, as soon as, before, after, until/till, while: After you **arrive**, we'll have a welcome party.*
- However, in the other clause, we use *will*. In other words, the sentence structure is very similar to the first conditional: ***As soon as** they get here, we'**ll have** lunch.*
- As with the first conditional, we can change the order of the clauses. We don't use commas when the time clause comes second: *We'll have a welcome party after you arrive.*

▶ **See Grammar reference, Unit 9,** page 157

1 **Write a word from the box in each gap. Sometimes more than one answer is correct.**

after	before	soon
until	when	while

1 A few minutes ___________ we set off, we'll check all the bikes' brakes and tyres.

2 Straight ___________ we come back, we'll clean the bikes and lock them up.

3 As ___________ as I pass this cycling course, I'll be able to ride my bike to school.

4 I won't listen to music ___________ I'm cycling, as it's dangerous.

5 I won't be able to ride on the road ___________ I take a cycling safety course.

6 I'll get a new bike ___________ I've saved up enough money.

REMEMBER

- We can use *once* to mean *when*, *after*, or *as soon as*: ***Once** I figure out the rules, we'll start!*

2 **The words in bold in each sentence are incorrect. Rewrite them correctly in each gap.**

1 We won't start until you **will get** here. ___________

2 **I call** you as soon as we leave the sports centre. ___________

3 Once we **found** the golf ball, we'll be able to continue! ___________

4 While I **will be** taking part in the bike race, my friends will be on holiday. ___________

3 **Complete the second sentence so that it has a similar meaning to the first sentence. Use no more than three words in each gap.**

1 I have to finish my homework before I'm free to play football.
I won't be free to play football until ___________ my homework.

2 I'll practise a bit more and then I'll try that jump.
I'll try that jump after ___________ a bit more.

3 We'll set up the net and then we'll start immediately.
We'll start as soon as ___________ up the net.

4 I'm going to do gymnastics tonight, and my parents are going to the theatre.
While ___________ gymnastics tonight, my parents will be at the theatre.

5 Emma will come back from athletics training and then we'll have dinner.
We'll have dinner once Emma ___________ from athletics training.

6 Once you show you're good enough, I'll put you in the swimming team!
I won't put you in the swimming team ___________ you're good enough!

Flipped classroom

1 **Watch the *Talk2Me* video and answer the questions.**

1 Why does Jamie laugh?
2 How many push ups did Jamie do at school last week?
3 What is Maddy's cousin good at / not good at?

2 **Watch the video again. Underline the phrases in the *Phrase expert* box that you hear on the video.**

> **PHRASE EXPERT**
> I never …, but (my best friend) does. | I don't think I've ever …, but (my best friend) has. | Take my (brother/sister), for example | I / (S)he … all the time | I / (S)he absolutely loves / quite likes / can't stand … | I'm / (S)he's a keen (athlete / gymnast).

3 **In pairs or as a group, answer the questions.**

1 How competitive are you?
2 Do you prefer team games or individual sports?

> **EXAM SKILL**
> ### Talking about other people
> - If you can't answer a question with a lot of information about yourself, talk about someone you know, e.g. *I'm not very competitive, but my brother's a keen cyclist and he gets really upset if he doesn't win a race.*
> - In an exam you may need to talk about your friends and family, so think about any vocabulary you may need. For example, if a friend does an interesting sport which you don't know the name of, ask your teacher what it's called in English or find out online.

4 3.07 **Listen to a student answering personal questions. Number the questions in the order that you hear them being answered.**

Question ____ Do any members of your family like doing or watching a sport that you don't like?
Question ____ Do any members of your family like doing unusual or dangerous sports?
Question ____ How often do you play games with your friends just for fun?
Question ____ Are any of your friends more competitive than you?

5 **How would you answer these questions about yourself and the people you know?**

6 **Look at the questions in Exercise 7 and make notes. Remember to talk about someone you know if the question isn't really relevant to you.**

> **OPTIMISE YOUR EXAM**
> ### Questions
> - Don't memorise answers, but think about your answers to typical questions in advance; for example, in many exams they ask you about your interests and what you do in your free time. Think about those ideas and make sure you know the vocabulary you will need to answer them.

7 **In pairs or as a group, ask and answer these questions. Use your notes from Exercise 6.**

1 What's your favourite sport to play or do? How often do you play games with your friends just for fun?
2 What's your favourite sport to watch? Do any members of your family like doing or watching sports that you don't?
3 What's the most extreme or unusual sport you've tried? Do any members of your family like doing unusual or extreme sports?
4 Do you like playing team games? Are any of your friends more competitive than you?

 ▶ **Workbook Unit 9:** Speaking, pages 72–73, exercises 1, 2, 3

1 **In pairs or as a group, ask and answer the questions.**

1 Do you know how to juggle? If you do, who taught you? If you don't, would you like to try?

REMEMBER

- The verbs *include*, *contain*, *consist* and *involve* have similar meanings, but they're not exactly the same.
- *Contain* means 'have something physical inside': *Many sports drinks* ***contain*** *sugar.*
- *Include* means 'be a part of a group/idea/thing': *The entrance fee* ***includes*** *use of the sauna and gym*. For something that means 'physically in, and part of, something else', you can sometimes use *contain* or *include*: *The booklet* ***contains/includes*** *full instructions.*
- *Involve* means 'need to include as part of an event/activity/situation': *Sky-diving* ***involves*** *jumping out of a plane.*
- *Consist* is followed by *of*, and means 'be made of particular parts or things': *A football team* ***consists of*** *11 players.*

2 **If a word in bold is correct, put a tick. If it's incorrect, write the correct word.**

1 The game **contains** both luck and skill. ______
2 The box **includes** everything you need to get started. ______
3 The box **involves** everything you need to get started. ______
4 Famous tennis players **consist of** Andy Murray and Serena Williams. ______
5 Each team **consists of** two or three players. ______

3 **In pairs or as a group, discuss the differences in meaning between the words in bold.**

1 **activity/hobby/sport**
2 **see/imagine/dream of/view** something
3 **catch/kick/hit/throw** a ball

4 **Quickly read the text in Exercise 5 and complete the chart below.**

Name of sport	
Number of teams in a game	
Number of players in each team	
Other sports it has similarities with	
Object placed between the teams	
Each player has in their hands	
What a player has to do when they get the ball	

OPTIMISE YOUR EXAM

4-option multiple-choice cloze

- Sometimes the correct answer depends on small differences in meaning between the possible choices.
- Read the words around the gap carefully to understand which particular meaning is correct.

5 **Choose the correct word to fill each gap.**

Introducing jollyball!

Have you ever heard of the **(1)** ____ of jollyball? It's not very surprising if you haven't, because not many people **(2)** ____ it, but if you like juggling, it's lots of fun!

Jollyball is a cross between juggling and volleyball. In a jollyball **(3)** ____ , two teams battle against each other. Each team **(4)** ____ of two or three people. It's sometimes played on a badminton court, or players sometimes play in an empty room. They might use chairs to hold the net up!

So, **(5)** ____ a table tennis or badminton net between the two teams. The game is a bit like tennis, but instead of a racket, each player holds two juggling balls in their hands. They only use their hands in the game, not a racket or their feet. When the ball comes over the net, they have to juggle with it and the other two balls before **(6)** ____ it back over the net.

	A	B	C	D
1	**A** play	**B** event	**C** game	**D** competition
2	**A** compete	**B** have	**C** go	**D** play
3	**A** match	**B** activity	**C** hobby	**D** sport
4	**A** includes	**B** contains	**C** consists	**D** involves
5	**A** see	**B** imagine	**C** dream	**D** view
6	**A** catching	**B** kicking	**C** hitting	**D** throwing

▶ **Workbook Unit 9:** Language in Use, page 73, exercises 1, 2

1 In pairs or groups, answer the questions.

1 Which of these activities have you tried before: table tennis, bowling, volleyball, ice-skating, skateboarding?
2 Which of these activities do you think are suitable for a charity event? Why?

EXAM SKILL

Expressing preferences

- In emails, you sometimes express a preference. To do this you can use *I'd prefer … to …*, or *I'd rather …*
- Always try to give a reason for your preference. For example, *I'd rather play volleyball than go ice-skating because I prefer to do team sports.*

2 Read the email. What three things does the class need to choose?

From: Mrs Bates
Subject: Charity fitness day

Dear Class,

I'd like our class to participate in the charity fitness day organised by the local youth centre next Saturday. *(Great!)*

There are many events to choose from: bowling, table tennis, volleyball, basketball and a dance marathon. Which event would you prefer to take part in? *(Say which you prefer)*

We should all practise our chosen activity before Saturday. Which day after school would be better, Wednesday or Friday? *(Choose)*

Our class's team will need a name. Any suggestions? *(Suggest …)*

Let me know!

Fiona Bates

3 Read Adam's reply ignoring the gap and answer the questions.

From: Adam
Subject: Charity fitness day

Dear Mrs Bates,

Thank you for your email. You suggested participating in the charity fitness day. Personally, I think that's a great idea and I'm sure the class will love it!

I'd rather take part in the basketball competition, because I prefer it to table tennis. Also, I can't dance and I've never tried bowling before. I think team sports are more exciting.

__________________ because we always have to do a lot of homework on Wednesday evening.

I think we should call our team the Best of Bates! The fitness day is going to be so much fun and it's great to do it for charity!

All the best,

Adam

1 What day does Adam prefer?
2 What reason does he give?

4 Write a word from the box to complete the phrases that fill the gap in Exercise 3.

prefer | rather | than | to

1 I'd prefer Friday (__________ Wednesday)
2 I'd __________ to go on Friday (rather __________ on Wednesday)
3 I'd __________ go on Friday (than Wednesday)

OPTIMISE YOUR EXAM

An email

- When writing an email in an exam, use your imagination to think of preferences and reasons.
- Remember, you can invent your preferences and reasons. They don't have to be true.
- Use a variety of words and phrases to express preference, for example *I prefer …*, *I'd rather …*, *My preference is …*, and to give reasons such as *because …*, *as …*.

5 **Look at this writing task and make notes to answer the questions.**

Read this email from your English teacher Mr Miller and the notes you have made.

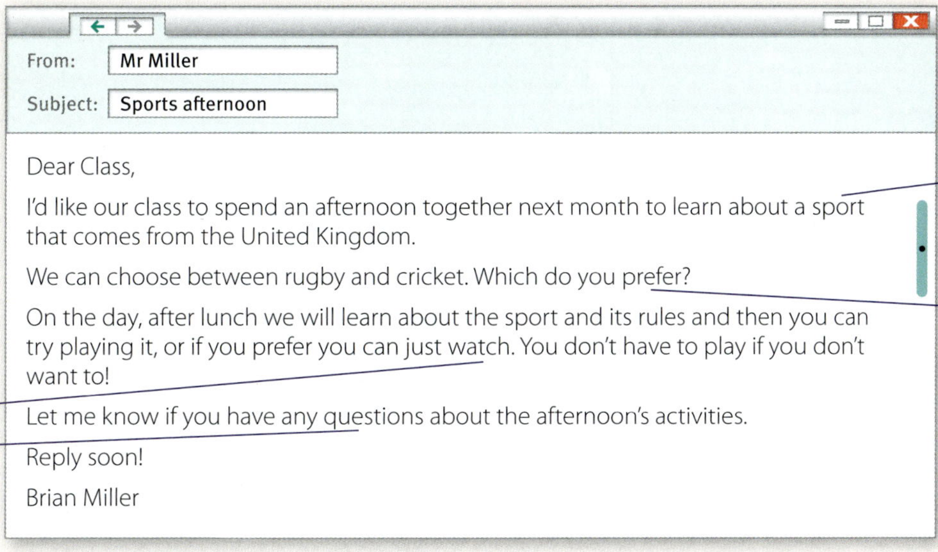

From: Mr Miller

Subject: Sports afternoon

Dear Class,

I'd like our class to spend an afternoon together next month to learn about a sport that comes from the United Kingdom.

We can choose between rugby and cricket. Which do you prefer?

On the day, after lunch we will learn about the sport and its rules and then you can try playing it, or if you prefer you can just watch. You don't have to play if you don't want to!

Let me know if you have any questions about the afternoon's activities.

Reply soon!

Brian Miller

Exciting!

Explain

Say which you prefer

Ask Mr Miller

Write your **email** to Mr Miller using **all the notes**.

1 Do you prefer to learn about rugby or cricket? ______________ Why? ______________________________

2 Would you prefer to try the sport or just watch? ______________ Why? ______________________________

3 What three questions can you ask Mr Miller? ____

6 Plan Make a paragraph plan.

Part	Purpose	Useful phrases	My notes
First line	greet the person you are writing to	*Dear …,*	
Paragraph 1	thank the other person for their email and write about the first note on the email	*Thank you for …, That's …!*	
Paragraph 2	write about the second note on the email	*You asked …, I think … is more interesting because …*	
Paragraph 3	write about the third note on the email	*Personally, I prefer …,* *I'd rather … because …*	
Paragraph 4	write about the fourth note on the email	*What …?* *Do we have to …?* *Will we …?*	
Closing expression	say goodbye	*Best wishes, Many thanks, All the best,*	
Your name	first name		

7 Write **Write your email to Mr Miller in an appropriate style. Use all the notes. Write about 100 words.**

8 Check **Before you hand in your email, complete this checklist.**

Checklist ✓

- ◯ I've started and ended my email the right way.
- ◯ I've expressed a preference.
- ◯ I've given a reason for my preference.
- ◯ I've asked Mr Miller some questions.
- ◯ I've written about 100 words.
- ◯ I've checked my spelling, grammar and punctuation.

▶ **Writing reference,** page 173 ▶ **Workbook Unit 9:** Writing, page 74, exercises 1, 2, 3, 4 and Progress check 9, page 75

10 All in good fun!

READING | Gapped text | A blog post

1 In pairs or as a group, answer the question.

Describe what you do with films and music videos on social media. Use the words in the box.

comment | download | like | post | upload

2 Read the text quickly, ignoring the gaps and the removed sentences. Decide if the statements are T (True) or F (False).

1 Motion capture is used in different types of films. T / F
2 Motion capture is a way of filming actors. T / F
3 With motion capture, an actor playing a monster must dress as a monster. T / F
4 Motion capture is only used in films. T / F

EXAM SKILL

Understanding linking words and phrases

- Linking words and phrases such as *for example*, *because*, *in other words*, *also*, *so*, *of course*, etc. help us understand the logic of a text more easily.
- It's important that you know what they mean or refer to. For example, *because* introduces a reason and *so* introduces a result. If a sentence starts with *Instead*, you should ask yourself: 'Instead of what?'

3 Find these words and phrases in the sentences in Exercise 4. Decide what we use them for.

1 **In other words**
 a) explains the same point again
 b) introduces a new point

2 **Take**
 a) makes a suggestion
 b) introduces an example

3 **Instead**
 a) introduces a different way of doing something
 b) gives more information

4 **However**
 a) introduces a contrast
 b) asks a question

5 **Of course**
 a) introduces an idea that is strange or unexpected
 b) introduces an idea that is obvious or expected

OPTIMISE YOUR EXAM

Gapped text

- When you've completed the text with the removed sentences, read the full text again, including the missing information.
- Ask yourself if the text makes logical sense.
- As a final check, look at the three sentences you didn't choose. Check that they couldn't fit logically in any of the gaps.

WE ♥ HOLLYWOOD

FREDDIE WOOD'S FILM BLOG

HOME | WHAT'S NEW | POSTS

SUBSCRIBE | CONNECT | FOLLOW | LIKE

7TH JULY

Motion capture – making movie magic!

Hulk in *The Avengers*. The Na'vi in *Avatar*. King Kong in *Skull Island*. What do these have in common? All of these characters were animated using 'motion capture'.

With motion capture, an actor wears sensors on their body. A special camera records the movement of each sensor and a 3D moving 'skeleton' is then made. After filming, animators can 'hang' any 'skin' they like on it. (**1**) ____

Back in 1937, the Disney cartoon *Snow White* used a low-tech form of motion capture. Today, film-makers use more advanced technology. (**2**) ____ **Take** Gollum in *The Lord of the Rings* films. If they'd drawn him as a cartoon, he wouldn't have seemed as real. And if the actor, Andy Serkis, had worn special make-up, he wouldn't have looked so unusual. **However**, with motion capture, the film-makers captured Andy's expressions and movements, and then added the animation of Gollum's appearance.

Motion capture can make life easier for actors. Think about the alien Maz Kanata in *Star Wars: The Force Awakens*. If Lupita Nyong'o, who played Maz, had had to put on make-up every day to get ready for filming, it would have taken her hours. (**3**) ____ They captured her expressions via a computer program, and special effects experts added the character's unique face afterwards. It would also have been difficult for animators to draw the penguins dancing in *Happy Feet*. (**4**) ___ **Instead**, they filmed real dancers first to create the penguins' dances.

Motion capture is also used in both video games and pop videos. The Coldplay video for *Adventure of a Lifetime* took six months to make because it used motion capture. The band members appear as chimps having fun in the jungle. (**5**) ____

What's your favourite motion capture movie, video game or pop video? Who's your favourite character?

Capcom Motion-Capture Studio, Japan

4 3.08 **Read the text again. Five sentences have been removed from the text. For each question, choose the correct answer. There are three extra sentences which you do not need to use.**

A Take the latest *Star Wars* movie.
B Instead, she acted wearing a special suit, with tiny white dots on her face.
C In other words, they can make the actor look like a penguin or a chimp, or even a monster.
D So she decided to do it differently.
E Of course, if they had worn costumes, we wouldn't have seen their expressions.
F However, they didn't do that.
G They will also save money doing it this way.
H This makes modern characters look incredibly realistic.

5 **Write a word or phrase from the text in each gap.**

1 a film or TV show which is drawn: ____________

2 what actors sometimes wear to make themselves look different: ____________

3 the fictional people in a story: ____________

4 completely different from anything else, very special: ____________

5 people who make movies: ____________

THINK | RESEARCH | CULTURE | LEARN | ME

In pairs or as a group, discuss the questions at the end of the blog post. Then write a comment to post on the blog.

10 GRAMMAR 1 | Conditionals (2): third conditional

Grammar in context

Look at these sentences from the blog post on page 103 and answer the questions.

If they'd drawn him as a cartoon, he wouldn't have seemed as real.

1 Did they decide to draw him as a cartoon?

2 Did he seem real?

If Lupita Nyong'o, who played Maz, had had to put on make-up every day to get ready for filming, it would have taken her hours.

3 Did Lupita Nyong'o put on make-up?

4 Did it take her hours each day to get ready?

REMEMBER

- The third conditional is *If* + past perfect, *would have* + past participle (*done*, *seen*, *gone*, etc.).
- We use it to describe a hypothetical situation in the past and its hypothetical result, in other words, a past situation and a result that didn't happen.
- For example, in the sentence *If **I'd known** about the show, **I'd have bought** tickets.*, the speaker didn't know about the show, and didn't buy tickets.

▶ **See Grammar reference, Unit 10,** pages 157–158

1 Rewrite the sentences as factual statements.

Example: If Lupita Nyong'o had worn make-up, it would have taken hours to get ready.
Lupita Nyong'o didn't wear make-up so it didn't take her hours to get ready.

1 If Andy Serkis had worn a rubber suit, he wouldn't have looked so unusual.

____

____

2 If they hadn't filmed real dancers for *Happy Feet*, illustrators would have drawn the dancing penguins.

____

____

3 If they hadn't used motion capture, we wouldn't have been able to see their expressions.

____

____

2 Choose the correct word or phrase to make sentences using the third conditional.

1 If our teacher **hadn't explained** / **doesn't explain** the third conditional to us, I'd have been confused!

2 Would you have looked at the Grammar reference at the back of the book if you **haven't** / **hadn't** understood the third conditional?

3 If they **hadn't** / **had** learnt English, their holiday in the UK would have been very challenging!

4 If you **were** / **had been** in school yesterday, you'd **find** / **have found** the lesson about motion capture really interesting.

5 If I **hadn't** / **haven't** read the blog post about motion capture, I **won't** / **wouldn't** have learnt about it.

6 I **will think** / **would have thought** Gollum was wearing make-up if I **didn't hear** / **hadn't heard** about motion capture.

3 Read the text and complete the sentences.

FACT FILE Jade Hameister

Millions of people post selfies on Instagram every day, and Jade Hameister is no exception. She's also a celebrity – but not because of fashion or music. In her photos, she's usually in extreme conditions. Jade is the youngest person ever to reach the North Pole, which she succeeded in doing at the age of 14. She's also skied across Greenland and to the South Pole. Jade decided to go on this adventure after meeting Vilborg Arna Gissurardóttir, the first Icelandic person to ski across Antarctica to the South Pole. Jade's dad Paul is a famous climber, which is perhaps how she managed to climb Mount Kosciuszko at the age of six, and reach Everest Base Camp at the age of 12.

1 We wouldn't have been able to see Jade's selfies if she (**post**) ____________ them online.

2 If Jade had been in fashion or music, she (**take**) ____________ photos in extreme conditions.

3 If Jade hadn't succeeded in getting to the North Pole, she might not (**decide**) ____________ to ski to the South Pole.

4 If Jade (**meet**) ____________ Vilborg Arna Gissurardóttir, she wouldn't have decided to go on this adventure.

5 Jade might not have managed to climb Mount Kosciuszko at the age of six if her father (**be**) ____________ a famous climber.

6 If I (**go**) ____________ with Jade to the North Pole, I (**feel**) ____________ very cold!

Words connected with *people in the media*

1 3.09 **Write a word from the box in each gap. Listen and check.**

actor | author | celebrity | DJ | journalist | musician | performer | presenter

1 I play the violin and piano, and I really want to be a professional ___________ when I'm older.
2 The editor of the magazine sent a ___________ to interview David Guetta, the famous French ___________ and record producer.
3 What's the name of the ___________ of the quiz show *The Chase*?
4 Eddie Redmayne is a great ___________ – he was amazing in *Fantastic Beasts*!
5 Who is the ___________ of the *Divergent* books?
6 She's a really talented ___________ – she can act, sing and dance.
7 When you're a ___________ , photographers follow you everywhere.

cinema | festival | gallery | museum | stage | studio | theatre | venue

8 Two of my aunt's paintings are in our local art ___________ .
9 They hold an outdoor music ___________ near here every summer.
10 As I walked out onto the ___________ , all my nerves disappeared!
11 The band are making their next album in a recording ___________ in New York.
12 The film starts at eight, so let's meet inside the ___________ at quarter to.
13 We're going to the ___________ tonight to see a play.
14 When we visit the science ___________ next week, you'll see a dinosaur skeleton!
15 The Grafton Centre is a great ___________ for concerts, shows and parties.

Phrasal verbs

2 3.10 **Replace the word in bold in each sentence with a phrasal verb from the box. Write the correct answer in each gap. Listen and check.**

come out | log onto/into | log out of | put on | shut up | turn down | turn up | write back

1 Enter your username and password to **enter** the site. ___________
2 We're going to **hold** a school play at the end of term! ___________
3 When I wrote a fan letter to J.K. Rowling, I didn't expect her to **reply**, but she did! ___________
4 If you don't **finish using** Facebook on a public computer, someone might post a joke comment or status update pretending to be you! ___________
5 Can you **decrease** the volume? It's too loud! ___________
6 Can you **increase** the volume? I can't hear it! ___________
7 I hate it when people talk in the cinema. Why can't they just **stop talking** and watch the film? ___________
8 The two comics I buy every week **are first sold** on a Friday. ___________

Word patterns

3 3.11 **Choose the correct word or phrase. Listen and check.**

1 How did you *manage* **getting** / **to get** tickets to the opening night of the show?
2 Are you *able* **to come** / **coming** with us to the cinema on Friday?
3 Ella's definitely *capable* **of winning** / **to win** the talent show.
4 The school play is a great *chance* **to show off** / **of showing off** your acting skills.
5 What are my *chances* **to get** / **of getting** a main part in the play?
6 I don't think my parents will *let* me **go** / **to go** to the music festival next weekend.
7 I don't think my parents will *allow* me **go** / **to go** to the music festival next weekend.
8 I don't think I'll *be* **allowed** / **let** *to go* to the music festival next weekend.

SAY IT RIGHT

Resource centre: Unit 10
/j/ before vowels

▶ Vocabulary reference, page 167 ▶ **Workbook Unit 10:** Vocabulary, pages 78–79, exercises 1, 2, 3

10 LISTENING | Gap fill

1 **In pairs or as a group, answer the questions. Use the words in the box to help you.**

backstage | cast | costumes | director hold auditions | lighting | programme rehearsals | set design | tickets

1 If a school is putting on a school play or concert, what do they need to arrange?
2 Would you like to be in a school musical?

EXAM SKILL

Selecting relevant information

- When you listen and take notes, you have to decide what to write down and what not to write down.
- Only write down the information you need. Don't write extra, unnecessary information.

2 3.12 **Listen to Amy talking about a school play. Choose the best word or phrase to complete the notes.**

Amy's feelings: excited and (1) **nervous / nervous too, of course**

The (2) **director was lovely / director**: Mrs Nowak

Place where Amy learnt her lines: her (3) **bedroom / bedroom for hours and hours**

Costumes not provided by: the (4) **school / school didn't have any**

Person who made the costume: Amy's (5) **neighbour / my neighbour: Mrs Davis**

3 **In pairs, discuss your answers to Exercise 2.**

OPTIMISE YOUR EXAM

Gap fill

- Before you listen, read through the notes and try to predict the words and phrases that might fill each gap.
- Ask yourself what kind of information you might hear, for example, a day, a number, a name, etc.

4 3.13 **You are going to listen to someone talking about a school production. For each question, write the correct answer in the gap. Write one or two words or a number or a date or a time.**

SCHOOL PRODUCTION	
Type of production:	(**1**) ____________
Title:	*Disco Inferno*
Mr Taylor:	director
Mrs Patel:	musical director
Mr Farah:	(**2**) ____________
Auditions:	in the (**3**) ____________ , next Weds and Thurs
Number of nights:	(**4**) ____________
Rehearsals:	Thursday evenings
Visit of professional photographer:	4th of (**5**) ____________
Price per ticket:	(**6**) £____________

5 3.13 **Listen again and check your answers.**

THINK | RESEARCH | CULTURE | LEARN | ME

Which would you rather do: have a small/main part in a school play, help backstage, direct, be involved with set design, help with costumes or design the programme?

 ▶ **Workbook Unit 10:** Listening, page 80, exercises 1, 2

GRAMMAR 2 | The causative

Grammar in context

Read these extracts from the audio in the listening lesson on page 106 and choose the correct word or phrase.

1 I ***was*** / ***had*** my dress made by my neighbour, Mrs Davis.

2 We're going to get programmes ***printing*** / ***printed*** …

3 Actors will have ***their photo taken*** / ***taken their photo*** for the programme by a professional photographer …

REMEMBER

- The **causative form** is *have*/*get* + object + past participle (*done*, *made*, *cleaned*, etc.). *Have* is more formal than *get*.
- We use it to talk about **getting**, **asking** or **paying someone else to do something for us**.
- We can also use it to describe things that happen to us, for example: *I **had my phone stolen** last week.* We don't usually use *get* with this meaning.
- As with the passive, we can use *by* to show who does it: *She **got the book signed** by the author.*

▶ **See Grammar reference, Unit 10,** page 158

1 Match sentence beginnings (1–6) to endings (a–f) to make sentences.

1 I got all of ____
2 When did you have your ____
3 Are you going to get ____
4 I'm never going ____
5 My dad had one of his teeth ____
6 All the celebrities had their photographs ____

a) your hair cut before the party?
b) the posters printed yesterday.
c) bedroom redecorated?
d) taken on the red carpet.
e) taken out last week.
f) to get my ears pierced!

2 Put the words and phrases in the correct order to complete these causative sentences about Ralph Fiennes in the *Harry Potter* films.

1 **completely changed / by / his appearance**
He had ______________________ make-up artists.

2 **have / shaved / his eyebrows**
He didn't ______________________ .

3 **covered / had / his eyebrows and forehead**
Instead, he ______________________ with gelatine.

3 Complete the second sentence so that it has a similar meaning to the first sentence, using the causative form.

1 When you see him in the films, it's clear they've changed the shape of his nose.
When you see him in the films, it's clear he's ______________________ .

2 Did they put in false teeth? Yes, they did!
Did he ______________________ ?
Yes, he did!

3 'Now we're going to lighten his skin,' said one of the make-up artists.
'Now he's going to ______________________ ,' said one of the make-up artists.

4 I'm not sure if they put false fingernails on his fingers.
I'm not sure if he ______________________ on his fingers.

THINK | RESEARCH | CULTURE | **LEARN** | ME

How easy or difficult do you find it to understand and use the causative?

Do you have any grammatical structures similar to the causative in your first language? How similar/different are they?

▶ **Workbook Unit 10:** Grammar 2, page 79, exercises 1, 2

That sounds like fun.

Flipped classroom

1 Watch the *Talk2Me* video and answer the questions.

1 What made Jamie's granny angry?
2 What do Angus and Maddy both promise?
3 Who does Angus describe?
4 Why do they decide to play *Snap!*?

2 Watch the video again. Underline the phrases in the *Phrase expert* box that you hear on the video.

PHRASE EXPERT

Really? | I never thought of that. | That's interesting! | That sounds like fun. | Same here. | I think you're right. | I completely agree. | I see what you mean, but … | I'm not sure I agree. | That isn't quite how I see it.

3 In pairs or as a group, answer the questions.

1 Do you like reading?
2 What kind of things do you and your friends often read?

EXAM SKILL

Listening and responding

- In a discussion, listen carefully when someone else speaks.
- Then respond to what they say to show that you've understood. Good phrases for responding include *Really?*, *That's interesting!* and *That sounds like fun.*
- You can then go on to give your own ideas.

4 3.14 Listen to two students having a discussion. For each extract, choose the question they are discussing.

1 **a)** What kind of books do you like reading?
b) What's your favourite book? Why?
2 **a)** What kind of things do you read online?
b) Do you prefer to read paper books or e-books?
3 **a)** How important is it for teenagers to read regularly?
b) What are the best kinds of books for teenagers?

5 3.14 Listen again and note down the words and phrases from the *Phrase Expert* box, they use to respond to each other.

____
____
____

OPTIMISE YOUR EXAM

General conversation

- Make sure that you and your partner speak equally during the discussion. Remember to ask questions and let your partner speak. How you interact with your partner is as important as what you say.

6 In pairs, discuss these questions.

1 What kind of books do you like reading?
2 What's your favourite book? Why?
3 How often do you buy magazines?
4 What kind of things do you read online?
5 Do you like comics?
6 Do you prefer to read paper books or e-books?
7 Do you ever decide to stop reading a book before you've finished it?
8 What are the best kinds of books for teenagers?
9 How important is it for teenagers to read regularly?

 ► **Workbook Unit 10:** Speaking, pages 80–81, exercises 1, 2, 3

LANGUAGE IN USE | Open cloze

1 **In pairs or as a group, ask and answer the questions.**

1 People sometimes make mistakes and have accidents. What kind of things do people regret doing, for example, dropping a phone and breaking it?

2 What kind of things do people regret NOT doing (e.g. not telling someone the truth)?

REMEMBER

- We can use *wish* and *if only* to describe hypothetical situations in the past, now and in the future. The verb tenses we use are the same as in conditionals.
- To talk about a hypothetical past, we can use the **third conditional**: *If I had entered the competition, I would have won.*
- We can emphasise this by using *only*: *If **only** I had entered the competition, I would have won.* We can also leave out the result clause when it's clear what the context is: *If only I had entered the competition.*
- We can also use *wish*: *I **wish** I had entered the competition.*
- To talk about a hypothetical present or future, we can use the **second conditional**: *If I had enough money, I'd buy tickets to the concert.*
- We can emphasise this by using *if only*: ***If only** I had enough money, I'd buy tickets to the concert.* We can also leave out the result clause: *If only I had enough money.*
- We can also use *wish*: *I **wish** I had enough money.*

2 **Complete the second sentence so that it has a similar meaning to the first sentence.**

1 I don't have a new smartphone.
I wish I ______________ a new smartphone.

2 What a shame I didn't see that programme last night.
I wish I ______________ that programme last night.

3 Ed lied to Julie and now he regrets it.
Ed wishes he ______________ to Julie.

4 My mum didn't let me go to the music festival, so I missed my favourite band.
If only my mum ______________ me to go to the music festival.

5 Sue's upset because she can't go to the concert.
Sue wishes she ______________ go to the concert.

OPTIMISE YOUR EXAM

Open cloze

- Remember that this task usually tests grammar.
- Think very carefully about verb tenses, verb patterns, prepositions, articles and quantifiers.

3 **Write one word in each gap to complete the text.**

Last week I won a ticket to the premiere of the new *Star Wars* film! All the stars were going to be there! Unfortunately, on **(1)** __________ day of the event, several things went wrong.

I ended up leaving home late because I couldn't find my ticket. I wish I'd been more organised! I ran to the bus stop, but just missed the bus. If **(2)** __________ it had waited for me! When I finally arrived at the cinema, all the stars were already inside.

Anyway, the film was brilliant. Afterwards, I waited outside, hoping I'd manage **(3)** __________ take a selfie with Daisy Ridley (my favourite actress!). She was there, but people **(4)** __________ in front of me and I couldn't see her. If only I was taller!

I wish I **(5)** __________ the chance to do it all again and I wish I had **(6)** __________ able to say hi to Daisy. Maybe another time!

THINK | RESEARCH | CULTURE | LEARN | ME

Think of three things you wish you had done in the past year, and three things you wish you hadn't done. Write sentences with *If only* …

1 In pairs or groups, answer the questions.

1 Do you ever make short videos or audio files to share with your friends?

2 Do you know what a 'podcast' is? Have you ever downloaded one and listened to it?

EXAM SKILL

Describing how to do something

- In an article, you sometimes have to give instructions to the reader on how to do something.
- Use a variety of phrases and structures. For example, you can use the imperative: *Think of an interesting topic.* / *You have/need to* (e.g. *You need to speak clearly.*) / *You should* / *Remember to* / *Don't forget to* / *It's important to*, etc.

2 Read this article. In pairs or groups, answer the questions.

Podcast fun!

Do you listen to podcasts? They're audio blogs you can download. They're easy and fun to make. You just need a smartphone or computer that can record audio.

You can make a podcast by yourself, but I think it's more fun to make one with friends. Before you start, think of an interesting topic to discuss.

When you record, remember to speak clearly. It's important to make it interesting and entertaining, so be enthusiastic!

Afterwards, don't forget to give it an interesting title. Then you can share it using social media or a podcast app. It's great to make one regularly – perhaps once a month. Your friends will love them! Good luck!

1 What equipment do you need to make a podcast?

2 Does the writer prefer to make podcasts alone or with others?

3 What should you decide on before you start recording?

4 What advice does the writer give about recording a podcast?

5 What advice does the writer give about after you've recorded it?

3 Each word or phrase in bold is incorrect. Rewrite it correctly in each gap.

1 **Make you** sure you choose a subject people will be interested in. ________________

2 **Not to talk** for too long. Ten minutes is perfect! ________________

3 You **should to** check that the microphone is the right distance from you. ________________

4 **Remember that** to listen to it before you share it. ________________

5 If you don't like what you recorded, just **you delete** it and start again! ________________

6 It's important **of asking** your friends if they enjoyed it. ________________

OPTIMISE YOUR EXAM

An article

- When you write an article, it's important to interest the readers.
- A good way to do that is to start by asking a direct question, such as *Do you listen to podcasts?* or *Have you ever thought of making a podcast?*
- Another way to get your readers interested is to start with a sentence that makes them want to read more.

4 **Look at this writing task. Match each event (1–5) to a piece of advice (a–e).**

You have seen this notice on a website for teenagers.

> As part of our *How to …* series, we're looking for short articles giving advice about how to put on a play, concert or talent show with your friends, how to perform a magic show for your friends or family, or how to organise a surprise party for someone. Choose one of them and give us your ideas!

Write your **article**.

1 play ____ **2** concert ____ **3** talent show ____ **4** magic show ____ **5** surprise party ____

a) Look on YouTube for some great card tricks to learn.
b) Don't forget to think about costumes for the actors.
c) Remind everyone to keep it a secret!
d) Try to include some singing, some dancing, maybe even some comedy and magic.
e) Ask your friends what musical instruments they can play, and who can sing.

5 **Choose one event from Exercise 4 and write the four most important pieces of advice.**

Type of event: ....
Advice 1: ....
Advice 2: ....
Advice 3: ....
Advice 4: ....

6 **Plan** **Make a paragraph plan.**

Part	Purpose	Useful phrases	My notes
Title	explain what the article is about, and interest the reader		
Paragraph 1	introduce the subject	*Do you …? Have you ever …?* *I've always wanted to be a magician, so …*	
Paragraph 2 **Paragraph 3** **Paragraph 4**	give your advice in the order in which they should do the things	*Don't forget to …, It's important to …* *You can …, Then you should …* *It's great if you can …, Remember to …*	

7 **Write** **Write your article in an appropriate style. Write about 100 words.**

8 **Check** **Before you hand in your article, complete this checklist.**

Checklist

- ◯ I've given my article a title.
- ◯ I've started my article in an interesting way.
- ◯ I've explained clearly what to do and think about.
- ◯ I've used friendly, conversational language.
- ◯ I've used different phrases to introduce advice.
- ◯ I've checked my spelling, grammar and punctuation.

▶ **Writing reference,** page 170 ▶ **Workbook Unit 10:** Writing, page 82, exercises 1, 2, 3, 4 and Progress check 10, page 83

PROGRESS CHECK UNITS 9–10

GRAMMAR AND VOCABULARY

1 If a word or phrase in bold is correct, put a tick. If it's incorrect, rewrite it correctly in each gap.

1 If a player gets the ball in the net, they **would score** three points. ______________
2 If you **practise** more, you would be a much better player. ______________
3 If you had more money, **do** you go to concerts more often? ______________
4 I **wouldn't want** to be a chaser if I played quidditch. ______________
5 What **do** you do if you have free time at the weekend? ______________
6 If tonight's match isn't on TV, we **would listen** to it on the radio. ______________

__/6

2 Write a word from the box in each gap.

catch | come | knock | log | put (x2) | send | turn

1 I don't think your idea for 'tennis on ice' will ever __________ on!
2 I tried to __________ onto the ticket website for over an hour.
3 Why did the referee __________ you off during the match?
4 We're going to __________ a show on for other pupils in the school gym.
5 Could you __________ the TV up? I can't hear a thing.
6 Because of the rain, the match has been __________ off until next week.
7 Just one more point and he will __________ his opponent out of the competition!
8 When does Taylor Swift's new album __________ out?

__/8

3 Complete the sentences using the correct form of the verbs in brackets.

1 I wish I ______________ (**have**) more money. Then I could buy myself a new tablet.
2 If only you ______________ (**be**) taller! Then you could be in the basketball team.
3 When it started to rain, I wished I ______________ (**bring**) my umbrella.
4 I wish I ______________ (**go**) to see the new film last night.
5 If only Sam and Harry ______________ (**be**) in our team last Saturday!
6 The film was terrible! I wish I ______________ (**not agree**) to take my little sister to see it.

__/6

4 Choose the correct word.

1 I would love to **go** / **play** windsurfing and see what it's like.
2 How did you **manage** / **succeed** to get tickets for tonight's show?
3 How long have you been **doing** / **going** gymnastics?
4 Will your mum and dad **allow** / **let** you to go to the concert on your own?
5 I'm sorry, but I won't be **able** / **capable** to go to the cinema this evening.
6 I don't know whether to **do** / **play** athletics or yoga this year.

__/6

5 Complete the sentences with the correct causative form using the verb in capitals.

1 When did you ______________ your hair ______________ ? It suits you. **CUT**
2 Our neighbours ______________ their car ______________ bright pink last week! **PAINT**
3 Did it hurt when you ______________ your ears ______________ ? **PIERCE**
4 I need to ______________ my photo ______________ for my new passport. **TAKE**
5 I think I'll ______________ flowers ______________ to Mum for her birthday. **DELIVER**
6 Have you ever ______________ your eyes ______________ ? **TEST**

__/6

6 Complete the sentences using the correct form of the verbs in brackets.

1 When we ______________ (**get**) to the beach, we ______________ (**call**) you.
2 I ______________ (**keep**) trying until I ______________ (**learn**) how to skateboard perfectly.
3 As soon as we ______________ (**arrive**) at the cinema, I ______________ (**buy**) you some popcorn.
4 They ______________ (**continue**) with the match once it ______________ (**stop**) raining.
5 Don't worry – I ______________ (**look after**) your bike while you ______________ (**shop**).
6 I'm sure the players ______________ (**not/start**) celebrating before the match ______________ (**be**) over.

__/6

7 Match each person to a word connected to what they do.

1 gamer ___	a) circus
2 presenter ___	b) book
3 acrobat ___	c) bike
4 author ___	d) computer
5 cyclist ___	e) team
6 captain ___	f) quiz show

__/6

8 Choose the correct word or phrase.

1 If we **didn't score** / **hadn't scored** in the last second, we would have lost the match!
2 I **would help** / **would have helped** you if I had known you had a problem.
3 It would have been a good film if the acting **had been** / **has been** better.
4 What would you **do** / **have done** if you had been me in that situation?
5 My parents wouldn't have let me go to the show if I **was** / **had been** on my own.
6 She wouldn't **become** / **have become** champion if she hadn't practised for years.

__/6

Total score __/50

EXAM SKILLS

Tick the statements that are true for you. Review the skills in the unit if you need more help.

I can …	**Unit/page**
☐ understand implication in an online article	Unit 9 p92
☐ identify why some answers are incorrect in multiple-choice listening tasks	Unit 9 p96
☐ talk about other people and their habits in an interview	Unit 9 p98
☐ understand different forms of verbs and use them in multiple-choice cloze activities	Unit 9 p99
☐ use the correct language to express preferences in an email	Unit 9 p100
☐ understand linking words and phrases in a blog post	Unit 10 p102
☐ select relevant information in a short talk	Unit 10 p106
☐ listen to my partner and respond appropriately in a conversation	Unit 10 p108
☐ understand and form conditionals and use them in open cloze activities	Unit 10 p109
☐ give instructions in an article	Unit 10 p110

11 Curious minds

READING | Matching | An online guide

1 **In pairs or as a group, answer the questions.**

1 Have you ever got a certificate or an award for doing something? Explain what it was for.

2 Explain the difference between these words. Use a dictionary if necessary.

certificate	degree	diploma	qualification

____

____

____

____

2 **For each pair, decide which word or phrase (a or b) is more specific.**

		a)	b)
1	____	**a)** social media	**b)** Facebook
2	____	**a)** performing	**b)** acting
3	____	**a)** a trip to a castle	**b)** tourism
4	____	**a)** canoeing	**b)** water sports
5	____	**a)** online media	**b)** videos
6	____	**a)** culinary school	**b)** pastry school
7	____	**a)** technology	**b)** software
8	____	**a)** audience	**b)** public

EXAM SKILL

Understanding specific information

- When reading for specific information, think about finding synonyms in the text. For example, if the text talks about *pupils*, another way of saying this is *students*.
- You should also think about how information can be more specific. For example, if the text talks about *learning a musical instrument*, a more specific way of saying this might be *having piano lessons*.

OPTIMISE YOUR EXAM

Matching

- Part of the information about someone may match with more than one of the paragraphs. For example, if someone in Exercise 3 likes performing, they might match with either D, E or H.
- Read all the other information carefully to choose between the possible answers.

Summer Camp

Our guide to unusual ways to spend your summer!

A Robotics Camp
Robotics Camp is fun and **educational**, all at the same time! Students choose to work alone or in pairs to build and program a robot. With sessions for different levels of ability, you'll learn how to use the right software and how to construct your robot. Please note that students are not allowed to keep any of the materials used at the camp.

B Camp BizSmart
At Camp BizSmart, we'll give you all kinds of tips about starting and running your own business. You'll get **experience** in working with successful people and working in teams. You'll **graduate** from camp with your own business plan ready to go! One recent visitor said she had learnt more in a week here than in a year at her school!

C Kids' Culinary Academy
Kids' Culinary Academy is perfect for young people who either want to learn the **basics** or develop their skills. Each day is a new adventure in learning about a different type of cuisine. It is easy to **enrol** and our excursions in the local area include trips to well-known foodie destinations, as well as other tourist attractions.

D Camp Kids 'N Comedy
If you want to put up a tent, climb trees and learn how to survive in the wild, then Camp Kids 'N Comedy isn't for you! But if you're full of opinions, we'll take you and turn you into a confident performer. Our **experts** will help you write material and practise your show. You'll soon have the audience laughing!

E Camp Jam
From songwriting to playing as a band, Camp Jam will **guide** you every step of the way. You'll perform live and make recordings that are yours to keep. Not only that, but we'll also teach you all you need to know about getting more fans and surviving in the music industry.

F Plantation Farm Camp
We all need a break from our smartphones, and Plantation Farm Camp offers exactly that. With no electricity, the camp allows young people to get away from the pressures of their online lives and make friendships that last a lifetime. By growing and preparing your own food, you'll connect with nature and with each other.

G Camp Can-Aqua
Camp Can-Aqua is the perfect place to learn water sports. Students select different activities each day to develop their own individual skills. You'll also get the chance to go on a three-day canoe trip, where you'll learn to rely on those around you. Older students can attend leadership camps, where they may get a certificate in important skills!

H Hollywood Stunt Camp
You need to be fit for Hollywood Stunt Camp! You'll need all your energy as you learn how to fall, fight and jump off a building! **Professionals** will take you all the way from the basics to appearing in a short movie. The camp ends with a stunt show, where you can show off what you've learnt!

3 3.15 **Decide which camp would be the most suitable for the people below.**

1 Ricardo enjoys performing and likes writing too. He loves telling jokes! However, he's not very keen on music and doesn't want to go camping. ____

2 Natasha really likes cooking and loves being outdoors. She's not interested in sightseeing, and wants a camp where she can forget about social media while she's there. ____

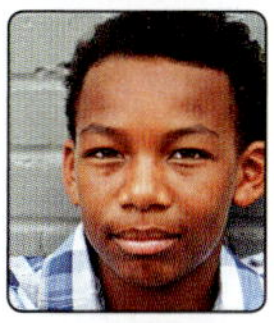

3 Marcus likes adventure and going on trips. He loves trying new things, but likes to choose what he does. He'd like to get a qualification at the end of the camp. ____

4 Maria doesn't want to do anything that looks dangerous. She loves music and is keen on performing. She'd like a camp where she can learn about a future career and take something home at the end. ____

5 Dylan loves cooking and eating, and wants to learn more about food preparation and places that particular foods come from. He needs to stay in touch with his family using social media while he's at camp. ____

4 **Find words and phrases in the text which match these definitions.**

1 people who are good at something and do it as a job: ____________
2 people who know a lot about a subject: ____________
3 teaching you something: ____________
4 the most important things you need to learn first: ____________
5 knowledge and skill from doing something: ____________
6 join a course or become a student at a place: ____________
7 help someone learn something: ____________
8 complete a course, often at college or university: ____________

THINK | RESEARCH | CULTURE | LEARN | **ME**

Which camp from the text would you like to go to and why?

11 GRAMMAR 1 | Reported speech

Grammar in context

Read this sentence from the online guide on page 115. Match the sentence to the correct form of direct speech.

One recent visitor said she had learnt more in a week here than in a year at her school! ____

a) 'I have learnt more in a week here than in a year at my school!'

b) 'She learns more in a week here than in a year at her school!'

REMEMBER

- We use reported speech to describe what someone said, without giving their exact words.
- Compared to direct speech, reported speech generally uses different tenses. For example: *'I **am going** to Camp Jam,'* Layla said. ➔ Layla said she ***was going*** to Camp Jam.
- Modal verbs are also used differently in reported speech. For example: *'It'**ll** be fun!' Oliver said.* ➔ *Oliver said it **would** be fun.*
- Some other words which refer to time, place and people are used differently in reported speech. For example: *'**My** brother loved summer camp **last year**,' Joe said.* ➔ *Joe said **his** brother had loved summer camp **the year before**.*

▶ **See Grammar reference, Unit 11,** page 159

1 Choose the correct word or phrase.

1 'Everyone is enjoying Robotics Camp,' Lucy said.
Lucy said everyone **enjoyed** / **was enjoying** Robotics Camp.

2 'It's important to learn the basics,' the tutor said.
The tutor said it **was** / **will be** important to learn the basics.

3 'Lilly stayed at Hollywood Stunt Camp,' Ravi said.
Ravi said Lilly **was staying** / **had stayed** at Hollywood Stunt Camp.

4 'I've been thinking about going to summer camp,' Alex said.
Alex said he **had been thinking** / **was thinking** about going to summer camp.

5 'You'll have a great time at Camp Kids'N Comedy!' Harry said to me.
Harry said I **could** / **would** have a great time at Camp Kids'N Comedy.

6 'Summer camp was very educational last year,' Joel said.
Joel said summer camp **has been** / **had been** very educational the year **before** / **ago**.

7 'They taught me a lot at Camp Jam,' Oli said.
Oli said they **have taught him** / **had taught him** a lot at Camp Jam.

8 'We had fun at camp last summer,' Mia said.
Mia said **they have had** / **they had had** fun at camp the summer **before** / **last**.

2 Rewrite each sentence using reported speech.

1 'It's the best summer camp ever!' Priya said.
____

2 'We're having a great time here!' Zoe said.
____

3 'Jack gave me a few camping tips,' Nadia said.
____

4 'We've been here for over a week,' Sam said.
____

5 'I can cook really well after a few lessons,' Joshua said.
____

6 'You'll love it here,' Fatima said to me.
____

3 Read the sentences in reported speech and write what they said.

1 Ryan said he'd never been to a summer camp before.
'____________________,' Ryan said.

2 Luke said he was feeling better now he had made a few friends.
'____________________,' Luke said.

3 Alina said she had gone to the same camp that year as the year before.
'____________________,' Alina said.

4 Leah said she had been having canoe lessons since the summer before.
'____________________,' Leah said.

THINK | **RESEARCH** | CULTURE | LEARN | ME

Think of a person you admire (a celebrity, someone in the media, etc.). Find a quote that they said and turn it into reported speech. Read both to your class.

Words connected with *studying*

1 3.16 **Write a word from the boxes in each gap. Listen and check.**

lesson	subject

1 A school ___________ is a period of time when you are in the classroom.
2 A school ___________ is an area of study, like maths, English or history.

read	study

3 When you ___________ , you try to learn something.
4 When you ___________ , you look at letters on a page to see what they mean.

primary	secondary

5 In the UK, you go to ___________ school between the ages of 5 and 11.
6 In the UK, you go to ___________ school between the ages of 11 and 18.

pass	take

7 You ___________ or sit an exam when you try to answer the questions on an exam paper.
8 You ___________ an exam when your mark is high enough.

pupil	student

9 A ___________ is someone at primary or secondary school, but not university.
10 A ___________ is someone at school, at college or at university.

Phrasal verbs

2 3.17 **Match to make sentences. Use the words in italics to help you. Listen and check.**

1 Our teacher asked us to *copy* ____
2 Our school *breaks* ____
3 We have to *hand* our homework ____
4 We asked the teacher to *go* ____
5 My brother was at college but he *dropped* ____
6 Make sure you study or you'll *fall* ____

a) *up* for the holidays on Friday!
b) *out* because he didn't like it.
c) *in* on Monday morning.
d) *out* the vocabulary from the textbook.
e) *behind* the other students.
f) *over* the explanation one more time.

Idioms for *education and learning*

3 3.18 **Choose the correct definition for each idiom. Listen and check.**

1 'You always *have your nose in a book*! You should go outside for some fresh air.'
a) read
b) play

2 'We have to *learn* these words *by heart*. And we've only got two days to do it!'
a) study and remember
b) read and write

3 'Congratulations. You've *passed* the test *with flying colours*!'
a) with a low mark
b) with a high mark

4 'How are we going to solve the problem? We'll have to *put our thinking caps on*.'
a) ask someone for help
b) consider something carefully

5 'When I started my new job, it didn't take long to *learn the ropes*.'
a) know what to do
b) get bored

6 'Ben's always playing tricks on me. I'm going to *teach* him *a lesson*!'
a) take someone to school
b) punish someone so they behave better

4 **Choose four idioms from Exercise 3. In pairs, write a short dialogue that includes those idioms. Perform your dialogue for the class.**

'Hi, Dan. Do you want to come and play football?'

'No, I have to ***learn*** *these pages* ***by heart****. We're having a test on Monday.'*

'Oh, you've always ***got your nose in a book****. Why don't you …'*

THINK | RESEARCH | CULTURE | **LEARN** | ME

Writing your own dialogues is a great way to learn new vocabulary. Try writing a short dialogue using some of the phrasal verbs from Exercise 2. Vote to choose the best dialogue!

1 In pairs or as a group, answer the questions.

1 What do you think the best and worst things about working as a teacher are?
2 Would you like to work as a teacher? Why / Why not?

EXAM SKILL

Understanding implication

- You don't always hear everything explicitly. You have to use logic to work out the answer.
- For example, in Exercise 3, question 1, the three pictures show a maths lesson, a science lesson and a geography lesson. When you listen to the recording, you won't hear those exact words.
- Think about the words you do hear and use logic to decide what the school subject is.

2 Read what these teachers say and decide what subject each one is teaching. Explain how you know.

1 OK, class. Now, last time we were thinking about safety and using the equipment properly. Now it's time to get into teams and start practising.

2 Right, everyone. I hope you've all studied the text I asked you to look at. What did you learn from the soldier's diary? What did he think about what was happening in 1940?

3 Now, let's go over this again. The climate in this part of the world is very wet, so they grow rice instead of wheat. Daisy, what do the farmers do to help it grow?

OPTIMISE YOUR EXAM

3-option multiple choice (pictures)

- You might be able to decide that one picture is definitely wrong, even if you're not sure which picture is the right answer.
- Cross that picture out and choose between the other two. If you're really not sure, make a guess. Don't leave any questions blank.

3 3.19 Listen to the extracts and choose the correct answers.

1 What subject is the teacher teaching?

A B C

2 Where is Callum now?

A B C

3 What does the girl want to learn?

A B C

4 How did Mike get to school today?

A B C

4 3.19 Listen again and check your answers.

THINK | RESEARCH | CULTURE | LEARN | ME

What is your favourite school subject? What do you like about it? Are there any subjects you don't like?

 ▶ **Workbook Unit 11:** Listening, page 88, exercises 1, 2

GRAMMAR 2 | Reported questions

Grammar in context

Look at these sentences in reported speech from the audio in the listening lesson on page 118. Match the sentences to what the girl's mum said.

1 *My mum asked how much the course was.* ____

a) 'How much the course is?'

b) 'How much is the course?'

2 *And she asked if I needed to buy anything.* ____

a) 'Do you need to buy anything?'

b) 'If you need to buy anything?'

REMEMBER

- With reported *wh-* questions (*what, who, how*, etc.), we repeat the question word and change the tense and the word order: *'What are you reading?'* → *She asked me what I was reading.*
- With reported *yes/no* questions, we use *if* or *whether* and change the tense and the word order: *'Do you wear a school uniform?'* → *She asked me **if** we wore a school uniform.*
- We also change time and place words like we do in reported statements.

▶ **See Grammar reference, Unit 11,** page 159

1 Read these sentences. If the second sentence is correct, put a tick. If it is incorrect, underline the mistake and rewrite it correctly on the line.

1 'Do you go to your local secondary school?'
She asked me if I had gone to my local secondary school. ______________________

2 'Who was your teacher last year?'
He asked me who my teacher had been the year before. ______________________

3 'Have you forgotten your homework?'
She asked me whether I have forgotten your homework. ______________________

4 'Where did you put your pencil case?'
He asked me where I did put my pencil case.
____

5 'How much did you spend on your uniform?'
She asked me how much did I spend on my uniform. ______________________

6 'When will your sister graduate from college?'
He asked me when my sister would graduate from college. ______________________

2 Write a word or phrase in each gap.

1 'What's your favourite subject at school?'
He asked me ____________ my favourite school subject ____________ .

2 'Where have you been?'
She ____________ where ____________ .

3 'Have you ever passed a test with flying colours?'
He ____________ I ____________ a test with flying colours.

4 'Can you help me study for the test?'
She ____________ I ____________ study for the test.

5 'How did you pass the test without doing any revision?'
He ____________ me how I ____________ passed the test without doing any revision.

3 Complete what Bethany says about Li's questions.

To: Bethany Subject: Your school

Hi Bethany!

I'm doing a project on education and I have a few questions.

What school do you go to? When did you start there? Does your school have a uniform? What's it like? Does everyone have to wear it? Can students wear their own clothes? Do you think a school uniform is a good idea?

Write soon!

Li

Bethany's Blog!

HOME | ABOUT ME | **POSTS** | LINKS

Posted at 7:30 pm

I got an email from my friend Li, who lives in China. He asked me a few questions.

He asked (**1**) ______________________ .
Then he asked (**2**) ______________________ .
He also asked (**3**) ______________________
and (**4**) ______________________ .
Then he asked (**5**) ______________________ .
He asked (**6**) ______________________ .
Finally, he asked (**7**) ______________________ .
I'll let you know my answers next time!

SAY IT RIGHT

Resource centre: Unit 11
/s/ and /ʃ/

11 SPEAKING | Extended turn (photos)

Talk 2 Me
I'm not sure, but ...

Flipped classroom

1 **Watch the *Talk2Me* video and answer the questions.**

1 What school subjects does each friend have homework for?
2 True or false? Shakespeare said 'Now I shall go to sleep. Goodnight.'
3 Apart from nuts, what was in the cake Maddy's mum made?

2 **Watch the video again. Underline the phrases in the *Phrase expert* box that you hear on the video.**

PHRASE EXPERT

I'm not sure, but … | I guess/imagine/suppose … | It looks like/as if … | They seem to be … | Maybe/Perhaps they're … They could/might/may be … | It's possible that … | It could be that … | It isn't clear whether they're … or …

3 **In pairs or as a group, answer the questions.**

1 Describe what's happening in the photo.
2 Have you ever been on a school trip? What was it like and what did you learn?

EXAM SKILL

Expressing uncertainty

- If you're not sure what's happening in a photo, don't worry! You don't need to be certain. Guessing information about the people and the situation will give you a lot more to say about the photo.
- To show that you're not certain, use words and phrases like *perhaps*, *I think …* or *it looks like …*, e.g. *It looks like they're on a school trip. Perhaps they're learning about history.*
- You can also use modal verbs to express uncertainty, e.g. *might*, *may* or *could*.

4 3.20 **Listen to a student describing this photo. In your own words, explain the points that the student made.**

5 3.20 **Listen again and write a word in each gap to complete the phrases you hear.**

1 It looks ____________ if …
2 I ____________ she wants …
3 It ____________ to me that …
4 I ____________ they could be …
5 I ____________ they're all …

OPTIMISE YOUR EXAM

Extended turn (photos)

- If you run out of ideas, but you still have time left, don't just stop talking.
- Go back to something you have already mentioned and talk about it in more detail. Keep speaking until the examiner tells you to stop.

6 **Describe this photo. Try to speak for at least one minute.**

1 In pairs or as a group, answer the questions.

1 Describe what you can see in the photo.
2 What's the average time it takes for you and your classmates to get to school? Who has the longest journey?

REMEMBER

- Some nouns have similar meanings. For example, we can say *The* ***problem*** *with* … or *The* ***trouble*** *with history is all the dates to remember.*
- Which one we use sometimes depends on grammar. We can say *a problem* but we can't say *a trouble* because *trouble* is uncountable.
- Sometimes it depends on collocation: you *get into trouble* but you don't *get into problem*.
- Sometimes it depends on meaning: you have *problems* to solve in maths, but not *troubles*.

2 Choose the correct word.

1 I've had some **problem** / **trouble** with my phone recently.
2 There's a **variety** / **collection** of different activities to choose from.
3 Who's your favourite pop **champion** / **star**?
4 It **took** / **became** a long time for me to do all my homework.
5 The film was a box office **bestseller** / **success**.
6 It doesn't **matter** / **mind** if you write in pen or pencil in the test.

3 Quickly read the text in Exercise 4 and answer the questions.

1 Why is the School of the Air necessary?
2 What did pupils do until the 1950s?
3 What's the problem with doing lessons by post?
4 How does the School of the Air work?

OPTIMISE YOUR EXAM

4-option multiple-choice cloze

- When you've chosen all your answers, read the text again with the missing words inserted.
- For each word, check that the meaning makes sense. Ask yourself if it sounds natural, if it fits grammatically and if it is part of a phrase or collocation which you know.

4 Choose the correct word to fill each gap.

School of the Air

Australia is a huge country, and many children live in remote areas, which can create a **(1)** ____ because those young people still need to be taught. The solution is the School of the Air.

Until the 1950s, the **(2)** ____ for pupils living far from a school was either to live away from home or **(3)** ____ their lessons by post. This made learning difficult because of the length of time it **(4)** ____ to get an answer to questions.

The first School of the Air started in the 1950s and quickly became a **(5)** ____ . Using two-way radios, young people could finally have daily contact with their teacher and other students.

Today, there are around 16 Schools of the Air, offering both primary and secondary education. The School of the Air is proof that it doesn't **(6)** ____ where children live in Australia – they can all go to school.

	A	B	C	D
1	**A** trouble	**B** mistake	**C** problem	**D** fault
2	**A** variety	**B** election	**C** collection	**D** choice
3	**A** do	**B** make	**C** gain	**D** read
4	**A** became	**B** took	**C** had	**D** was
5	**A** star	**B** winner	**C** champion	**D** success
6	**A** matter	**B** mind	**C** bother	**D** worry

11 WRITING | An email

1 **In pairs or as a group, answer the questions.**

1. Imagine you are not at school because you're ill. How can you make sure you don't miss anything important in the lessons?
2. What can you do to pass the time at home?

EXAM SKILL

Understanding the notes

- Notes on emails may ask you to respond to information, make a suggestion, express a preference, give information, ask questions, give a reason, etc.
- For each note, look at the word in the note and the word(s) it is connected to. Pay attention to any question words used. Then ask yourself: What does the note want me to do? What words and phrases can I use to do that?

2 **Read the email and notes and answer the questions.**

From: Maria
To: Ellie
Subject: Notes from school

Hi Ellie,

How are you? As you know, I didn't come to school today because I'm ill. I've got a really bad cold. I hope it goes away soon! — *Me too!*

Tell Maria — What work did I miss? Was it important?

Can I borrow any notes you took to see what I've missed? You could email them to me or bring them round to my house, whatever you prefer. — *Say what you prefer*

I'm so bored at home. Any ideas what I should do to pass the time? — *Suggest …*

Write soon!

Maria

1. Does the first note mean 'I'm also ill.' or 'I also hope you get well soon.'?
2. For the second note, what do you have to tell Maria?
3. For the third note, what options do you have?
4. For the fourth note, what things could you suggest?

3 **Read Ellie's reply to Maria and choose the best response to each note. Give reasons for your answers.**

From: Ellie
To: Maria
Subject: RE: Notes from school

Hi Maria,

Thanks for your email. Sorry to hear you're ill. (**1**) ____

(**2**) ____ We also had PE but we didn't do anything important.

Yes, of course you can have my notes. (**3**) ____ It'll be nice to see you!

I'm sorry you're bored. (**4**) ____

See you later!
Ellie

1. **a)** I hope it goes away soon!
   b) I hope you get better soon too!
2. **a)** You missed a maths test, and we did an interesting experiment in physics which you need to know about.
   b) Don't worry! I'll tell Maria that you've missed some work.
3. **a)** I'm not free this evening so I'll email them to you now.
   b) I don't have plans for this evening so I'll bring them round at about six.
4. **a)** How about starting a big jigsaw? Have you got one?
   b) Why don't you go for a long walk outside?

OPTIMISE YOUR EXAM

An email

- With some notes, you can use the same words in the note. For example, if the note says *Great!*, you could write *That's great news!* You can also express the same idea with a synonym, for example: *That's fantastic news!*
- With other notes, you can't use the same words because they're instructions. For example, *Tell Maria*, *Explain*, *Suggest …*

4 Look at this writing task and decide if the statements are T (True) or F (False).

Read this email from your friend Pete and the notes you have made.

From: Pete

Subject: Summer camp!

Hi!

I'm thinking of going to a summer camp in Germany for the last two weeks of July. They have lots of activities, including canoeing and rock-climbing. — *Amazing!*

Can you come too? It would be great to have a friend with me. — *No, because …*

After the camp I am going on holiday with my family. What are your plans for August? Are you doing anything fun? — *Tell Pete*

Let's have a video call sometime this weekend if you're free! — *Suggest …*

Bye for now!

Pete

Write your **email** to Pete using **all the notes**.

1 You think the camp and activities sound fun. **T / F**

2 You're able to go to the camp with Pete. **T / F**

3 For the third note, you have to think of your own ideas. **T / F**

4 For the fourth note, you're going to suggest some videos for Pete to watch. **T / F**

5 Look at the notes in the email in Exercise 4 again and answer the questions to expand on the notes. Use your imagination!

1 Why can't you go to the camp with Pete? ______________________

2 What are your plans for August? ______________________

3 When's a good day and time to have a video call with Pete? ______________________

6 Plan Make a paragraph plan.

Part	Purpose	Useful phrases	My notes
First line	greet the person you are writing to	*Hi …, Hi …! Dear …,*	
Paragraph 1	thank the other person for their email and write about the first note on the email	*Thanks for …* *The camp sounds …*	
Paragraph 2	write about the second note on the email	*I'd love to come too but …* *Unfortunately, I'm …*	
Paragraph 3	write about the third note on the email	*I'm not sure yet …* *We've already planned to …*	
Paragraph 4	write about the fourth note on the email	*How about …? What about …?* *Are you free on … at …?*	
Closing expressions	say goodbye/express friendship	*Bye for now! Talk soon!* *Love, Lots of love, All the best,*	
Your name	First name		

7 Write Write your email to Pete in an appropriate style. Use all the notes. Write about 100 words.

8 Check Before you hand in your email, complete this checklist.

Checklist

- ◯ I've given a reason why I can't go to the camp.
- ◯ I've told Pete what my plans are for August.
- ◯ I've suggested a day and time for a video call.
- ◯ I've checked my spelling, grammar and punctuation.

▶ **Writing reference,** page 173 ▶ **Workbook Unit 11:** Writing, page 90, exercises 1, 2, 3, 4 and Progress check 11, page 91

12 Our wonderful world

READING | 3-option multiple choice | Short messages

1 In pairs or as a group, discuss the questions.

1 What can you see in the photos?

2 Which of the following do you do to help the world around you? Make notes and say why.

clean the beach | not use plastic bags
recycle paper/glass/tins | use water carefully
walk or ride a bike to school

EXAM SKILL

Understanding instructions

- Short messages often ask or tell people to do things.
- Look for verbs in the imperative and for phrases such as *please, could you …, will you …, you should …*, etc.

2 Read the instructions and choose the correct answers.

1 Contact tim@riverways.org.
   a) You should send an email.
   b) You should send a text.

2 Ring or text me before 6 tonight.
   a) You have to make a phone call.
   b) You can choose how to communicate.

3 You should call before 5.
   a) Phone before 5 o'clock.
   b) Text before 5 o'clock.

4 Mum asks if you'll take us there tomorrow morning.
   a) Please drive us.
   b) Please call Mum.

5 Get in touch with holly@postbox.com.
   a) Send an email.
   b) Write a letter.

3 Read the short messages quickly and answer these questions.

1 What project does Holly take part in?

2 What does she decide to do after this project?

1

RIVER CLEAN-UP!

Help the environment – collect litter!
Saturday 9 am, Stonebridge.
Equipment provided but bring refreshments.
For transport, contact tim@riverways.org

2

From: Holly To: Katie

It's the clean-up tomorrow! Text me before 6 pm if you want to go with me and Mum. If not, we'll take someone else.
Holly

3

15:33
Online
Dad
79%

We'll have collected 50 bags of rubbish by the time we finish! Mum's asking if you'll drive us there tomorrow morning as she's busy!
Holly

4

Holly,
The local radio rang! They want to interview you about helping with pollution problems. They said you should phone them to arrange a time.
Mum

5

NEW CLUB

Help local wildlife through clean-up projects!
Come along with your ideas!
For details of the first meeting, contact
holly@postbox.com

OPTIMISE YOUR **EXAM**

3-option multiple choice

- For a possible answer to be correct, all parts of it must be correct.
- Look for words like *and*, *both* or *all* in the possible answers. They might mean there is more than one part to the answer. For example, in Exercise 4, question 1 A says 'You have to take your own lunch and your own equipment.' Both parts must be correct to make A the correct answer.

4 3.21 **Read the text again. For each question, choose the correct answer.**

1
A You have to take your own lunch and equipment.
B You have to travel to Stonebridge by yourself.
C You have to send an email if you need help getting there.

2
A Katie should tell Holly if she wants to travel with her.
B Katie needs to go to Holly's house before 6 o'clock.
C Katie has to find someone to go with Holly and her mum.

3
A Holly wants her dad to join them the following day.
B Holly needs her dad to help them take the rubbish away when they finish.
C Holly asks her dad if he can drive them there the next day.

4
A Holly should ring her mother to discuss a radio interview.
B Holly needs to visit the local radio station to be interviewed.
C Holly must call the local radio station about doing an interview.

5
A New club members should decide where to have the first meeting.
B People interested in the club should contact Holly to find out more.
C People who want to join the club should send suggestions to Holly by email.

5 **Write words from the texts that match the definitions.**

1 Find a word that means *pieces of paper, etc., that people drop on the floor in public places*: ____________
2 Find a word that means *the natural world around us*: ____________
3 Find a word that means *things you throw away because they're no longer useful*: ____________
4 Find a word that means *things that have a harmful effect on the natural world, such as chemicals*: ____________
5 Find a word that means *animals, birds and plants that live in the natural world*: ____________

▶ **Workbook Unit 12:** Reading, pages 92–93, exercises 1, 2, 3, 4

Grammar in context

Read this sentence from the text message on page 125 and choose the correct meaning.

We'll have collected 50 bags of rubbish by the time we finish!

a) We will finish and then we will collect 50 bags of rubbish.

b) Before we finish, we will collect 50 bags of rubbish.

REMEMBER

- The **future perfect** is *will* + *have* + past participle: *will have done, will have made*, etc.
- We use the future perfect to talk about actions completed at some time between now and a point in the future:
  - we can use *might* in the future perfect to mean *will possibly: We **might have discovered** life on other planets by 2050.*
  - we can use *should* in the future perfect to mean *will probably: He **should have recovered** from his injury by the next game.*
  - we often use *by* and *by the time* with the future perfect: *I won't have cooked dinner **by** 6 o'clock. / I will have cooked dinner **by the time** Mum gets home from work.*

▶ **See Grammar reference, Unit 12,** page 159

1 If a sentence is correct, put a tick. If it's incorrect, underline the mistake and rewrite it correctly in each gap.

1 I will have finish reading this book by dinner time. ____________

2 At the end of the month, I will had my new smartphone for a year. ____________

3 How many text messages will you have sent by the end of today? ____________

4 Hurry up or the concert might has started by the time we get there! ____________

5 I've got so much homework I won't have finished it all by bedtime! ____________

6 Stop or you'll have eat all the snacks before the guests arrive! ____________

7 If we don't leave now, they will have clean up the river without us! ____________

8 This article is really interesting. I'll have learnt a lot about local wildlife by the time I've finished.

____

SAY IT RIGHT

Resource centre: Unit 12
Pronunciation of *have* in the future perfect

2 Read this extract from a newspaper and explain what a 'bioblitz' is. Choose the correct words to complete the text.

TEENS COUNT LOCAL WILDLIFE

By the end of Saturday, teenagers will (1) **has / have** collected dozens of plants and insects from the local park. That's because they are doing a 'bioblitz'. By the time they finish, they will have (2) **record / recorded** all the plants and creatures in a small area to help scientists. And they only have one day to do it! By the end of the day, they (3) **will / shall** have found lots of common creatures, but they might (4) **had / have** discovered some rare ones too! By the end of the year, hundreds of teens across the country will have (5) **take / taken** part in bioblitzes. When scientists finish studying all the information, they should have (6) **learn / learnt** a lot.

3 Write a verb from the box in the correct tense in each gap.

do | find | happen | help | learn | take

Inside Ed's Head: my blog

Home **Posts** Archive Links

By the time you read this, I (**1**) ____________ part in my second bioblitz! They're awesome! And I (**2**) ____________ so much by the end of the day about nature where I live. Over a dozen bioblitzes (**3**) ____________ in my area by the end of the year. That'll be a lot of help to scientists, even though they (**4**) ____________ every different type of creature that lives around here – there are so many!

I'm really proud that by the end of the week, I (**5**) ____________ this and I (**6**) ____________ to clean up the river! I guess that officially makes me a nature lover!

THINK | **RESEARCH** | CULTURE | LEARN | ME

Choose a garden, a field or a park near where you live. See how many different types of plants, insects and animals you can find there. Tell your class.

Words connected with *natural habitats*

1 3.22 **Complete the table with the words in the box. Some animals may belong in more than one habitat. Add two more animals to each category. Use a dictionary if necessary. Listen and check.**

camel | dolphin | elephant | giraffe | gorilla | lion | lizard | monkey | shark | snake | tiger | whale | zebra

rainforest	desert	ocean	grassland

Phrasal verbs

2 3.23 **Complete the sentences with the correct form of the phrasal verbs in the box. Listen and check.**

bring up | cut up | end up | fill up | grow up | keep up | split up | wake up

1 Nocturnal animals __________ at night and sleep during the day.

2 Camels can live without water for up to eight days before they need to __________ again.

3 Male penguins can __________ a baby penguin until the mother returns.

4 Salmon are born in rivers, then swim downstream and __________ in the ocean.

5 Beavers and wolves mate for life but other animals __________ after mating.

6 We should support the WWF so they can __________ their good work with animals.

7 This bear has __________ in a zoo and so can't live in the wild.

8 Rabbits have sharp teeth and can __________ most plants and trees.

3 **Write the correct form of a phrasal verb from Exercise 2 in each gap to complete the text.**

Snow monkeys are from Japan and live in groups in forests. As babies they are (**1**) __________ on milk, but when they are older they use their teeth to (**2**) __________ seeds, trees and small insects as food. They take four years to (**3**) __________ into adults. They are very intelligent animals and can live for over 30 years. However, they usually (**4**) __________ living for around seven years in the wild.

Adjectives and nouns

4 3.24 **Complete the sentences with the correct form of the word in brackets. Listen and check.**

1 I find bugs and worms absolutely __________ ! (**disgust**)

2 What's the __________ (**explain**) for the peacock's amazing tail feathers?

3 The __________ (**nature**) world is amazing and I love learning about animals.

4 Some of the frogs in the rainforest are __________ (**poison**).

5 The __________ (**scene**) and the views on safari in Africa are incredible.

6 A bioblitz is much simpler than a proper __________ (**science**) study.

7 Almost all plants need __________ (**sun**) to grow.

8 Many __________ (**tropic**) birds and fish are very colourful.

THINK | RESEARCH | CULTURE | LEARN | ME

If you could be any animal, what would you be and why?

12 LISTENING | Multiple choice (single extract)

1 In pairs or as a group, answer the questions.

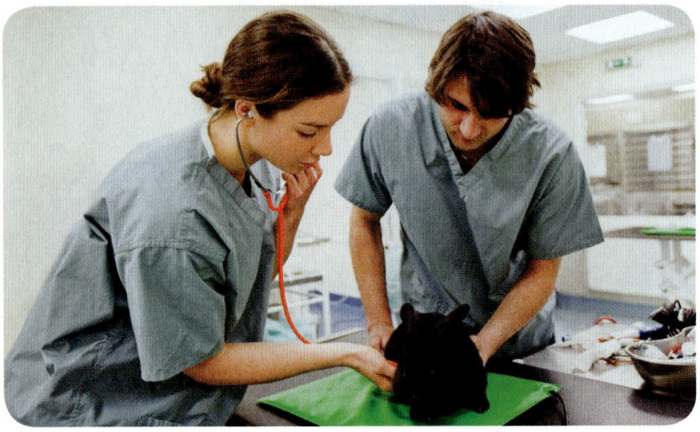

1 Describe what is happening in the photo.
2 What do you think are the best and worst things about working as a vet?

EXAM SKILL

Thinking logically

- When you listen, you often have to think about the logic of what you hear. This might mean taking a fact you hear and thinking about the logical result of that fact.
- For example, if you hear *I lived on a farm when I was growing up.*, then it's logical to conclude that the person saw and learnt about animals as a child.

2 Read this extract from a conversation. Tick the statements which must be logically true.

Erin: Hi, Reece. Did you find out what the problem was with Harry?

Reece: Oh, hi, Erin. He was fine. I thought he might have a problem with his legs, but the vet said he needs to get more exercise. I should have realised hamsters need more exercise when he started putting on weight.

1 Reece recently took her pet to the vet's. ☐
2 Harry is the name of Reece's vet. ☐
3 Reece has a pet hamster called Harry. ☐
4 The vet thinks Harry needs to lose weight. ☐
5 Reece's vet has put on weight recently. ☐

OPTIMISE YOUR EXAM

Multiple choice (single extract)

- If you are not sure of an answer, it's better to guess than to leave it blank.
- Think about what answer might be logical, based on what you've heard in the rest of the audio.

3 3.25 **For each question, choose the correct answer.**

1 What problem did Reece's hamster, Harry, have?
A It had a broken leg.
B It wasn't exercising enough.
C It was starting to lose weight.

2 *The Supervet* is about a vet who
A deals with very difficult cases.
B works with many other vets.
C likes to treat unusual animals.

3 Noel Fitzpatrick is well known for helping animals that
A have been involved in different kinds of accidents.
B are born without any feet.
C are special to their owners.

4 Erin thinks that because Noel grew up on a farm,
A he was bullied.
B he had problems reading and writing.
C he became a vet.

5 Where does Noel work now?
A in America
B in Ireland
C in England

6 How does Erin feel about Noel Fitzpatrick?
A She thinks he works too hard.
B She thinks his ideas about treating animals are correct.
C She would like to be as famous as him.

4 3.25 **Listen again and check your answers.**

GRAMMAR 2 | Modal perfect

Grammar in context

Read these sentences from the audio in the listening lesson on page 128 and answer the questions.

Oscar's owners must have been really pleased.

1 Does the speaker think Oscar's owners were pleased?

2 How certain is the speaker? **very / not very / not at all**

I should have realised hamsters needed more exercise when he started putting on weight.

3 Is the speaker talking about the past or the present?

4 What mistake does the speaker think he made in looking after his pet?

REMEMBER

- The **modal perfect** is modal + *have* + past participle: *must have done, should have done*, etc.
- When we make deductions about the past, we use different modals to show we think our deduction is:
  - **certain** *(must, can't, couldn't)*: *You* ***must have felt*** *happy when you passed all your exams!*
  - **probably correct** because that's what usually happens *(should, ought to)*: *It's 4 o'clock, so Jack* ***should have left*** *school by now.*
  - **possibly correct** *(may, might, could)*: *Ali's late. He* ***might have forgotten*** *about our meeting.*
- We use *should (not)* and *ought (not) to* to criticise someone's past actions: *You* ***shouldn't have told*** *Lucy my secret!*
- We use *could, might* and *would* to describe a hypothetical past (which didn't happen): *I* ***would have gone*** *on the trip but I didn't have enough money.*

▶ **See Grammar reference, Unit 12,** page 160

1 **Choose the correct word or phrase to complete each sentence.**

1 Oh, no, I can't find my phone! I ____ my bag on the bus!
a) must leave **b)** must have left

2 I'll help you look for your dog. He ____ far.
a) can't have gone **b)** shouldn't go

3 You ____ your homework by now. It's almost midnight!
a) could be finished **b)** should have finished

4 You really ____ have spoken to Julie like that! She's very upset.
a) ought not **b)** ought not to

5 Thanks for the tips. I ____ have passed my French test without your help.
a) must **b)** couldn't

6 I ____ have bought you a present but I forgot to take any money!
a) would **b)** must

2 **Read the situations and then complete the sentences using the modal perfect.**

1 Your mum asks where your dad is. You see that the car isn't there, so you are certain he has gone out.
'He ______________________.'

2 You think it's possible that your friend forgot to call you.
'She ______________________.'

3 You think your cousins have probably arrived home now after visiting you.
'They ______________________.'

4 Your friend fails a test because she didn't study and you want to tell her what she did wrong.
'You ______________________.'

5 You think your friend was wrong to invite Tom to the party.
'You ______________________.'

3 **Complete the dialogue using the verbs in brackets in the correct form. Use the modal perfect.**

Paige: Hey, Ryan! How was your trip to Iceland? You **(1)** ____________ **(be)** back for long. I saw your post online from the National Museum in Reykjavík only yesterday.

Ryan: We got back last night. It was fantastic! We travelled around a lot and saw the Northern Lights!

Paige: That **(2)** ____________ **(be)** amazing!

Ryan: It was! The sky was full of green and purple.

Paige: How long did each light show last?

Ryan: They **(3)** ____________ **(last)** for at least an hour. I **(4)** ____________ **(video)** it, but I forgot my phone.

Paige: Oh, no! I wish I **(5)** ____________ **(be)** there.

Ryan: Yes, you **(6)** ____________ **(come)** with us! Maybe next time.

Paige: I hope so!

12 SPEAKING | Discussion (pictures)

Flipped classroom

1 **Watch the *Talk2Me* video and answer the questions.**

1 Where would Maddy go on her dream holiday?
2 Which friend is good at: sports, pop music and fashion, history?
3 Does Angus' Mum want to take him on a skiing holiday, a shopping trip or a walking holiday?

2 **Watch the video again. Underline the phrases in the *Phrase expert* box that you hear on the video.**

PHRASE EXPERT

So which one do you think we should choose? | Shall we make a final decision? | I'd choose … | My first choice would be … | Of all the options, I think … is the best. | I'd also choose … | We agree, then. | That sounds like a good decision. | I think we agree with each other.

3 **In pairs or as a group, look at these photos and answer the questions.**

1 What are the people in the photos doing?
2 Which of these activities would you enjoy more? Why?

EXAM SKILL

Negotiating agreement

- When you have discussed each option, you need to try to reach a decision with your partner.
- You can do this by asking a question such as *So which one do you think we should choose?* Then say whether you agree or not. Remember to explain your choice.
- Remember that there are no right and wrong answers – it doesn't matter which option you choose. The important thing is to show how good your English is!

4 **Look at the pictures in Exercise 7. Would they be good places to visit? Write any good or bad points you can think of for each place.**

____

____

____

5 3.26 **Listen to two students doing the task in Exercise 7. Tick the points from your answers in Exercise 4 that the students also mention.**

6 3.26 **Listen again and write one word in each gap.**

1 What do you enjoy __________ ?
2 So how __________ the zoo?
3 So __________ do you think we should choose?
4 I think we __________ with each other …
5 My first __________ would be …
6 I was __________ to say that too.

OPTIMISE YOUR EXAM

Discussion (pictures)

- When your partner asks you a question, you might need a second or two to think about your answer.
- You can give yourself a little time to think by saying *That's a good question. Let me see …, Well, I think …* You can then give your opinion.

7 **In pairs, do the task.**

You both love nature. You are thinking of going on a weekend trip together. Look at the pictures below and talk together about the different places you could visit and then decide which two would be best.

LANGUAGE IN USE | Open cloze

1 **In pairs or as a group, answer the questions.**

1 What causes problems like this?
2 What effect does pollution like this have on wildlife?

REMEMBER

- Auxiliary verbs are used in *different tenses*, in *questions*, in *negatives* and in the *passive voice*.
- *be* is used in continuous tenses and in the passive voice: *Where **are** you going? / Some animals don't like **being** kept in zoos.*
- *do* is used in questions and negatives: *What **do** you think the solution is? / People **don't** care enough.*
- *have* is used in perfect tenses: *I **had** never seen so much pollution!*

2 **Find and underline where a word is missing from each sentence. Write the missing word in each gap.**

1 We had swimming for a while before we saw all the rubbish in the lake. __________
2 The beach is a mess because people been leaving litter all along it. __________
3 When they going to start cleaning up the rivers around here? __________
4 What you think the biggest challenge for the environment is? __________
5 Too many plastic bottles being used every day around the world. __________
6 The council done a good job of cleaning up our town. __________

3 **Write an auxiliary verb in each gap and then ask and answer the questions in pairs.**

1 __________ you ever been somewhere and been surprised by the amount of pollution?
2 How __________ you feel when you see people drop litter in the street?
3 Why __________ some people seem to care very much about their environment?
4 What __________ you think we can do to reduce the amount of rubbish we produce?

OPTIMISE YOUR EXAM

Open cloze

- Auxiliary verbs are often tested in this type of task. When you look at each gap, think about tenses, questions, negatives and the passive voice to see if you need an auxiliary.

4 **Write one word in each gap to complete the text.**

The Great Pacific Garbage Patch

Where **(1)** __________ all the plastic things we throw away end up? The answer is the middle of the Pacific Ocean. In 1997, Charles Moore **(2)** __________ crossing the Pacific Ocean when he noticed something strange. Miles from land, there was lots of rubbish floating on the water. This collection of plastic **(3)** __________ now known as the Great Pacific Garbage Patch.

Plastic enters our seas and gets broken down into smaller pieces as **(4)** __________ travels around the world. This can take some time. Rubbish from North America, for example, does not become part of the Patch until around six years after entering the sea. Most of the plastic is too small to **(5)** __________ seen without special equipment. It's a kind of plastic 'soup', which is harmful to sea creatures. There is no obvious solution, although the problem is **(6)** __________ studied by scientists at the moment.

THINK | RESEARCH | CULTURE | LEARN | ME

What do you think we should do about the Great Pacific Garbage Patch?

1 **In pairs or as a group, answer the questions.**

1 What is happening in the photos?
2 How do you think the animals in these photos feel?
3 What other jobs can animals do?
4 Have you ever been to a zoo or safari park? Did you enjoy it? Why / Why not?
5 Have you ever been to a circus? Did you enjoy it? Why / Why not?

EXAM SKILL

Giving reasons

- It is very important to give reasons for your opinions.
- You already know how to use *because* to give a reason. However, try not to use *because* all the time. Learn different phrases such as the ones in Exercises 3 and 4.

2 **Read the essay and answer the questions.**

I believe that dolphin shows should not be allowed. The main reason for this is that it is cruel to train dolphins to perform. They should be allowed to live in the wild.

Dolphins are wild animals and they do not enjoy being kept in pools. This is because they are not able to hunt fish and live a normal life.

Another reason dolphin shows are wrong is that dolphins in shows die at a young age. So, they die younger than wild dolphins just to provide entertainment for people.

In conclusion, I would like to see all dolphin shows closed down because dolphins should live free in the ocean.

1 Which of these questions is the writer answering?
 a) 'Dolphins are beautiful, intelligent creatures.' Do you agree?
 b) 'Everyone should go on a trip to see dolphins.' Do you agree?
 c) 'It's acceptable to use dolphins in shows for entertainment.' Do you agree?
2 Does the writer agree or disagree with the statement?
 ____
3 Which of these reasons does the writer give for their opinion?
 a) Training dolphins is cruel. ☐
 b) Dolphins don't like living in pools. ☐
 c) People don't like these shows. ☐
 d) Dolphins in shows don't live as long as they should. ☐

3 **Look at the essay in Exercise 2 again and complete these phrases for giving reasons.**

1 The main ____________ for this is that …
2 This is ____________ …
3 ____________ reason … are wrong is …

4 **Underline the words and phrases in these sentences that you can use to give reasons.**

1 Because of this, I do not think dolphin shows should be allowed.
2 For this reason, I am completely against dolphin shows.
3 People should not visit dolphin shows as they are cruel.

OPTIMISE YOUR EXAM

An essay

- Remember that an essay is a formal piece of writing, so you should use a formal style.
- This means you should avoid contractions (use *should not* instead of *shouldn't*, etc.). You should also try to use more formal vocabulary. For example, try to use words like *acceptable* instead of *good*, or *harmful* instead of *bad*, etc.

5 **Look at this writing task and read the post and the two opinions. Say which person you agree with and explain why.**

In your English class you have been talking about animals and tourism. Now your English teacher has asked you to write an essay for homework.

> **'It's acceptable to use animals to entertain tourists.' Do you agree?**
>
> **Notes**
>
> Write about:
>
> 1. animals in the wild and animals in parks/zoos/circuses
> 2. benefits for people and animals
> 3. .... (your own idea)

Write your essay using **all** the notes and giving reasons for your point of view.

I think it's cruel to use animals in the tourist trade because they are often badly looked after. It should stop now!

Abby Johnson | Like | Reply

I think it is perfectly acceptable to use animals in the tourist trade. It is usually harmless fun. Tourists pay to see the animals so they are looked after properly.

Jamie Wright-Brown | Like | Reply

6 **Plan** **Make a paragraph plan.**

Part	**Purpose**	**Useful phrases**	**My notes**
Paragraph 1	introduce the subject and state your opinion in general	*I believe that ...* *My opinion is that ...* *From my point of view, ...*	
Paragraph 2	give one key point and explain the reason	*The first reason for that is ...* *... because ...* *... as ...*	
Paragraph 3	give another key point and explain the reason	*Another reason for that is ...* *Because of this, ...* *For this reason, ...*	
Paragraph 4	conclude with a summary and what you believe should happen	*In conclusion, ...* *To conclude, ...* *I believe we should (not) ...*	

7 **Write** **Write your essay in an appropriate style. Write about 100 words.**

8 **Check** **Before you hand in your essay, complete this checklist.**

Checklist ✓

- ◯ I've given my opinion clearly.
- ◯ I've given reasons for my opinion.
- ◯ I've used a formal style.
- ◯ I've followed my paragraph plan.
- ◯ I've written about 100 words.
- ◯ I've checked my spelling, grammar and punctuation.

PROGRESS CHECK UNITS 11–12

GRAMMAR AND VOCABULARY

1 Write one word in each gap.

1 We have to learn 100 words by ___________ before Monday!
2 Lena's a very good student and she often passes tests with flying ___________ .
3 I'm sure we can find a solution if we put our thinking ___________ on.
4 Tim loves reading and he's always got his ___________ in a book.
5 Once you ___________ the ropes, this job isn't very difficult.
6 Ben's so mean! It's time someone taught him a ___________ .

__/6

2 Choose the correct word.

1 Animals that wake **in** / **on** / **up** when night falls are called nocturnal.
2 Please don't forget to hand your homework **on** / **off** / **in** on Monday morning.
3 Did he split **off** / **out** / **up** with her or was she the one who left him?
4 Every year, many orangutans end **around** / **up** / **off** losing their habitat due to deforestation.
5 I spent the night before the test copying **in** / **out** / **over** some of my notes.
6 You're doing really well. Keep **up** / **back** / **over** the good work!
7 Did your sister drop **down** / **off** / **out** halfway through her medical degree?
8 Will you please go **in** / **on** / **over** the plan just one more time?
9 Her parents brought her **away** / **up** / **out** to be a global citizen.
10 Sanjay missed a week of school and he fell **back** / **behind** / **off** the others.

__/10

3 Choose the correct answer.

1 'You have half an hour to do the test,' our teacher said.
Our teacher said we ______________ half an hour to do the test.
a) will have **b)** had **c)** have had

2 'You'll see lots of animals on safari,' the guide said.
The guide said we ______________ lots of animals on safari.
a) would see **b)** will see **c)** will have seen

3 'I've been learning the guitar for over a year,' Luca said.
Luca said he ______________ the guitar for over a year.
a) was learning **b)** has been learning **c)** had been learning

4 'What are you doing this evening?' my best friend asked me.
My best friend asked me ______________ doing that evening.
a) what am I **b)** whether I was **c)** what I was

5 'Have you ever been to the zoo before?' the zookeeper asked us.
The zookeeper asked us ______________ been to the zoo before.
a) if we had ever **b)** if have we ever **c)** whether we are

6 'Where were you going when I saw you?' the police officer asked.
The police officer asked where I ______________ when she saw me.
a) would be going **b)** had been going **c)** had gone

__/6

4 Write a form of the word in capitals in each gap.

1 I didn't understand the teacher's ___________ so I asked her to repeat it. **EXPLAIN**
2 Olivia has a lot of ___________ in herself and always thinks she'll do well. **BELIEVE**
3 I saw a great TV show about a ___________ study of the everyday lives of cats. **SCIENCE**
4 Many animals are suffering from the ___________ of their habitat. **LOSE**

5 It's important that we look after the ___________ world. **NATURE**
6 What are your ___________ on protecting the environment? **THINK**
7 What's in this soup? It tastes absolutely ___________ ! **DISGUST**
8 The party was a great ___________ ! Everyone had a wonderful time. **SUCCEED**

__/8

5 **If a word or phrase in bold is correct, put a tick. If it's incorrect, rewrite it correctly in each gap.**

1 Many animals **will have disappeared** by the middle of the century. ______________
2 I love the present, but you really **shouldn't bought** me anything. ______________
3 It **must has been** amazing to see lions in the wild. ______________
4 It's half past eleven, so Alysia's piano lesson **should finish** by now. ______________
5 By the end of the month, I **will have sit** ten exams! ______________
6 I **would have called** you last night but I didn't know your number. ______________

__/6

6 **Read the definitions and write the correct words. The first letters have been given.**

1 the kind of school you go to aged 11–18 s_ _ _ _ _ _ _ _ _
2 a very large animal that lives in the ocean w_ _ _ _ _
3 pieces of paper, etc., people drop on the floor in public places l_ _ _ _ _ _
4 someone at school but not someone at university p_ _ _ _ _
5 an African animal with a very long neck g_ _ _ _ _ _ _
6 someone who is good at something and does it as a job p_ _ _ _ _ _ _ _ _ _ _ _ _ _
7 an area of study, like maths, English or history s_ _ _ _ _ _ _
8 complete a course, often at college or university g_ _ _ _ _ _ _ _

__/8

7 **Write an auxiliary verb in each gap.**

1 I ___________ been to a zoo since we ___________ shown around London Zoo last year.
2 What ___________ you think of the way animals ___________ treated in most safari parks?
3 People ___________ care enough about the way we ___________ damaging the environment.
4 Rory ___________ taken part in a few bioblitzes that have ___________ organised in his area.
5 What ___________ you ___________ doing before this photograph ___________ taken?
6 I ___________ had a great time on holiday, although we ___________ seen much wildlife.

__/6

Total score __/50

EXAM SKILLS

Tick the statements that are true for you. Review the skills in the unit if you need more help.

I can …	Unit/page
☐ understand specific information in an online guide	Unit 11 p114
☐ understand implication in short extracts	Unit 11 p118
☐ use phrases to express uncertainty when talking about photos	Unit 11 p120
☐ differentiate words with similar meanings in multiple-choice cloze activities	Unit 11 p121
☐ understand the notes in an annotated email	Unit 11 p122
☐ understand instructions in short messages	Unit 12 p124
☐ think logically about a listening text to find out other information	Unit 12 p128
☐ negotiate an agreement in a discussion	Unit 12 p130
☐ use auxiliary verbs in open cloze exercises	Unit 12 p131
☐ give reasons for opinions in an essay	Unit 12 p132

OPTIMISE YOUR EXAMS | Reading

OPTIMISE

The reading exam has six parts. You get one mark for each correct answer. You have 45 minutes to complete all the parts.

In **Part 1**, there are five short texts. These are usually signs, short messages or notes. There are five questions. You need to choose one option (A, B or C).

In **Part 2**, there are eight short texts and five descriptions of people. You need to match these descriptions to five of the texts. There are three texts you do not need to use.

In **Part 3**, there is one long text in which the writer expresses an opinion. There are five questions. You need to choose one option (A, B, C or D).

In **Part 4**, there is one long text with five sentences removed. You need to choose the correct option from eight sentences to complete each gap. There are three sentences you don't need to use.

In **Part 5**, there is one text with six gaps. You need to choose the correct word (A, B, C or D) to complete each gap.

In **Part 6**, there is one text with six gaps. You need to decide what the correct word is to complete each gap, but you are not given any options.

1 **Look back at the Reading and Language in Use pages in Units 1–12. Find one activity that practises each part of the exam (1–6).**

OPTIMISE

In **Part 1**, read each short text carefully and decide what kind of text it is. Look for important words, for example *noticeboard*, *party*.

Read the questions and options. Be careful – don't just look for similar words. You need to understand the meaning of the whole sentence.

2 **Read the two texts carefully. Then answer the questions about each text.**

Natasha
I was walking past the noticeboard when I saw the perfect accommodation advert!
When are you free to see the rooms?
Adriana

House-warming Party

7:30 pm Thursday

Refreshments provided but numbers are limited because of space, so please let us know if you can make it.

Natasha & Adriana

1 What kind of text is it?
2 Who is it from and to?
3 What is the main function?

3 **Read the two Part 1 questions. Look at the underlined words and find similar words and phrases in the texts.**

1

A Natasha and Adriana are looking for a place to put up a notice.
B Natasha and Adriana are looking for a place to live.
C Natasha and Adriana are looking for a new hobby.

2

A According to the invitation, guests must bring food and drink.
B The invitation asks guests to arrive at 7:30 pm.
C The invitation says that there won't be room for a lot of people.

4 **Now read the texts again carefully and choose the correct answers (A, B or C). Why aren't the other answers correct?**

OPTIMISE

In **Part 2**, read the descriptions of the people first and think about the main ideas. Then read the eight short texts and look for ideas in the texts that match the ideas in the descriptions.

Be careful! You may find the same word in a text and a description, but it doesn't always mean that they contain the same idea. Always read the whole sentence.

5 Read about three students who want to go to a summer camp. Then answer the questions below with the names of the students.

1 Maya is interested in robots and software, and likes working in groups. In the future, she'd like to set up a company and be her own boss. When she leaves the camp, she hopes to have some ideas for her company.

2 Carlos is already good at performing in front of a live audience and wrote his band's first album. He wants to learn how to become popular with bigger audiences and manage a competitive business.

3 Rebecca has played in a band and made her own recordings. She knows exactly what she wants: her dream is to perform on stage, entertaining people and telling jokes. She gets nervous before she performs and wants to feel more relaxed.

Which teenager

1 knows how to write songs? ____________

2 wants to make people laugh? ____________

3 likes technology? ____________

4 wants to feel less shy on stage? ____________

5 wants to have a lot of fans? ____________

6 wants to start a business? ____________

6 Now read the texts about the summer camps on **page 115****. Decide which summer camp (A–H) would be the most suitable for each student (1–3).**

1 ____ 2 ____ 3 ____

7 Find words or phrases in the texts that have similar meanings to phrases in the descriptions.

Maya 'Maya […] likes working in groups' 'You'll get experience in […] working in teams'

OPTIMISE

In **Part 3**, the text expresses opinions or attitudes – either those of the author or of another person.

The first four questions usually ask you about specific information. The last question will ask you about the whole text.

8 Quickly read two paragraphs from a Part 3 text. What type of text is it and what is it about?

Remmi, who lives in the USA, is just 16. She has already starred in two cookery shows and has published a book of healthy recipes. From the age of four, Remmi helped in the kitchen by preparing vegetables. By the age of seven, Remmi was a real foodie who could cook complete meals for her family.

That show focused on Remmi's main interest, which is getting teenagers to take healthy eating seriously. She believes that when young people make their own food, they care more about what they eat. Remmi works with a company in the USA which shows her videos in school cafeterias. About 3.5 million students watch her every day!

9 **Look at questions 2 and 3 and options A–D quickly. Which question asks about an opinion? Choose the correct answer (A–D) for each question.**

2 What does the writer say about Remmi as a child?

A She enjoyed cooking at home more than cooking on TV.
B Her book of healthy recipes was very popular.
C She loved food and was able to cook whole menus.
D She could prepare vegetables with some help.

3 What does Remmi think about teenagers?

A They prefer watching videos to cooking.
B Cooking for themselves encourages them to eat well.
C They don´t want to spend a lot of money on food.
D Most of them want to learn to cook healthy food.

10 **Read question 5, which asks you about the whole text. Choose the answer (A–D) which you think fits best according to the text. Then read the whole text on page 59 to check your answer.**

5 What might Remmi write in a blog about her attitude to cooking?

A I help my mum a lot in the kitchen and we've written a great recipe book together. I love cooking because it's sociable.

B On my TV show, I always cook healthy dishes. It's important for young people to learn to eat well without having to spend much money.

C I like cooking for my family but I prefer making videos. It´s great having my own TV show. My cooking is very popular and I always cook with strawberries.

D If you make videos when you cook, it's much more interesting. You can put them online and become famous.

OPTIMISE

In **Part 4**, think carefully about the type of information needed in each gap. Read the sentences before and after the gaps. Do they contrast the information before the gap or add more details?

11 **Read through sentences A–E. Find three phrases that introduce contrasting information. Find one phrase that gives extra information.**

12 **Three sentences have been removed from the text below. For each question, choose the correct answer. There are two extra sentences which you do not need to use.**

Motion capture has, in the past, been an expensive way for Hollywood to make animated characters look realistic using special sensors and cameras. (**1**) ____ *Rokoko*, a Danish company, has designed a suit called the *Smartsuit Pro*. It is different from traditional methods, as it can capture an actor's movements wherever they are and without cameras. (**2**) ____ This is an advantage for projects without a lot of money.

The *Smartsuit Pro* is a full-body suit containing 19 sensors that follow your movements. The sensors send the data to a computer in real time. *Rokoko's* suit is almost as precise as traditional and more expensive methods of motion capture. (**3**) ____ Film-makers can use it to quickly test out an early version of a character and make changes without having to leave their desks.

A In addition to this, the suit is much cheaper.
B It is also easy to set up and use.
C However, the suit they produce is still very accurate.
D On the other hand, it costs a lot more money.
E But a new small business is looking to change this.

OPTIMISE

In **Part 5**, look at each gap carefully and think about what tense or form of the word you might need. Do you know any collocations or phrasal verbs that use the words before or after the gaps?

13 **Read the text quickly and then think about what word or type of word might fit each gap.**

14 **For each question, choose the correct answer.**

Drinking tea around the world

For many people around the world, tea isn't (**1**) ____ a drink, it's a way of life. However, there are many different types of tea and many different ways of drinking it.

Tea (**2**) ____ from China where it was first used as a medicinal drink. It wasn't until the 17th century that it became (**3**) ____ in Britain and today it is considered the national drink. Over 165 million cups of tea are drunk in Britain each year!

People still drink a lot of tea in China, with *Oolong*, *Jasmine* and *Gunpowder* being some of the most well-known. In India, *chai* tea is considered to be the national drink, with the black tea infused with spices being (**4**) ____ to most guests.

How do you drink tea in your country?

	A	B	C	D
1	just	always	now	still
2	became	came	discovered	brought
3	general	popular	full	liked
4	used	produced	drunk	offered

OPTIMISE

In **Part 6**, make sure you read the text after you have completed it to ensure it makes logical and grammatical sense. Check that your spelling is correct.

15 **Think about what prepositions can join with *get* and *look* to make phrasal verbs. What does each phrasal verb mean?**

16 **For each question, write the correct answer. Write one word for each gap.**

School holidays

by Ada Morris

What do you do in your school holidays? Some people work and some people go away.

I have (**1**) __________ most tiring holidays because I have to look (**2**) __________ my younger sister. She's only six, so she likes going to the park. Even though she's a lot younger than I am, we get (**3**) __________ really well because we both have a lot of energy and the same sense of humour.

I'd (**4**) __________ to go away in the school holidays rather than stay at home, though. Ideally, I'd like to travel around Europe for a few weeks with my friends.

OPTIMISE YOUR READING EXAM

Remember to …

- ☐ read all the instructions carefully.
- ☐ check you understand the general meaning of the text.
- ☐ read and understand the whole question or text – don't just match similar words.
- ☐ use your time well. If you can't answer a question, leave it and return to it later.

OPTIMISE YOUR EXAMS | Writing

OPTIMISE

The writing exam has two parts. You have 45 minutes to complete two tasks.

In **Part 1**, you read an email with notes. Then you write a response to it in about 100 words. Make sure you answer all the notes.

In **Part 2**, you have a choice of two tasks. You can write either an article or a story in about 100 words.

Each task carries equal marks. Marks are given for …

Content: Does your answer include a response to all the notes? Is the information relevant?

Communication: Is your answer clear? Is the style appropriate? Does it begin and end in an appropriate way?

Organisation: Are your ideas in a logical order? Are they connected with linking words, for example *and*, *but* and *because*?

Language: Are the vocabulary, grammar, spelling and punctuation generally correct? Is there a good variety of words, phrases and structures?

OPTIMISE

In **Part 1**, read the question and the four notes carefully. You must respond to all the notes in your email. Spend about five minutes planning your answer and 15 minutes writing and checking it.

1 Read Part 1 of the exam below and answer the questions.

1 What type of message do you have to write?
2 Who are you writing to?
3 Which notes do you need to respond to?
4 How many words should you write?

Read this email from your English friend Darrell and the notes you have made.

Write your **email** to Darrell using **all the notes**.

Write about **100 words**.

From: Darrell
Subject: Race next Friday

Hey Alex,

Remember the charity race I told you about? I can't do it because I've hurt my leg! (A) I fell off my bike yesterday. I don't think my leg's broken, but it's difficult for me to walk. I'm not sure what to do about it. (B)

Could you run in the race for me please? (C) I know you're a good runner and it's only 200 metres. It starts next Friday at 3 pm. (D)

Thanks so much,

Darrell

2 Look at notes 1–4 and then match them to A–D in the email in Exercise 1.

1 Reply
2 Terrible!
3 Suggest …
4 Where?

3 Read two answers to Part 1 of the exam. Which is better? Why? Think about content, communication, organisation and language.

A

Hey Darrell,
I'm sorry to hear that. That's terrible about your leg and it's a shame you can't run in the charity race. I hope it doesn't hurt too much.
Yes, I'm quite a good runner, so I can run in the race for you on Friday. Where is it?
I think you should rest your leg when you can. If you walk too much, then it won't get better! You could put some ice on it if it's really painful. If it still hurts next week, you should go to the doctor.
Take care!
Alex

B

Dear Darrell,
Sorry you hurts your leg. That's terrible. You can go to the doctor for your leg, if it hurts a lot.
I like running and I can run 200m. I'll run in the race on Friday, OK?
Get better soon!
Bye bye
Alex

OPTIMISE

In **Part 2**, you need to choose only ONE of the tasks.

When you write your **article**, make sure you include all the necessary information in the prompts.

When you write your **story**, you must include the sentence you are given.

Remember to use a range of structures and tenses and an appropriate style.

Try to include a relevant title for your article or story that is interesting for the reader. Sometimes, starting an article with an opening question is also a good way to engage the reader.

Spend about five minutes planning your answer and 15 minutes writing and checking it.

4 **Read the first question for Part 2 of the exam and then complete the sentences.**

You see this announcement on a website for young people learning English.

Articles wanted!

HOW DO YOU RELAX?

Write an article telling us what you like to do to relax.

Do you think it's important to spend a lot of time relaxing? Why?

The best articles will be published next month.

Write your **article**.

1 I'm writing an ______________ .
2 I'm writing about ______________________________ .
3 The three questions I need to answer are: ______________________________
____
____

5 **Read the sentences about relaxing and choose the best linking word.**

1 I think relaxing is important **but / because** studying can be very stressful.
2 I'm always really busy studying **because / so** I like relaxing with my friends when I can.
3 It's important to relax **so / but** it's also important to work hard.
4 To relax, I like to play sport, **however / because** I don't often find the time!

6 **Now write your article in about 100 words.**

7 **Look at the second question for Part 2 of the exam. Does the sentence need to go at the start or end of the story?**

Your English teacher has asked you to write a story.

Your story must begin with this sentence.

It was midnight, so why was the phone ringing?

Write your **story**.

8 **Read the student's story below. Find one example of each of the following tenses: past simple, past continuous, present continuous, past perfect simple and past perfect continuous.**

The surprise phone call

It was midnight, so why was the phone ringing? I had been working hard all day and I was trying to sleep, so I was annoyed too. Who is calling me so late? I thought. I had left my phone in the living room so I needed to get out of bed to answer it.

'Hello?' I answered. At first, I couldn't hear anything. Then I heard a noise. 'Hello?' I said again, a bit angrily.

'Hello! Happy birthday!' the person shouted, happily.

It was my sister calling from another country – it was already the morning where she was.

I'd completely forgotten it was my birthday!

9 **Now write your story. Write about 100 words. Use as many tenses as you can.**

OPTIMISE YOUR WRITING EXAM

Remember to …

- [ ] read all the instructions carefully.
- [ ] plan your ideas before you start writing your answer.
- [ ] include all the points in the question.
- [ ] organise your writing clearly.
- [ ] write your answers on the answer sheet.
- [ ] leave five minutes to check your writing at the end of the exam.

OPTIMISE YOUR EXAMS | Listening

OPTIMISE

The listening exam has four parts.
The exam is 30 minutes long. There is one mark for each correct answer. You need to write your answers on the question paper first. You will have six minutes at the end of the exam to write them on your answer sheet.

The audio for each part of the exam is played twice.

In **Part 1**, you listen to seven short extracts. You need to choose one picture for each extract (A, B or C).

In **Part 2**, you listen to six short separate extracts. There are six questions. You need to choose one option (A, B or C).

In **Part 3**, you listen to one long extract, such as a radio advertisement or recorded message. You need to complete six gaps in a page of sentences or notes.

In **Part 4**, you listen to an interview. There are six questions. You need to choose one option (A, B or C).

1 Read the sentences about the listening exam. Choose the correct option.

1 The exam is about **6** / **30** minutes long.
2 You get **one mark** / **two marks** for each correct answer.
3 You **should** / **shouldn't** write your answers on the question paper before you write them on the answer sheet.
4 You hear each part **once** / **twice**.

OPTIMISE

In **Part 1**, first listen to get a general idea. Who is talking? Where? What about? Then listen for more specific information. Be careful! The speakers often mention all three pictures.

2 Look at the pictures from a Part 1 question. What can you see in each picture?

In picture A, there's a tennis racket on the back seat of a car.

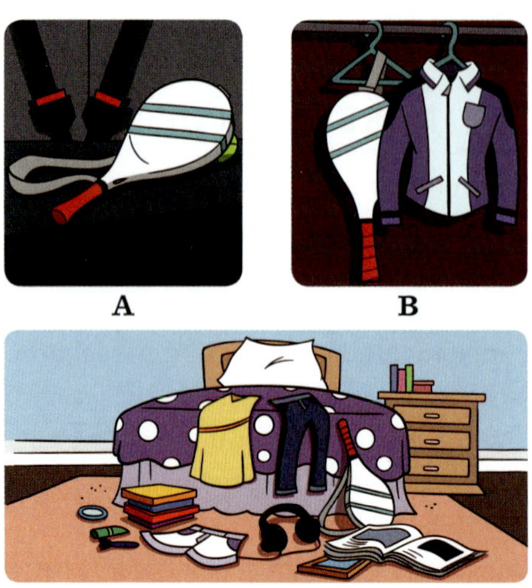

3 3.27 **Listen to the extracts. Answer the questions.**

1 Who is speaking?
2 What about?
3 Where are they?
4 Do they talk about all three pictures?

4 3.27 **Where is the girl's tennis racket? Listen again and choose the correct picture A, B or C.**

OPTIMISE

In **Part 2**, read the questions and options carefully.

Underline any important words, including words like *always*, *all*, *main*, *very* and *only*. These may be very important.

Remember that the speakers won't always use the words in the questions.

5 3.28 **Look at two Part 2 questions. Then listen. Can you hear words or phrases with a similar meaning to the underlined words and phrases in the questions?**

For each question, choose the correct answer.

---

1 You will hear two friends talking about a show at the theatre.

Why didn't the boy go?

A He doesn't like musicals.

B He was tired.

C He didn't get a ticket in time.

2 You will hear two friends talking about being in a band.

The girl suggests the boy should

A listen to more types of music.

B go on a TV programme.

C practise alone more.

6 3.28 **Listen again and choose one answer for each question. Why are the other options incorrect?**

OPTIMISE

In **Part 3**, write the exact words or number(s) that you hear (one or two words or numbers).

Before you listen, think about what word(s) could complete the sentences, or if you might need to write a number, date or time instead.

Be careful! You may hear information that you do not need.

Remember to check your spelling. It doesn't matter if you make a spelling mistake with most words, as long as the reader can understand the word. If the spelling of the word is dictated in the audio, then you need to spell it correctly to get the mark.

7 **Look at some sentences from a Part 3 task. What kind of information do you need to complete each gap (a number, a name, etc.)?**

The types of celebration offered are parties and (**1**) ___________ .

The cost of hiring the Stanlow Room on a Saturday is (**2**) £___________ .

The website address is (**3**) www.______________.co.uk.

The phone number is (**4**) _____________ .

8 3.29 **Listen and complete the notes. Then listen again and check your answers.**

OPTIMISE

In **Part 4**, you will hear speakers express opinions and attitudes. Read through options A–C before you listen the first time.

Then, try to understand the main ideas. What are the speakers talking about? Do they agree with each other? The second time, listen for more detailed information.

9 3.30 **Read options A–C and underline the important words. Listen to the extract and decide what the speakers are talking about. Then listen again. For each question, choose the correct answer.**

You will hear an interview with a student called Jenny.

1 What does Jenny think about the quantity of maths homework?

A Students have the right amount to prepare them for exams.

B Students have too much to prepare them for exams.

C Students don't have enough to prepare them for exams.

2 Jenny feels that group work is

A an efficient way of learning.

B not suitable for students who prefer to work on their own.

C only useful when you do a project.

OPTIMISE YOUR LISTENING EXAM

Remember to …

- ☐ read all the instructions and questions carefully before you listen.
- ☐ make notes on the exam paper the first time you listen.
- ☐ keep calm if you can't answer a question the first time you listen. Try again the second time.
- ☐ report your answers carefully onto the answer sheet at the end of the exam. You will have six minutes to do this.

OPTIMISE YOUR EXAMS | Speaking

OPTIMISE

The speaking exam has four parts. You take the exam with another student or sometimes with two other students.

In **Part 1**, the examiner asks you personal questions.

In **Part 2**, you each describe a photograph on your own.

In **Part 3**, you talk with your partner about some pictures related to a situation and try to reach a decision together.

In **Part 4**, you answer some questions about topics related to the discussion in Part 3. You may be asked to answer on your own, or to discuss with your partner.

OPTIMISE

In **Part 1**, the examiner asks you for some personal information.

You also answer questions on personal topics, for example, your likes and dislikes; your hobbies and interests; studying English; holidays; your family and friends; etc.

1 **Watch Part 1 of the video. Tick (✔) the questions you hear.**

A Tell us about your school. ____
B Where did you go on your last holiday? ____
C Do you like your teacher? ____
D Tell us something about someone in your family. ____
E Who do you live with? ____
F What did you do on your last birthday? ____

2 **Match answers 1–5 to one of the questions (A–F) in Exercise 1.**

1 **Anfisa:** Umm … I tell about my mum. Her name is Lana. She's 50 years old … err … and she does her business. ____
2 **Teresa:** I was in Germany … err … in a boarding school and I was new so yeah I was like I didn't have many friends but like the girls there like made an effort and they baked me something so it was nice but … ____
3 **Anfisa:** On my last holiday, I went to Greece. Err … we went with my parents … to the sea at hotel … and we spent a really great time. ____
4 **Teresa:** I go to a German school so I study German, and it's not a really big school, like we don't have any sports centre or anything … ____
5 **Teresa:** I live with my family. I have two brothers. We live together. One is 27 and the other one is 15. ____

3 **Look at the answers in Exercise 2 again and answer the questions.**

1 Can you correct any mistakes in Anfisa's answer in 3?
2 What other type of information could Anfisa give in 1 and Teresa give in 4?
3 Watch the video again to check your ideas in question 2.

OPTIMISE

In the exam, you get a mark for pronunciation. This includes:

individual sounds (for example /æ/ in *cat*)

word and sentence stress (for example *<u>ta</u>ble, nice to <u>meet</u> you*)

intonation (for example *How are you?*)

4 **Watch the video again, paying attention to Anfisa and Teresa's pronunciation. Is it easy to understand what they say? Give each student a mark from 1 to 4 (1 = not at all; 2 = not always; 3 = most of the time; 4 = always).**

OPTIMISE

In **Part 2**, you talk about a photograph for one minute. The examiner will tell you when to stop.

Describe the photograph in detail. Imagine you're describing the photograph to someone who can't see it. Say what you can see, where things are, what people are doing, etc.

5 **Work in pairs.**
Student A: look at photograph A.
Student B: look at photograph B.
Spend one minute making notes about your photograph.

6 **Now show your notes to your partner. Look at your partner's photograph and see if you can add any more ideas to their notes.**

A

B

OPTIMISE

In the exam, you get a mark for grammar and vocabulary.

Use verbs in the correct tense and form (for example *she's writing; I can see a kitchen*).

Use a variety of adjectives (for example *she has light brown curly hair*).

Use prepositions to say where people and things are (for example *on the table; in the background*).

7 **Read Anfisa and Teresa's descriptions of their photographs. Think of one word to complete each gap. Then watch the video. Did you use the same words?**

Anfisa:

Um, I can see a girl doing her **(1)** ___________ . I think she's **(2)** ___________ in the kitchen, and, um, I think she tries to write something. So, I think she uses the **(3)** ___________ because I can see an iPad near her. I think it's an **(4)** ___________ because the kitchen's quite white, so it's the **(5)** ___________ there. So, I think she's in home, 'cause she **(6)** ___________ her home clothes, a red T-shirt. Er, maybe she's **(7)** ___________ doing it for long 'cause she has like water here, so she drinks sometimes. Maybe her mum does something behind her because I can see someone's **(8)** ___________ and some vegetables and things.

Teresa:

In the photograph I can see a group of people. They are … I think they are like 15 or 16 years old and they are eating pizza. And I also can see some juice, I think it's **(1)** ___________ juice. It's really … you can see a lot **(2)** ___________ light so I think they are having **(3)** ___________ . And they are in a really **(4)** ___________ house **(5)** ___________ I can see some **(6)** ___________ behind so I guess it's like a two-floor house. And they are like, erm …, they are sitting **(7)** ___________ a **(8)** ___________ and I can see a television so maybe it's the, the salon … and, um …, maybe because, err …, they are like, maybe they are in the school break and they've decided to have some good time, go to house, like relax and eat some pizza or maybe they're in the weekend and they're gonna do something and first they are having lunch together.

8 **Look at the blue words and phrases in the students' answers. Can you find and correct the grammar and vocabulary mistakes?**

OPTIMISE

In **Part 3**, the examiner describes a situation to you, and gives you some pictures with ideas to help you.

Look at the pictures and talk about them with your partner for 2–3 minutes.

Don't just give your own ideas – ask for and respond to your partner's ideas too.

Try to reach an agreement but not too early. Remember to talk about all the pictures first.

9 Read the instructions for Part 3. Complete them with the words from the box.

camp | could | interesting students | there

I'm going to describe a situation to you.

Some **(1)** ___________ are going on a school summer **(2)** ___________ . Here are some activities they could do **(3)** ___________ . Talk together about the different activities they **(4)** ___________ do together at the summer camp and decide which would be the most **(5)** ___________ .

Alright? Now, talk together.

10 Work in pairs. Look at the pictures. Make notes about the different activities you can see. Which do you think would be the most interesting? Why?

11 ▷ **Watch the video and note down words and phrases that Anfisa and Teresa use to talk about the activities. Did you have any of the same ideas?**

OPTIMISE

In the exam, you get a mark for interaction.

Listen carefully to your partner. Make sure you both speak.

Ask your partner about their ideas.

Give your opinion on your partner's ideas. You can agree or disagree.

12 ▷ **Watch the video again. Answer the questions about Anfisa and Teresa.**

1 Who starts the discussion and how does she start it?
2 Which student interrupts the other more often?
3 Do they agree or disagree on the following activities: **a)** swimming, **b)** drawing, **c)** looking at animals?
4 Do they come to a final decision at the end? If so, what is their decision? If not, how could they reach an agreement?

13 Look at some of the things that Anfisa and Teresa said in the Part 3 task. Match sentences 1–5 to functions A–E.

1 OK, but I think we are like two hours from the lake so I think that's a little bit difficult. ____
2 Maybe they can also do fishing if there is lake. ____
3 I think that's a great idea actually. ____
4 I think that's exciting because they get some knowledge and get to know the nature. ____
5 … but at the same time it's quite dangerous. ____

A Giving a reason
B Making a suggestion
C Agreeing
D Disagreeing
E Contradicting

OPTIMISE

In **Part 4**, you and your partner answer some questions related to the topic from the collaborative task in Part 3. The examiner may ask a question to you or your partner individually, or you may be asked to talk together.

Answer the questions with more than one sentence; share your opinions and give examples.

Use a variety of words and phrases to express likes, dislikes and opinions.

14 **Read the questions below. Then watch the video and make notes of the students' answers.**

1 Does your school organise trips or summer camps?
2 What do you need to take with you when you go on a summer camp or school trip?
3 Is it better to go on trips with friends or family?
4 What kind of activities would you like to do on a summer camp?
5 Which is more fun: going on a summer camp in the countryside or doing a school trip in a city?

OPTIMISE

In the exam, you get a mark for what you say, how fluently you speak and how you organise your ideas.

Answer all the questions logically and give examples.

Try not to pause too often. If you need time to think, use filler words and phrases, for example, *well, …, let me think.*

Connect your ideas with linking words, for example, *because, and, but, so.*

You may need to answer a question individually, or the examiner may ask you to discuss your answer with your partner. When you answer the question together, remember to ask your partner questions and keep the conversation going.

15 **Look at the table and decide if Anfisa and Teresa did these things well. Watch the video again and make notes on how they could improve. Then compare your notes with a partner.**

	Anfisa	Teresa
Speak clearly		
Use linking words		
Give examples		
Use filler words and phrases		
Ask their partner questions		

OPTIMISE YOUR SPEAKING EXAM

Remember to …

- ☐ listen to all the examiner's instructions carefully.
- ☐ speak clearly.
- ☐ speak in complete sentences and use linking words.
- ☐ listen to and interact with your partner.
- ☐ give reasons and examples to support your ideas.
- ☐ ask the examiner or your partner to repeat anything you don't understand (*Sorry, can you say that again, please?*).

GRAMMAR REFERENCE

GRAMMAR REFERENCE | Unit 1 | Present simple, present continuous, stative verbs

Present simple

FORM: *I/You/We/They* ***laugh / don't laugh …***

He/She/It ***laughs / doesn't laugh …***

Do *I/you/we/they* ***laugh …?*** ***Does*** *he/she/it* ***laugh …?***

! We add *-s* to the verb to form the third person singular. Irregular verbs change spelling.

Isa usually ***goes*** *to the pool on Sundays.*

I ***have*** *ten points and Mark* ***has*** *eight.*

! We form the emphatic present simple with *do/does:*

I can't believe it! Karen ***does speak*** *Chinese!*

USE: to talk about: **1** general truths and facts, **2** current habits, **3** how often things happen, **4** permanent situations, and **5** states:

1	*The Sun* ***rises*** *in the east.*
2	*I* ***play*** *the violin in the school orchestra.*
3	*Phil* ***goes*** *swimming every Thursday evening.*
4	*My dad* ***works*** *as a car mechanic.*
5	*Susie* ***has*** *long hair.*

Present continuous

FORM: *I* ***am/'m not laughing*** *… You/We/They* ***are/ aren't laughing*** *… He/She/It* ***is/isn't laughing*** *…*

Am *I* ***laughing*** *…?* ***Are*** *you/we/they* ***laughing*** *…?* ***Is*** *he/she/it* ***laughing*** *…?*

USE: to talk about: **1** actions happening now, **2** temporary situations, **3** changing and developing situations, **4** temporary series of actions, and **5** annoying habits (+ *always*):

1	*I****'m doing*** *my homework.*
2	*What* ***are*** *you* ***doing*** *in chemistry this week?*
3	*Mobile phones* ***are becoming*** *cheaper.*
4	*We****'re doing*** *lots of tests at school this week.*
5	*Jack****'s always laughing*** *at us!*

Stative verbs

USE: to refer to states rather than actions. Stative verbs include verbs about thinking (*believe, know, think*, etc.), existence (*be, exist*, etc.), emotions (*love, like, hate*, etc.), human senses (*hear, see, smell*, etc.), appearance (*appear, look, seem*, etc.) and possession or relationships between things (*belong to, have, include*, etc.).

! Some verbs can refer to either states or actions, but their meaning changes. (for example *feel, have, imagine, look, see, smell, think* and *taste*).

Does Anne ***have*** *dark hair?* (state)

Are *we* ***having*** *pizza for dinner?* (action)

GRAMMAR REFERENCE | Unit 1 | Quantifiers

USE: to talk about numbers and amounts

- with a singular countable noun (*each, every, a little, the, a, an, one*)
- with a plural countable noun (*all, both, little, a lot of, lots of, enough, many, most, some, the, two/three/etc., a number of, a few, few, how many*)
- with an uncountable noun (*enough, little, a little, a lot of, lots of, most, much, how much, some, a piece of, an amount of*)

Common quantifiers include: *all, both, each, every, enough, little, a little, a lot of, lots of, many, most, much, how much, some, the, a, an, one/two,* etc, *a number of, a few, few, how many, a piece of, an amount of.*

! See Grammar reference, Unit 3 for more information on countable and uncountable nouns.

! Quantifiers with *of the* take a plural verb: *Most of the books* ***are*** *old.* The exception is *each of the,* which takes a singular verb: *Each of the boxes* ***is*** *empty.*

! *all* = generally *(****All*** *people eat food.), all of* = specific *(****All of*** *the kids in my class like pizza.)*

GRAMMAR REFERENCE | Unit 2 | Past simple and past continuous

Past simple

FORM: Regular verbs in the past simple end in *-ed* (*played, closed, lived,* etc.); irregular verbs don't follow a pattern (*got, had, said, taught, went,* etc.). You need to learn the past simple of irregular verbs.

USE: to talk about: **1** single completed actions in the past, **2** main events in a story, **3** habits and repeated actions in the past, **4** permanent situations in the past, and **5** general truths and facts about the past:

1	*Jay and I* ***played*** *a game of volleyball.*
2	*The woman* ***closed*** *the door,* ***sat*** *down and* ***opened*** *the letter.*
3	*We always* ***went*** *on holiday to Spain when I was very young.*
4	*My grandparents* ***lived*** *in a house on top of a hill.*
5	*The Ancient Egyptians* ***built*** *the pyramids.*

! We form the emphatic past simple with *did:*

I ***did*** *tidy my room!*

! When we repeat a verb in the past simple, we usually just use the auxiliary verb. We don't repeat the main verb:

✔ *Ella spent a lot of money but I* ***didn't****.*

✘ *Ella spent a lot of money but I* ***didn't spend****.*

Past continuous

FORM: *I* ***was/wasn't reading*** *... You* ***were/weren't reading*** *... He/She/It* ***was/wasn't reading*** *...*
Was *I* ***reading*** *...?* ***Were*** *you* ***reading*** *...?*

Was *he/she/it* ***reading*** *...?*

USE: to talk about: **1** an action in progress at a specific time in the past, **2** background information or description in a story, **3** an action in progress in the past when another thing happened (possibly interrupting it or stopping it), **4** two situations in progress at the same time, and **5** temporary situations in the past:

1	*At five o'clock this morning, I* ***was sleeping****!*
2	*It* ***was raining****. I put on a coat and left the house.*
3	*When you called, I* ***was having*** *a shower.*
4	*Mum* ***was watching*** *TV while Dad* ***was reading*** *a book.*
5	*Before he found a flat, Josh* ***was staying*** *with a friend.*

! The past continuous is not used to talk about repeated actions in the past:

✔ *My team* ***played*** *three football matches this week.*

✘ *My team* ***was playing*** *three football matches this week.*

! When we repeat a verb in the past continuous, we usually just use the auxiliary verb. We don't repeat the main verb:

✔ *Jamie was reading but I* ***wasn't****.*

✘ *Jamie was reading but I* ***wasn't reading****.*

GRAMMAR REFERENCE | Unit 2 | *used to* and *would*

used to

FORM: *used to* + bare infinitive

Grandad ***used to*** *play with us in the garden.*

I ***used to*** *be frightened of cats.*

USE: to talk about past habits and past states (particularly the distant past)

! For negative statements with *used to*, we can use *never used to* or *didn't use to*:

I ***never used to*** *like olives but I do now.*

I ***didn't use to*** *like olives but I do now.*

! For questions with *used to*, we use *did ... use to ...?*:

Did *you* ***use to*** *have long hair?*

would

FORM: *would* + bare infinitive

Grandad ***would*** *play with us in the garden.*

USE: to talk about past habits (particularly the distant past).

! We can't use *would* to talk about past states:

✔ *I* ***used to*** *have a pet hamster.*

✘ *I* ***would*** *have a pet hamster.*

GRAMMAR REFERENCE | Unit 2 | Result clauses

so and *such*

USE: to talk about amounts, and their results and effects:

so + adjective/adverb + (*that*) clause	*It's **so hot** I can't work!* *He worked **so hard** that he got the top mark.*
so + *many/much* + noun + (*that*) clause	*I've got **so many** books I can't carry my bag.* *He's got **so much** money that he can buy anything.*
such + *a(n)* + adjective + singular noun + (*that*) clause	*It was **such a hot day** that we had a picnic.*
such + adjective + plural noun + (*that*) clause	*We have **such good teachers** that I love my school.*
such + *a lot of* + noun + (*that*) clause (= *so many/much*)	*I have **such a lot of homework** that I can't do it all!*

too

USE: to criticise, to say that something is negative or bad, or to show that something prevents us from doing something:

too + adjective/adverb + *for* (+ full infinitive)	*It's **too wet** for a picnic.* *It's raining **too hard** for a picnic.* *It's **too wet** for us to have a picnic.*
too many + plural countable noun	*We invited **too many** people to the party.*
too much + uncountable noun	*I've got **too much** work to do this weekend.*

! *too* is not followed by a *that* clause.

! When the meaning is positive, we don't use *too*. We use other words and phrases, such as *really* or *extremely* (with adjectives or adverbs) or *lots of* (with nouns).

enough

USE: *enough*: the right amount/number of;

not enough: less than the right amount/number of:

(*not*) *enough* + noun (+ full infinitive)	*I don't have **enough money** (to buy a game).*
(*not*) *enough* + noun + *for*	*Are there **enough people** for a game of football?*
(*not*) + adjective/adverb + *enough* (+ *for*) (+ full infinitive)	*Is the water **warm enough** for you (to swim)?*
(*not*) + *a(n)* + adjective + *enough* + singular noun	*It's not a **nice enough** day to go to the beach.*

! The word *enough* is not followed by a *that* clause.

GRAMMAR REFERENCE | Unit 3 | Present perfect simple and continuous

Present perfect simple

FORM: *have/has* + past participle

*I/You/We/They**'ve seen** / **haven't seen** …*

*He/She/It**'s seen** / **hasn't seen** …*

***Have** I/you/we/they **seen** …? **Has** he/she/it **seen** …?*

USE: to talk about the following situations: **1** situations that started in the past and are still true, **2** completed actions at a time in the past which is not mentioned, **3** completed actions where the important thing is the present result, and **4** a series of actions continuing up to now:

1	*I**'ve lived** here all my life.*
2	*I**'ve played** this game before.*
3	*She**'s** just **finished** her final exam.*
4	*So far this term in geography, we**'ve learnt** about Asia and Antarctica.*

We can also use the present perfect simple: **5** with words/phrases like *already, ever, for, just, never, since, so far, up to now, yet*, **6** with superlatives, and **7** with ordinal numbers:

5	*I**'ve already decided** what to get Dad for his birthday.*
6	*That's **the best** pizza I**'ve ever eaten**!*
7	*This is the **first** time I**'ve fallen asleep** at the cinema!*

! We use *for* + a period of time, and *since* + the moment when it started:

*I've had my bike **for four months** / **since last summer**.*

Present perfect continuous

FORM: *have/has* + *been* + *-ing*

*I/You/We/They**'ve been** / **haven't been waiting** …*
*He/She/It**'s been** / **hasn't been waiting** …*

***Have** I/you/we/they **been waiting** …?*
***Has** he/she/it **been waiting** …?*

USE: to talk about: **1** actions and situations (often temporary ones) continuing up to now, and **2** actions and situations (often temporary ones) that ended recently:

1	*You've **been playing** that game for hours.*
2	*She's **been working** all morning and she's only just finished.*

! Phrases used with the present perfect continuous include: *all day/week/morning*, etc., *for, just* and *since.*

GRAMMAR REFERENCE | Unit 3 | Countable and uncountable nouns

Countable nouns can be counted and have a singular and plural form *(one book, two books; one sheep, three sheep; a child, five children).*

Uncountable nouns are often abstract ideas (*truth, information,* etc.), materials *(iron, glass, water, wood,* etc.) and collections *(furniture, luggage, baggage, money,* etc.).

Nouns like these are followed by a verb in the singular, even if they're describing more than one object:

*The luggage **is** heavy.*

*All the furniture **is** made of wood.*

! See Grammar reference, Unit 1 for information on which quantifiers **(***much, many,* etc.) we use with countable and uncountable nouns.

! To talk about one object in a collection, we can use *piece of, sheet of, item of,* etc. and we can use plural verbs where appropriate:

*The answers are printed on a **sheet of** paper.*
*Two **pieces of** cake **are** enough.*

! Some nouns are both countable and uncountable. Often, this is because the word refers to a substance/material or a thing that's made of that substance:

- material/substance – uncountable: *glass, chocolate, coffee, paper,* etc.
- a thing containing that material/substance – countable: *a glass* (to drink from), *a chocolate* (one from a box), *a coffee* (a drink), *a paper* (a newspaper), etc.

GRAMMAR REFERENCE | Unit 4 | *will* and *be going to*

FORM: *will/be going to* + bare infinitive

Predictions

For a prediction saying what we think or guess will happen, we often use *will.*

*I think you **will** love your holiday in Turkey!*

For a prediction based on evidence seen at the time of speaking, we often use *be going to.*

*Watch out! You**'re going to** hurt yourself!*

For a prediction when we are not certain what will happen, we can also use *may/might* (possibility) *or should* (probability).

***Will** the weather be fine this weekend? It **might** be. After all, it's the summer!*

or

*It **should** be. The forecast was for good weather.*

Intentions

To talk about intentions (something planned but not yet arranged), we often use *be going to.*

*I'**m going to** start swimming lessons but I'm not sure when.*

Instant decisions

For decisions made at the moment of speaking, we often use *will.*

I'm not sure what to have. Oh, I know! I'll have spaghetti Bolognese.

Offers, requests, promises, suggestions

To make offers or requests, we use *will* or *shall. Shall* is quite rare except in questions.

*I'**ll** help you. **Will** you help me, please? **Shall** I help you?*

! We don't use *will* in questions to make offers.

✘ ***Will** I help you?*

To make promises, we use will.

*I **won't** be late.*

To make suggestions (for *I* and *we* only), we use *shall.*

***Shall** we go to the cinema tonight?*

! Sometimes *will* and *be going to* are both correct. In general, *be going to* is more informal and is common in speech.

*Ellie **will** drive you to the station. / Ellie **is going to** drive you to the station.*

GRAMMAR REFERENCE | Unit 4 | Present simple and present continuous for the future

Timetabled future events

To talk about things that happen according to a schedule, we often use the present simple.

*The train **arrives** in half an hour.*

! Words/phrases used with the present simple for the future include: *as soon as, before, once, the moment that, unless, until, when.*

Arrangements

To talk about arrangements (something agreed and arranged), we often use the present continuous.

***We're having** a vocabulary test on Monday morning.*

GRAMMAR REFERENCE | Unit 4 | *although, even though, despite, in spite of*

USE: to contrast one idea with another:

although / even though + clause, clause	***Although / Even though*** *Alex is young, he's very tall.*
in spite of / despite + *-ing*, clause	***In spite of / Despite*** *being young, Alex is very tall.*
in spite of / despite + *the fact that* + clause, clause	***In spite of / Despite*** *the fact that he's young, Alex is very tall.*
in spite of / despite + noun, clause	***In spite of / Despite*** *his age, Alex is very tall.*
However, clause	*Alex is young.* ***However****, he's very tall.*

GRAMMAR REFERENCE | Unit 5 | Modals (1): ability, obligation, advice, permission

FORM: Modals have only one form in the present and are followed by the bare infinitive:

*I/You/He/She/It/We/They **can** ride a bike.*

*I/You/He/She/It/We/They **must** be careful.*

USE: some modals (*can, could, may, might, must, should*) and semi-modals (*have to, ought to*) can express: ability, possibility, probability, advice or criticism, obligation and permission.

We can use the modals *shall, will* and *would* to talk about the future, to make offers and to talk about hypothetical situations.

Ability – *can/could*

To talk about ability now or generally: *I **can** play the piano.*

To make a decision now about future ability: *We **can** come to your house tomorrow.*

To talk about ability in the past: *I **could** ride a bike when I was three.*

! To talk about ability in the future, use *will be able to.*

*You **will be able to** swim two lengths of the pool in a few months.*

! We don't use *can* as an infinitive. We use *be able to.*

✔ *I'd love **to be able to** visit the USA.*

✘ *I'd love **to can** visit the USA.*

Obligation – *must / have/has to*

To talk about personal obligation now, in the future, or generally: *I **must** remember to call Meera this evening.*

To talk about external obligation now, in the future, generally or in the past: *I **have to** get up at 7 am on school days. Carl **had to** do lots of homework last night.*

! In formal and official language, *must* is sometimes used for external obligation.

*All students **must** attend the school assembly.*

! *Mustn't* and *don't have to* mean different things.

*You **mustn't** eat that!* = Don't eat that!

*You **don't have** to eat that.* = You can eat that if you want to but it's not necessary.

! *Must* cannot be used as an infinitive. Use *to have to.*

✔ *I'd hate **to have to** go to school on Sundays.*

✘ *I'd hate **to must** go to school on Sundays.*

Advice or criticism – *ought to / should*

To ask for or give advice, or to criticise someone, now, in the future, or generally:

*You **ought to** tell your mum.*

*You **shouldn't** watch that film – it's too scary!*

! *Should* is much more common in spoken and written English than *ought to.*

Permission – *can/could/may*

To talk about permission now, in the future, or generally.

***Can/Could/May** I invite Jenny round this evening?*

! *May* is more polite and formal than *could*, and *could* is more polite than *can*.

! To talk about permission in the past, we don't usually use a modal.

✔ *I **was allowed to** watch the movie.*

✘ *I **could** watch the movie.*

! *Could* might refer to permission in the past, in reported speech.

*Mum said I **could** have a birthday party.*

GRAMMAR REFERENCE | Unit 5 | Modals (2): possibility, probability, certainty

Possibility – *may/might/could*

To talk about possibility in the present, the future and generally.

*Alana **may/might/could** be at the cinema, but I'm not sure.*

Probability – *should/ought to*

To talk about what is probably true, or what will probably happen.

*Mum **should/ought to** come home in a few minutes.*

Certainty – *must/can't*

If we are certain that something is true, we use *must*.

*Living in Antarctica **must** be difficult.*

If we are certain that something is not true, we use *can't*.

*Living in Antarctica **can't** be easy.*

! We can also use a continuous infinitive to show that something is continuing.

*Sarah must **be flying** to Australia now.*

GRAMMAR REFERENCE | Unit 6 | Relative clauses

Relative clauses are often introduced by relative pronouns and adverbs.

Relative pronouns and adverbs

who – for people (and sometimes animals): *Jade, **who** is my best friend, lives next door to me.*

which – for things (and sometimes animals): *Paris, **which** is the capital of France, is a beautiful city.*

that – for people and things; in defining relative clauses only: *The shoes **that** I bought were uncomfortable.*

whose – possessive: *Mr Kapoor, **whose** daughter is in my class, lives at the end of our street.*

where – for places: *This is the house **where** my mum was born.*

when – for time: *I will never forget the day **when** my baby brother was born.*

Defining relative clauses

FORM: In defining relative clauses we:

- don't use a comma.

  *The person **who** you were talking to is my teacher.*
- can use *that* instead of *who* or *which*.

  *The person **that** you were talking to is my teacher.*
- often leave out the relative pronoun when it is the object of the clause.

  The person you were talking to is my teacher.

USE: to tell us exactly who or what we are talking about.

*Is your brother in this photo? Yes, he's the person **who** has short hair.*

! Notice that without the relative clause, the sentence doesn't really make sense.

✘ *Is your brother in this photo? Yes, he's the person.* (Which person? We need more information.)

Non-defining relative clauses

FORM: In non-defining relative clauses we:

- separate the relative clause with commas.

  My brother, who lives with me, is a doctor.
- can't use *that* as a relative pronoun.

✘ *My brother, that lives with me, is a doctor.*

- can't leave out the relative pronoun.

✘ *My brother, lives with me, is a doctor.*

USE: to give us extra information about who or what we are talking about.

Usain Bolt, who has won lots of gold medals, is from Jamaica.

! Notice that without the relative clause, the sentence still makes sense.

Usain Bolt is from Jamaica.

GRAMMAR REFERENCE | Unit 6 | Articles

Indefinite article (*a(n)*)

USE: with singular countable nouns (when we are not being specific or when we mention something for the first time): *I need **a** pen.*

! Whether we use *a* or *an* depends on the sound, not the spelling:

*Have you got **a euro**?*

*I've been waiting for **an** hour.*

Definite article (*the*)

USE: with singular countable nouns (specific or general): *Where's **the** book I gave you? **The** guitar is my favourite instrument.*

with plural countable nouns (when we are being specific): ***The** guests will be here any moment!*

with uncountable nouns (when we are being specific): *Thanks for **the** advice.*

! We usually use *the* when there is only one of something: ***the** sun, **the** sky, **the** internet,* etc.

No article

USE: with plural countable nouns (when we are talking generally): *Movies are very expensive to make.*

with uncountable nouns (when we are talking generally): *Water is necessary for life.*

! Notice how we use articles in these phrases:

time: *in **the** 2020s, in **the** morning, in July, on Tuesday, at night*

people and work: *work as **a** ..., have **a** job, go to work, **the** Queen, **the** Chinese*

places: ***the** Himalayas, **the** USA, **the** UK, Istanbul, Mexico*

entertainment: ***the** media, on **the** radio, on TV, go to **the** cinema*

organisations: ***the** army, **the** police, **the** fire brigade*

travel: *on **the** bus, catch **a/the** bus, take **a** taxi*

GRAMMAR REFERENCE | Unit 7 | Past perfect simple and continuous

Past perfect simple

FORM: *had* + past participle

*I/you/he/she/it/we/they **had/'d seen** the film before.*

*I/you/he/she/it/we/they **had not / hadn't seen** the film before.*

***Had** I/you/he/she/it/we/they **seen** the film before?*

*Yes, I/you/he/she/it/we/they. **had**. No, I/you/he/she/it/we/they **hadn't**.*

Irregular verbs

You need to learn the past participle of irregular verbs.

See the Irregular verbs reference, page 175.

USE: to talk about: **1** completed actions before a moment in the past, **2** situations and states before the past, and **3** completed actions where the important thing is the result at a moment in the past:

1	*They **had eaten** dinner by the time I got home.*
2	*I **had lived** in London for three years before I met Daniel.*
3	*I didn't hear the phone because I**'d** just **fallen** asleep.*

! Phrases such as *It was the first/second/*etc. *time ...* are followed by the past perfect simple.

*It was the first time I **had had** a banana milkshake.*

Past perfect continuous

FORM: *had been + -ing*

*I/you/he/she/it/we/they **had/'d been running**.*

*I/you/he/she/it/we/they **had not / hadn't been running**.*

***Had** I/you/he/she/it/we/they **been running**?*

*Yes, I/you/he/she/it/we/they **had**. No, I/you/he/she/it/we/they **hadn't**.*

USE: to talk about: **1** actions continuing up to a moment in the past, and **2** actions stopping just before a moment in the past:

1	*By six o'clock, we **had been playing** computer games for four hours.*
2	*I was hot because I **had been running**.*

GRAMMAR REFERENCE | Unit 7 | Comparatives and superlatives

FORM:

Type of adjective	Normal	Comparative	Superlative
Regular adjective (one syllable)	*fast*	+ *-er faster*	+ *-est fastest*
Regular adjective (one/two syllables) ending in *-e*	*nice*	+ *-r nicer*	+ *-st nicest*
Regular adjective (one syllable) ending in a vowel + consonant	*hot*	double the final letter + *-er hotter*	double the final letter + *-est hottest*
Regular adjective (two syllables) ending in *-y*	*happy*	replace *-y* with *-ier happier*	replace *-y* with *-iest happiest*
Other regular adjective (two or more syllables)	*interesting*	*more* + adjective *more interesting*	*most* + adjective *most interesting*
Irregular adjective	*good* *bad* *far* *little* *many/much*	*better* *worse* *farther/further* *less* *more*	*best* *worst* *farthest/furthest* *least* *most*

Regular adverb	Comparative	Superlative
loudly	*more/less loudly*	*most/least loudly*
Irregular adverb	**Comparative**	**Superlative**
hard	*harder*	*hardest*
early	*earlier*	*earliest*
well	*better*	*best*
badly	*worse*	*worst*
far	*farther/further*	*farthest/furthest*
fast	*faster*	*fastest*
late	*later*	*latest*
often	*more/less often*	*most/least often*

USE: We use **comparative** adjectives and adverbs to show that things or people are different or separate from each other:

*Marta is **better** at diving **than** me.*

*Marta dives **better than** me.*

We use **superlative** adjectives and adverbs to show that one member of a group is at the top or bottom of the group:

*Marta is **the best diver** in my swimming team.*

*Marta dived **the best** in the diving competition.*

! We don't always use *than* with comparatives:

*This is my **older** sister.* (the comparative describes the noun)

*In winter, the weather is usually **colder**.* (= colder than it is at other times)

! We don't always use *the* with superlatives:

*It was **my best** exam result ever!*

! We can use *even* and *much* with comparatives:

*I'm good at skateboarding, but Greg is **even/much** better!*

Other ways of comparing

as + adjective + *as*	To describe how things are the same in some way	*I am **as tall as** Rachel (is).*
not as/ so + adjective + *as*	To describe how things are different	*I'm **not as tall as** Linda (is).*

GRAMMAR REFERENCE | Unit 8 | The passive

FORM: *be* + past participle (+ *by/with/of*)

USE: We often use the passive: **1** when we don't know who 'does' the action, **2** when it's not important who 'does' the action, **3** when it's obvious who 'does' the action, and **4** for emphasis, or to sound more formal:

1	*My phone **has been stolen**!*
2	*Jeans **are made** in factories.*
3	*The students **were given** a test.*
4	*A new law **has been passed**.*

We use *by* to show who or what does the action: *This book was written **by** a teenager.*

We can use *with* for tools and equipment: *The window had been broken **with** a hammer.*

We can use *of* for materials: *My new shirt is made **of** silk.*

! We often don't use *by* if we don't know who does the action, if it's not important or if it's obvious:

The house was built in 1965.

! We don't use the passive in the present perfect continuous or past perfect continuous. We can use it in all other tenses, plus with modals, *-ing* forms and infinitives:

*Children **should be taught** to swim.*

*I like **being given** presents!*

*How did it feel **to be told** you had won?*

! Some verbs are not usually used in the passive. These include intransitive verbs (verbs which don't take objects), such as *appear* and *seem*, and some transitive verbs, such as *have* and *let*.

GRAMMAR REFERENCE | Unit 8 | Question tags

FORM: When the verb *be* is a main verb, we form the question tag with *be:*

*It's a nice day, **isn't** it?*

When *be*, *have* or *do* are used as auxiliary verbs, we form the question tag with the auxiliary:

*She **doesn't** look very old, **does** she?*

With other main verbs that don't have an auxiliary verb, we form the question tag with *do:*
*You **live** in Warsaw, **don't** you?*

*He **has** a nice smile, **doesn't** he?*

With modals, we form the question tag using the modal:

*You **can't** play the piano, **can** you?*

With *there*, we repeat *there* in the question tag:

***There** were lots of people at the party, weren't **there**?*

With *let's*, we form the question tag with *shall we:*

***Let's** go out to eat, **shall we**?*

With imperatives, we form the question tag using *will*:

***Lend** me a pen, **will** you?*

***Don't forget** to text me, **will** you?*

USE: to ask questions: **1** when we expect someone to agree with our opinion, **2** to express surprise or doubt about something, **3** to suggest doing something (*Let's* +), and **4** when we want someone to do something for us (an imperative +):

1	*It's really cold today, **isn't it?***	Our voice goes down at the end of the sentence.
2	*You're not American, **are you?***	Our voice goes up at the end of the sentence.
3	*Let's watch TV, **shall we?***	
4	*Open the window, **will you?***	

! With words like *never, no, nobody*, etc., we use a positive question tag: *He's **never** angry, **is** he?*

GRAMMAR REFERENCE | Unit 8 | *-ing* and full infinitive after verbs

Verbs/phrases usually followed by the full infinitive (+ *to*)

be able, agree, appear, arrange, ask, attempt, choose, decide, hope, manage, offer, plan, prepare, pretend, promise, refuse, seem, tend, want, would like

! Some of these verbs/phrases can be followed by an object before the full infinitive.

*Mum asked **me** to help cook dinner.*

Verbs/phrases usually followed by the *-ing* form

admit, appreciate, avoid, deny, discuss, dislike, enjoy, fancy, feel like, mention, mind, miss, practise, put off, risk, succeed, suggest, understand

! Some of these verbs and phrases can be followed by a possessive form (more formal) or an object (more informal) before the *-ing* form.

*The teacher didn't mention **my/me** being late.*

! Verbs and phrases with prepositions can often be followed by the *-ing* form.

*I finally **succeeded in scoring** a goal.*

Verbs/phrases usually followed by an object + bare infinitive

feel, hear, let, make, notice, see, watch

Verbs/phrases followed by the full infinitive or *-ing* form with little or no change in meaning

begin, continue, hate, intend, love, start

Verbs/phrases followed by the full infinitive or *-ing* form with a change in meaning

forget, like, remember, stop, try

forget + *-ing* = to forget a past event

I'll never forget meeting you.

forget + *full infinitive* = not do something you are/were planning to do

I forgot to call Dad!

like + *-ing* = enjoy

Do you like going to the theatre?

like + full infinitive = do as a useful habit

I like to brush my teeth after breakfast.

remember + *-ing* = remember that you have done something

I remember going to Paris.

remember + full infinitive = remember that you need/needed to do something

Did you remember to text Rachel?

stop -ing = stop an action

Please stop talking.

stop + full infinitive = interrupt an action to do something else

I saw my friends so I stopped to chat to them.

try + *-ing* = do something to solve a problem

It was hot so I tried opening the window but it was still hot!

try + full infinitive = make an effort to do something

I tried to open the window, but I couldn't.

GRAMMAR REFERENCE | Unit 9 | Conditionals (1): zero, first and second conditionals

Zero conditional

FORM: *If* + present simple, present simple

USE: general truths, scientific facts:

*If you **exercise** regularly, you **stay** fit and healthy.*

*You **stay** fit and healthy if you **exercise** regularly.*

! We can also use other present tenses in the *if* clause, depending on the meaning:

*If you**'re exercising** every day, **you need** to make sure you eat properly.*

First conditional

FORM: *If* + present simple, *will/won't* + bare infinitive

USE: possible or likely situations now, generally, or in the future:

*If you **work** hard, you**'ll pass** the exam.*

*You**'ll pass** the exam if you **work** hard.*

! We can also use other present tenses in the *if* clause, depending on the meaning:

*If you**'ve studied** hard, you'll do well in the exam.*

! We can also use other modals in the result clause, depending on the meaning:

*If you study hard all this week, you **might/may/could/should** pass the exam.*

! We can also use the imperative for commands, instructions and advice:

*If you see Liz, **tell** her about my party.*

Second conditional

FORM: *If* + past simple, *would/wouldn't* + bare infinitive

USE: impossible, unlikely or hypothetical situations now, generally, or in the future:

*If you **were** a Martian, you **would live** on Mars.*

*You **would live** on Mars if you were a Martian.*

! We can also use the past continuous in the *if* clause, depending on the meaning:

*If you **were watching** this film with me now, you **would be** very scared.*

! We can also use other modals in the result clause, depending on the meaning:

*If we **had** wings, we **could** fly.* (= would be able to)

! With the verb *be*, there are two forms with the second conditional:

*If I **were** you, I'd ...* (more formal and often used in writing)

*If I **was** you, I'd ...* (more informal and often used in speech)

unless, as long as

unless (= 'except if', and replaces *if not*).

***Unless** you work hard, you won't pass the test.* = ***If** you **don't** work hard, you won't pass the test.*

as long as (= 'if the following situation is true or happens', and replaces *if*).

***As long as** you work hard, you'll pass the test.* = ***If** you work hard, you'll pass the test.*

GRAMMAR REFERENCE | Unit 9 | Time clauses

USE: to talk about the future

FORM: As with *if* in the first conditional, we can use other time words/phrases + present simple (and NOT *will*) in a time clause. Time words/phrases include: *when, as soon as, once, before, after, until, till, while:*

*I'll do my homework **as soon as** I **get** home.*

***As soon as** I **get** home, I'll do my homework.*

! We can also use present continuous and present perfect in time clauses.

*I won't listen to music while **I'm doing** my homework.*

*I'll call you once **I've finished** my homework.*

GRAMMAR REFERENCE | Unit 10 | Conditionals (2): third conditional

USE: to talk about the hypothetical past (i.e. to imagine a past that didn't happen):

*If **I'd had** enough money, **I'd have bought** the shoes.* = *I didn't have enough money. I didn't buy the shoes.*

FORM: As with other conditionals, a third conditional sentence has two parts: the *if* clause and the result clause. We separate the clauses with a comma when the *if* clause comes first: *If you'd been there, you'd have enjoyed it. / You'd have enjoyed it if you'd been there.*

! Both clauses in the third conditional are hypothetical (i.e. they didn't really happen).

! Instead of *would*, we can also use *might* and *could:*

*If you'd entered the race, you **might/could** have won.*

! Be careful with verbs in the negative in third conditional sentences.

*She **wouldn't** have passed the test if she **hadn't** studied. = She did pass the test. She studied.*

*She **would** have passed the test if she **hadn't** made a mistake. = She didn't pass the test. She made a mistake.*

*She **wouldn't** have passed the test if she **had** made a mistake. = She passed the test. She didn't make a mistake.*

GRAMMAR REFERENCE | Unit 10 | The causative

USE: to talk about asking or paying someone else to do something for us. We can use it when the person who does the action is unimportant or obvious, in the same way as we can with the passive. We can also use the causative to put the topic (the thing we are talking about) first in a sentence and the new information later.

FORM: *have* (in the right form) + object + past participle

*I'm **having my eyes tested** next week.*

We can also use *get* instead of *have*. *Get* is less formal.

*Where did you **get** your family photo taken?*

! The causative can also be used to talk about (usually bad) things that happen to us, such as things being stolen, broken, etc. We don't usually use *get* with this meaning.

*Ellie **had her bike stolen** yesterday.*

The causative and the passive

The causative has a number of things in common with the passive.

- We use *by* to show who or what 'does' the action:

  *I had my bike repaired **by** a mechanic.*

- We can use *with* to describe tools and equipment:

  *They had their house painted **with** a special weatherproof paint.*

- We often don't use *by* if we don't know who 'does' it:

  Simon had his phone stolen ~~by someone.~~

- We often don't use *by* if it's obvious or not important who 'does' it:

  We're having our house painted this week ~~by a painter.~~

GRAMMAR REFERENCE | Unit 10 | *wish* and *if only*

USE: to talk about hypothetical situations generally, or in the past, present and future.

! *Wish* and *if only* mean the same thing, but *if only* is more emphatic than *wish*.

FORM: As with conditionals, you have to learn which tenses we use with *wish* and *if only*, because they're different to normal English:

	wish / if only +	
hypothetical situations now, in the future, or generally	past simple past continuous	*I wish I **had** a smartphone.* *If only I **had** a smartphone.* **(= I don't have a smartphone but I want one.)** *I wish you **were coming** with us.* *If only you **were coming** with us.* **(= You're not coming with us but I'd like you to.)**
hypothetical ability or permission now, in the future, or generally	*could*	*I wish you **could** come with us.* *If only you **could** come with us.* **(= You can't come with us but I'd like you to.)**
criticising or complaining about a situation now or generally	*would*	*I wish/If only you **would** be nice to your sister.* **(= You aren't nice to your sister but I'd like you to be.)** ! We only use this when talking about other people. We can't say *I wish I would …*
hypothetical situations in the past (regrets)	past perfect	*I wish/If only I **had bought** that T-shirt.* **(= I didn't buy that T-shirt and now I regret it.)**

! We use *wish* and *if only* for hypothetical situations only. If the situation isn't hypothetical, we often use *hope*:

*I **wish** Jan **could** come to the party.* (= hypothetical – she can't come)

*I **hope** Jan **can** come to the party.* (= real – maybe she can come)

GRAMMAR REFERENCE | Unit 11 | Reported speech

FORM: In reported speech, we don't use all the words and tenses of direct speech. Be careful with tenses and time/place words.

Direct speech	Reported speech
present simple *'I learn Japanese.'*	**past simple** *Emily said (that) she **learnt** Japanese.*
present continuous *'I am learning Japanese.'*	**past continuous** *Emily said (that) she **was learning** Japanese.*
past simple/present perfect simple/past perfect simple *'I learnt/have learnt/had learnt Japanese.'*	**past perfect simple** *Emily said (that) she **had learnt** Japanese.*
past continuous/present perfect continuous/past perfect continuous *'I was/have been/had been learning Japanese.'*	**past perfect continuous** *Emily said (that) she **had been learning** Japanese.*
will/can *'I will/can learn Japanese.'*	***would/could*** *Emily said (that) she **would/could** learn Japanese.*
must *'I must learn Japanese.'*	***had to*** *Emily said (that) she **had to learn** Japanese.*

! Time and place words are often different, because of the different perspective:

Direct speech	Reported speech
here	*there*
today	*that day*
now	*then / at that moment*
tomorrow	*the following/next day*
next week/month/year	*the following week/month/year*
yesterday	*the day before / the previous day*
last week/month/year	*the previous week/month/year*
ago	*before*
this/that + noun	*the/that*
this/that (subject/object)	*it*
these/those + noun	*the/those*
these/those (as a subject)	*they*
these/those (as an object)	*them*

GRAMMAR REFERENCE | Unit 11 | Reported questions

FORM: In reported questions the subject comes before the verb, we do not use auxiliary verbs or question marks.

With questions with *who*, *why*, *how*, etc., we repeat the question word and change the tense and the word order:

Direct question	Reported question
'What are you wearing to the wedding?' Dad asked me.	reporting verb + *wh-* word + subject + verb *Dad **asked** me **what I was wearing** to the wedding.*

With reported *yes/no* questions, we use *if* or *whether* and change the tense and word order:

Direct question	Reported question
'Do you have any money?' Kerry asked me.	reporting verb + *if/whether* + subject + verb *Kerry **asked** me **if/whether I had** any money.*

! We also change time, pronouns and place words like we do in reported speech:

*'Are **you** doing **your** homework **tonight**?'*
*Mum asked **me** if **I** was doing **my** homework **that** night.*

GRAMMAR REFERENCE | Unit 12 | Future perfect

FORM: *will/won't* + *have* + past participle (*will have drunk, won't have eaten,* etc.)

USE: to talk about actions completed at a time between now and a point in the future. This use is similar to how we use the present perfect to talk about actions completed between some point in the past and now and how we use the past perfect to talk about actions completed before a point in the past. (See Grammar Reference, Unit 3 and Grammar Reference, Unit 7).

*I don't have a lot of homework, so I **will have finished** it by six o'clock.*

! We can also use other modals in the future perfect, including *might* (possible actions) and *should* (probable actions).

*I **might not have finished** my homework by six o'clock. I'll text you and let you know.*

*I'm not sure, but I **should have finished** my homework by six o'clock. That's what I hope!*

! We often use *by* and *by the time* with the future perfect.

*I'll have cooked dinner **by the time** Mum gets home from work.*

GRAMMAR REFERENCE | Unit 12 | Modal perfect

FORM: modal + *have* + past participle (*would have gone, should have seen,* etc.)

USE: The modal perfect is used for a number of different purposes:

Deductions about the real past

Past situations which are almost certainly correct: *must, can't, couldn't*

*Courtney **must have lost** her phone. = I'm almost certain she's lost her phone.*

*Courtney **can't/couldn't have lost** her phone. = I'm almost certain she hasn't lost her phone.*

Past situations which are probably correct: *should, ought to*

*Let's go in. The lesson **should / ought to have finished** by now. = The lesson has probably finished.*

Past situations which are possibly correct: *may, might, could*

*Tim **may/might/could have hurt** his arm. = It's possible he's hurt his arm.*

Describing a hypothetical past

We use the modal perfect in this way in third conditional result clauses.

*You **would/could/might have won** if you had tried harder.*

! We use *could* + *have* + past participle to describe hypothetical past ability. For real past ability, we use *could* + bare infinitive:

*I **could talk** when I was just nine months old.*

Criticising past behaviour

We can use the modal perfect with *should* or *ought to* to criticise past action and behaviour. *You **should / ought to have trusted** me! = You didn't trust me and that was wrong.*

! Be careful with *should* + *have* + past participle because it can be used for situations which happened and didn't happen:

*Dad **should have left** work so he'll probably be home in a minute. = He's probably left work.*

*Dad **should have left** work but he hasn't. Maybe there's a problem. = He hasn't left work.*

GRAMMAR REFERENCE | Unit 12 | Auxiliary verbs

FORM: *be, do* and *have* in different forms. They are followed by another verb.

USE: to create tenses, form questions, in negatives and in the passive voice

be

be is used in continuous tenses and in the passive voice:

*What **is** Oliver doing here?*

*Photography **was** invented in the 19th century.*

do

do is used in questions and negatives:

*Where **do** you live?*

*You **don't** care about me!*

have

have is used in perfect tenses:

*I **have** been waiting for you for an hour.*

! We don't use *do/does* with *be* or *have got.*

VOCABULARY REFERENCE

Introduction

This *Vocabulary reference* contains all the target vocabulary from *Optimise B1* Student's Book. The words and phrases are arranged unit by unit, so you can refer to them as you work on vocabulary lessons throughout the book. You can also use the pages as a revision tool when you're preparing for a test or an exam.

The target vocabulary has been subdivided into six groups:

Topic vocabulary

The **Topic vocabulary** sections focus on language connected to the unit topic. Learning these words and being able to use them correctly will help you in your exams. Having a wide vocabulary is particularly relevant for Use of English, Speaking and Writing exams.

Word formation

The **Word formation** sections present you with all the different parts of speech – verbs, adjectives, nouns and adverbs – that come from root words that appear in *Optimise B1* Student's Book. Most exams will test your knowledge of word formation, so learning all the forms of a word is a good way to make sure you are well prepared for your exam.

Collocations

Collocations are phrases with combinations of words which naturally go together in English. Learning collocations will help you in exam tasks, such as open cloze, multiple-choice cloze and sentence transformations. It will also improve your productive English and therefore help you with speaking and writing.

Idioms

Idioms are common phrases in a language, whose meaning is often not literal, so can be difficult or impossible to guess. You will find a good knowledge of idioms is particularly helpful in sentence transformation tasks.

Word patterns

Word patterns are phrases which use specific grammatical structures. For example, phrases with dependent prepositions (*regardless of*), or phrases that require a certain verb form or sentence structure (*find* (sth) *strange* (+ *that*)).

Phrasal verbs

Phrasal verbs consist of a verb (*take, come, look*, etc.) plus a particle. The particle can be an adverb (*away, down*, etc.) or a preposition (*in, on*, etc.). Remember that some phrasal verbs have more than one meaning; in the tables, the meaning given for the phrasal verb always matches the one used in the unit.

These are the main types of phrasal verbs:

Type 1: the verb is transitive (has an object). When the object is a noun, we can put the particle before or after the noun:

*I'll **sort** the CDs **out**. / I'll **sort out** the CDs.*

And when the object is a pronoun, the pronoun **must** separate the two parts of the phrasal verb:

✔ *I'll **sort** them **out**.*
✘ *I'll **sort out** them.*

Type 2: the verb is intransitive (does not have an object) and you cannot separate the two parts of the verb:

✔ *It's hard to **get by** without a job.*
✘ *It's hard to **get** without a job **by**.*

! Some phrasal verbs may have different meanings when they are used transitively or intransitively:

*I started to **drop off** during the lesson. (= fall asleep)*

*I'll **drop** the money **off** at your house tomorrow. (= deliver)*

Type 3: the verb is transitive (has an object) but you cannot separate the two parts of the verb:

✔ *I **came across** some old photos in the cupboard.*
✘ *I **came** some old photos **across** in the cupboard.*

✔ *In the end Harley **went for** the black jeans.*
✘ *In the end Harley **went** the black jeans **for**.*

Type 4: the phrasal verb is three words – verb + adverb particle + preposition:

*Why do you **put up with** his behaviour?*

! These phrasal verbs are always transitive and you can never separate the words with an object or pronoun:

✔ *He **got away with** the robbery.*
✘ *He **got** the robbery **away with**.*

Throughout the *Vocabulary reference*, you will see various abbreviations. This key explains what they all mean.

KEY: adj = adjective; adv = adverb; n = noun; ex = exclamation; p = preposition; phr = phrase; pl = plural; sb = somebody; sth = something; swh = somewhere; US = American English; v = verb

UNIT 1

TOPIC VOCABULARY | Words connected with *personality*

Word	Example
creative (adj)	Tina's quite creative – she loves making things out of plastic bottles.
curious (adj)	Dan's very curious – he always asks questions starting with 'why'!
dependable (adj)	Amira's totally dependable – if she says she'll be there, then she will.
friendly (adj)	Our new teacher is very friendly, she always tries to help everyone.
generous (adj)	My uncle and aunt are quite generous – they always give me great birthday presents.
negative (adj)	Don't be so negative – we can still win the game!
polite (adj)	Jill's so polite – she always says 'please' and 'thank you' and never says rude words.
popular (adj)	Leila's very popular – she has lots of friends.
serious (adj)	Mr Black is very serious – he never smiles.
shy (adj)	Dana is quite shy and doesn't like talking to people at parties.
unreliable (adj)	Gareth's a bit unreliable, so he'll probably be late tomorrow.

PHRASAL VERBS

Phrasal verb	Meaning	Example sentence
look after (Type 3)	take care of	A babysitter usually looks after us on Friday evenings.
look forward to (Type 4)	be excited about something in the future	I'm really looking forward to my birthday!
look into (Type 3)	investigate	The police are looking into the cause of the accident.
look up (Type 1)	(try to) find information in a book, dictionary, etc.	If you don't know the meaning of the word, look it up in a dictionary.
turn into (Type 3)	change from one thing into another	It takes many years for a tiny acorn to turn into a big oak tree.
turn off (Type 1)	make a machine (e.g. a TV or computer) stop working temporarily	Turn off the computer when you've finished with it.
turn on (Type 1)	make a machine (e.g. a TV or computer) start working	Turn on the laptop, then enter your password.
turn over (Type 1)	proceed to the next page of a book or magazine	If you turn over the page, you'll see a map of Egypt.

COLLOCATIONS | Collocations with adjectives

Collocation	Example sentence
a long time	Have you lived in that house for a long time?
deep voice	My dad's got a really deep voice.
fast asleep	The cat was fast asleep in its basket when we got home.
feel small	I felt really small when my best friend told me I was selfish.
in big trouble	You'll be in big trouble if you don't tidy your bedroom soon!
wide awake	When I heard a noise downstairs, I went from being fast asleep to being wide awake in about one second!

WORD FORMATION | Nouns with *-ity / -ness*

Core word	Derivatives
create (v)	creative (adj), creation (n), creator (n), creativity (n), creatively (adv)
curious (adj)	curiosity (n), curiously (adv)
depend (v)	dependable (adj), (in)dependent (adj), dependability (n), (in)dependently (adv)
friend (n)	(un)friendly (adj), friendship (n), friendliness (n)
generous (adj)	generosity (n), generously (adv)
negative (adj)	negativity (n), negatively (adv)
person (n)	personalise (v), (im)personal (adj), personality (n), personally (adv)
polite (adj)	impolite (adj), politeness (n), (im)politely (adv)
popular (adj)	unpopular (adj), popularity (n), popularise (n), (un)popularly (adv)
rely (v)	(un)reliable (adj), (un)reliability (n), (un)reliably (adv)
serious (adj)	seriousness (n), seriously (adv)
shy (adj)	shyness (n), shyly (adv)

UNIT 2

TOPIC VOCABULARY | Words connected with *the house and home*

Word	Example sentence
attic (n)	Dad got a ladder and climbed up into the attic to find some old boxes.
balcony (n)	Juliet stood on the balcony and waved to Romeo.
basement (n)	I felt nervous as I went down into the basement because it was so dark and damp.
ceiling (n)	I looked up at the ceiling and noticed a big crack from one side of the room to the other.
chimney (n)	It was cold so Mum lit a fire and the smoke started to go up the chimney.
dining room (n)	When dinner was ready, we all went into the dining room and sat down.
fence (n)	We couldn't find the gate into the garden so we had to climb over the fence!
garage (n)	Mum was in the garage all day, trying to mend her car.
hedge (n)	I kicked the ball and it went over the hedge into next door's garden!
living room (n)	After doing her homework, Jessie went into the living room and turned the TV on.
roof (n)	There was a storm during the night and it almost blew the roof off the house!
study (n)	I like to go into the study when I want to read quietly by myself.

PHRASAL VERBS

Phrasal verb	Meaning	Example sentence
do up (Type 1)	repair, improve the appearance of	It took us a long time to do the house up but now it looks great!
move in (Type 2)	start living in a house	When we moved in, our new neighbours welcomed us.
move out (Type 2)	stop living in a house	When we moved out, it was very sad to leave the house we had loved so much.
pull down (Type 1)	demolish, knock to the ground	I can't believe they've pulled my primary school down!
put up (Type 1)	provide accommodation for	Could you put me up for a few days?
rent out (Type 1)	make available for others to live in for money	Mum is thinking of renting out the spare room to make a bit of money.
settle in (Type 2)	become comfortable in a new place	Has Alfie settled in at university yet?
tidy up (Type 1)	make neat and clean	I have to tidy my bedroom up once a week.

WORD PATTERNS

Core words	Example sentence
be worth (doing sth)	It's not worth travelling all the way to New York just for the weekend.
be keen on (doing sth)	My mum's not very keen on flying so she usually takes the train.
depend on	Your success in the test depends on how much work you do.
tell (sb) to (do sth)	Our teacher told us to write a letter to a friend.
stop (sb) from (doing sth)	The rain stopped us from going to the park.
make (sb) do	Dad made me do the washing up!

UNIT 3

TOPIC VOCABULARY | Words connected with *holidays*

Word	Example sentence
backpacker (n)	Lots of backpackers travel to Thailand each year.
business trip (n)	My dad's away on a business trip at the moment.
camping trip (n)	Let's go on a camping trip in the summer!
campsite (n)	We stayed at a lovely campsite by the beach.
cruise (n)	We're going on a two-week cruise around the Greek islands.
currency (n)	What currency do we need to take to the UK – British pounds or euros?
guest (n)	This hotel has rooms for 40 guests.
guidebook (n)	It says in the guidebook that this castle is 500 years old.
guided tour (n)	We went on a guided tour of the Acropolis – we learnt a lot about its history.
hostel (n)	Backpackers often stay in hostels rather than hotels as they're cheaper.
luggage (n)	How much luggage are you taking on this trip?
package holiday (n)	Package holidays are great because you don't need to book flights and accommodation separately.
passport (n)	You'll have to show your passport when you enter the country.
resort (n)	We stayed in a lovely holiday resort by the coast.
school trip (n)	We're going on a school trip next Thursday to see a play at a theatre.
sightseer (n)	Here's a list of the 10 most important things for sightseers to see in the city.
tour guide (n)	The tour guide told us everything about the history of the building.
tourist (n)	Nobody lives here in the winter, but lots of tourists come in the summer.

PHRASAL VERBS

Phrasal verb	Meaning	Example sentence
break down (Type 2)	stop working properly (a machine, vehicle, etc.)	Mum was late to work because her car broke down.
check in (Type 2)	register at an airport, hotel, etc.	Let's find the desk where we need to check in.
drop off (Type 1)	to take someone to a place (usually by car)	Could you drop me off outside the supermarket?
pick up (Type 1)	collect (in a vehicle)	Could you pick me up outside the post office in half an hour?
set off (Type 2)	start a journey	We'll have to set off at 5.30 in the morning.
speed up (Type 2)	increase speed	If we don't speed up, we'll be late for the show.
take off (Type 2)	leave the ground	I love watching planes take off and start flying.
turn up (Type 2)	arrive, appear	Jack just turned up at the door with two tickets for tonight's concert!

WORD PATTERNS

Core words	Example sentence
be interested in	Are you interested in going to the science museum?
be keen on	I'm not very keen on playing team games.
be ready for	Are you ready for the geography test?
have time to (do sth)	I didn't have enough time to revise last night.
look forward to (doing sth)	I'm really looking forward to seeing you next week!
make (sb) do	Never let someone make you do something you don't want to do.
prevent (sb) from (doing sth)	The security guards prevented everyone from entering the building.
spend time (doing sth)	Do you spend a lot of time playing video games?

WORD FORMATION | Adjectives with *un- / im- / il- / ir- / dis-*

Core word	Derivatives
able (adj)	(in)capable (adj), unable (adj), disabled (adj), (in)ability (n), capability (n)
certain (adj)	uncertain (adj), (un)certainty (n), certainly (adv)
comfortable (adj)	uncomfortable (adj), (dis)comfort (n), (un)comfortably (adv)
fair (adj)	unfair (adj), (un)fairness (n), (un)fairly (adv)
happy (adj)	unhappy (adj), (un)happiness (n), (un)happily (adv)
helpful (adj)	unhelpful (adj), helpless (adj), help (v/n), helper (n), (un)helpfully (adv), helplessly (adv)
honest (adj)	dishonest (adj), (dis)honesty (n), (dis)honestly (adv)
legal (adj)	illegal (adj), (il)legality (n), (il)legally (adv)
patient (adj)	impatient (adj), (im)patience (n), (im)patiently (adv)
popular (adj)	unpopular (adj), popularity (n), popularise (v), (un)popularly (adv)
possible (adj)	impossible (adj), (im)possibility (n), (im)possibly (adv)
responsible (adj)	irresponsible (adj), (ir)responsibility (n), (ir)responsibly (adv)
tidy (v/adj)	untidy (adj), (un)tidiness (n), (un)tidily (adv)

UNIT 4

TOPIC VOCABULARY | Words connected with *outdoor activities*

Word	Example sentence
hiking (n)	We went hiking in the mountains and got lost!
horse-riding (n)	Ryan went horse-riding and he fell off the horse five times!
ice-skating (n)	I would love to try ice-skating but there isn't an ice rink where I live.
rock-climbing (n)	The hardest thing about rock-climbing is building up the strength in your fingers.
sailing (n)	My family goes sailing around the Mediterranean every summer.
skiing (n)	The last time we went skiing, I broke my ankle!
snowboarding (n)	To be good at snowboarding, you need to have good balance.
sky-diving (n)	I don't think sky-diving is dangerous if you have training.

PHRASAL VERBS

Phrasal verb	Meaning	Example sentence
call off (Type 1)	cancel	The school sports day has been called off because of bad weather.
eat out (Type 2)	eat in a restaurant	Whenever we eat out, my little brother has pasta.
get together (Type 2)	meet	Why don't we get together on Saturday and go to the cinema?
go out (Type 2)	leave home to meet friends, etc.	Mum and Dad go out every Friday night with their friends.
sleep in (Type 2)	stay in bed in the morning	I had a late night, so I slept in the next day.
stay up (Type 2)	not go to bed	At the weekend, I stay up later than I do during the week.
take up (Type 1)	start doing something new regularly	I'm thinking of taking up ice hockey.
work out (Type 2)	exercise	Dan works out at the gym three times a week.

COLLOCATIONS | Collocations connected with *free time*

Collocation	Example sentence
have a go at doing (sth)	Why not have a go at a sport you've never tried before?
spend time with (sb)	It's important to spend time with your friends.
make time for (sb/sth)	Jasmine's very busy at school, but she always makes time for playing video games!
take a break from	Why not take a break from your busy life and come to sunny Jamaica?
have a good time	Did you have a good time at summer camp?
have the day off	Mum had the day off so she took us out for the day.

UNIT 5

TOPIC VOCABULARY | Words connected with *health and illness*

Word	Example sentence
ache (v/n)	I banged my finger a couple of days ago and it still aches.
ankle (n)	I fell over yesterday and twisted my ankle.
bandage (v/n)	The nurse wrapped a bandage around Jill's arm.
blood (n)	I cut my finger and got blood on my bedroom carpet.
bone (n)	There are more than 200 bones in the human body.
chin (n)	My dad's got a small beard on his chin.
cold (n)	I can't go swimming after school today because I've got a cold.
cough (v/n)	I've had a cough for three days so I'm going to start taking some medicine.
cut (v/n)	Put your finger over the cut until it stops bleeding.
flu (n)	My sister has flu so she's not going to school this week.
hurt (v)	Did you hurt yourself when you fell off your bike?
infection (n)	Take antibiotics for a week to stop the infection.
injure (v)	Lots of people injure themselves while doing sport.
knee (n)	I banged my knee on the desk and now it hurts when I walk.
medicine (n)	Buy some medicine for your cough from the pharmacy.
operation (n)	My grandma's just gone into hospital to have an operation.
pain (n)	If you feel any pain in your teeth, see a dentist immediately.
prescription (n)	The doctor gave me a prescription for antibiotics.
shoulder (n)	She was carrying a red bag over her left shoulder.
skin (n)	Skin burns easily in the sun, so put sun cream on before you go out.

PHRASAL VERBS

Phrasal verb	Meaning	Example sentence
cheer up (Type 3)	become happier	Cheer up! It's Friday!
cheer up (Type 1)	make sb happier	Arjun looks sad – let's cheer him up!
come down with (Type 4)	become ill with a disease	I feel a bit strange – I hope I'm not coming down with a cold.
feel up to (Type 4)	feel well enough, have enough energy	Tony's a bit better, but he still doesn't feel up to having visitors.
get down (Type 1 – usually with a pronoun)	make sad or miserable	It really got me down when my dog got lost.
get down (Type 3)	become sad/ miserable	I get down occasionally, but usually I'm a happy person.
get over (Type 2)	recover from	It took me about two weeks to completely get over my cold.
pass out (Type 3)	faint, become unconscious	It was so hot in the room, I nearly passed out.
put down (Type 1)	kill (a very old or sick animal)	Vets sometimes have to put animals down.
put on (Type 1)	gain, add extra	I've put on some weight recently, so I'm going to cut down on sugar.

COLLOCATIONS | Collocations with *have, take, make* and *do*

Collocation	Example sentence
do homework/ housework	Don't forget to do your homework this evening.
do your teeth/ hair	I always do my teeth after breakfast and before bed.
do/take some exercise	How much physical exercise do you do each week?
have flu or a cold/cough/ headache	Sam has a headache so I'm going to get some aspirin for her.
have surgery or an operation	My cousin's just gone into hospital to have surgery on her knee.
have/take a bath/shower	I'm going to take a quick shower before dinner.
have/take medicine	Take this medicine twice a day for a week.
make a mistake	If you make a mistake, cross it out and write it again correctly.
make an effort	When Lucas broke his leg, everyone made an effort to help him.
make fun of somebody	My older brother always makes fun of me – it's so annoying!
make up your mind	I can't make up my mind whether to buy the green T-shirt or the blue one.
make your bed	Don't forget to make your bed before you go to school.
make/take a decision	I've made a decision – I'm going to buy the green T-shirt.
take care of somebody	A nurse visits twice a day to take care of my granddad.

WORD FORMATION | Words formed from verbs

Core word	Derivatives
accommodate (v)	accommodation (n)
agree (v)	disagree (v), (dis) agreeable (adj), (dis)agreement (n), (dis)agreeably (adv)
amaze (v)	amazing (adj), amazement (n), amazingly (adv)
communicate (v)	(un)communicative (adj), communicator (n), communication (n), (un)communicatively (adv)
decide (v)	(in)decisive (adj), decision (n), (in)decisively (adv)
enjoy (v)	(un)enjoyable (adj), enjoyment (n)
entertain (v)	entertaining (adj), entertainer (n), entertainment (n)
equip (v)	equipment (n)
excite (v)	(un)exciting (adj), (un)excited (adj), excitement (n), (un)excitingly (adv), (un)excitedly (adv)
improve (v)	improving (adj), (un)improved (adj), improvement (n)
infect (v)	infected (adj), infection (n)
operate (v)	operating (adj), operator (n), operation (n)
organise (v)	(un/dis)organised (adj), organiser (n), organisation (n)
prescribe (v)	prescribed (adj), prescription (n)
protect (v)	(un)protected (adj), (un)protective (adj), protector (n), protection (n), protectively (adv)
treat (v)	(un)treatable (adj), treatment (n)

UNIT 6

TOPIC VOCABULARY | Words connected with *food*

Word	Example sentence
bake (v)	Why don't we bake a cake this afternoon?
barbecue (v)	When you barbecue the fish, make sure it doesn't burn.
bitter (adj)	I don't like the taste of dark chocolate – it's too bitter.
boil (v)	Let the water boil for a minute before you put the eggs in the pan.
fry (v)	Fry the potatoes in a little oil and then add salt and pepper.
grill (v)	Chop the tomatoes while I grill the chicken.
juicy (adj)	These oranges are nice and juicy.
microwave (v)	I microwaved my bowl of soup and it got too hot!
roast (v)	I'm going to roast some beef for Sunday lunch.
salty (adj)	I love salty food, such as anchovies and olives.
sour (adj)	Add a bit of sugar to the tomato sauce if it's too sour.
spicy (adj)	I need a glass of water – this curry is too spicy!
sweet (adj)	My mum says I shouldn't eat too much sweet food.

PHRASAL VERBS

Phrasal verb	Meaning	Example sentence
chop up (Type 1)	cut into small pieces	Chop the onion up into very small pieces.
cool down (Type 2)	become colder	Let your soup cool down before you eat it.
cut down on (Type 4)	eat less of something	I've cut down on bread and potatoes and I feel much better.
eat up (Type 1)	eat all of something	I didn't like the curry, but my brother ate up all of his.
give up (Type 1)	stop eating	My mum has given up fish, but I still eat it.
go off (Type 2)	begin to decompose	An orange has gone off in the fruit bowl and it smells terrible!
live off (Type 2)	survive by eating only something	My sister lives off peanut butter sandwiches!
warm up (Type 1)	make hotter	Why don't you warm up the pasta in the fridge for lunch?

WORD FORMATION | Adjectives/nouns/verbs

Core word	Derivatives
fry (v)	fried (adj), frying (adj)
mix (v)	mixed (adj), mixture (n), mixing (adj)
spice (n)	spicy (adj)
cream (n)	creamy (adj), creamed (adj)
blend (v)	blender (n)
boil (v)	boiling (adj), boiled (adj)
satisfy (v)	(dis)satisfied (adj), (un)satisfying (adj)
taste (n)	tasty (adj), tasteless (adj)

COLLOCATIONS

Collocation	Example sentence
a wide variety	This shop has a wide variety of things for sale – everything from food to bicycles!
fall ill	When our teacher fell ill, the headteacher taught us for the day.
have in common	My cousin and I have a lot in common, since we're both blond, tall and athletic.
in the opposite direction	Mum turned the car around and headed in the opposite direction.
look forward to	I'm looking forward to Katrina's party this weekend.
make a meal	Have you ever made a meal for your whole family?
set foot in	This is the last time I ever set foot in this restaurant!
the whole world	Apparently, this is the biggest cave in the whole world!

UNIT 7

TOPIC VOCABULARY | Words connected with *shopping*

Word	Example sentence
bargain (n)	Those shoes were a bargain – I should have bought two pairs!
brand-new (adj)	It's a brand-new video game – it only came out yesterday.
cash card (n)	I need to go to the cash machine but I can't find my cash card anywhere.
change (n)	Here's your receipt, and here's your change.
cost (v/n)	How much did your coat cost?
exchange (v)	I got a shirt for my birthday but it's too small so I'm going to exchange it for a bigger one.
half price (phr)	These jeans are normally €40 but I got them half price in the sales.
special offer (phr)	We've got this cheese on special offer this week – three packs for the price of two.
order (v)	We haven't got that book in stock, but we can order it for you.
rent (v/n)	My grandparents don't own their flat – they rent it.
return (v)	I got a shirt for my birthday but it's got a black mark on it so I'm going to return it.
second-hand (adj)	They have lots of nice second-hand furniture in that shop.
voucher (n)	My uncle usually sends me a gift voucher so I can choose my own birthday present.

PHRASAL VERBS

Phrasal verb	Meaning	Example sentence
add up to (Type 2)	form a total	If you get all these clothes, it'll add up to over €100.
get by (Type 2)	survive (with enough money)	It's difficult to get by if you can't find a job.
give away (Type 1)	to provide sb with something that you no longer want or need	These clothes are too small for Tomek now, so I'll give them away.
pay back (Type 1)	return money you have borrowed	I'll pay you back on Friday, I promise.
run out of (Type 4)	not have any left	We've run out of milk, so I'll go and get some.
save up (Type 1/2)	keep money until you have enough to buy something	I'm saving up for a new bike.
shop around (Type 2)	look in different shops	If you shop around, you might find the same phone cheaper.
take back (Type 1)	return	I bought a new shirt yesterday but it's got a black mark on it so I'm going to take it back.

IDIOMS | Idioms for *shopping and spending*

Idiom	Example sentence
be on sb	The meal's on me because I'm celebrating!
go on a spending spree	She won the lottery and went on a spending spree.
like a bull in a china shop	Calm down, George – stop rushing around like a bull in a china shop!
shop till (sb) drop(s)	We've got all day tomorrow, so we can shop till we drop!
window shopping	I haven't got any money, but I'm happy to go window shopping.

WORD FORMATION | Nouns connected with *people*

Core word	Derivatives
assistant (n)	assist (v), assistance (n)
buyer (n)	buy (v)
cashier (n)	cash (n)
customer (n)	custom (n)
electrician (n)	electric (adj), electrical (adj), electrify (v)
hairdresser (n)	hairy (adj), hair (n), haircut (n)
lawyer (n)	law (n)
librarian (n)	library (n)
manager (n)	manage (v), managing (adj)
mechanic (n)	machine (n), machinery (n), mechanism (n)
optician (n)	optic (adj), optical (adj)
owner (n)	own (v), ownership (n)
receptionist (n)	reception (n)
salesperson (n)	sale(s) (n), salesman (n), saleswoman (n)
seller (n)	sell (v), (un)sold (adj), sold (adj)
shopper (n)	shop (v/n), shopping (n), shopkeeper (n)
supervisor (n)	supervise (v), (un)supervised (adj), supervision (n)
visitor (n)	visit (v/n)
waitress (n)	wait (v), waiter (n)

UNIT 8

TOPIC VOCABULARY | Words connected with *clothes and accessories*

Word	Example sentence
belt (n)	I'm going to need a new belt for my trousers now that I've lost weight!
bracelet (n)	Molly bought herself a lovely silver bracelet.
button (n)	I've lost a button on my coat and now I can't fasten it.
cap (n)	Mohammed was wearing a cool baseball cap.
collar (n)	The wind started to get stronger so I put my collar up around my neck.
earring (n)	Your new gold earrings really suit you!
glove (n)	It's cold today so don't forget your hat and gloves.
handbag (n)	Amelia thought she'd lost her phone but it was in her handbag.
jewellery (n)	Mum doesn't wear much jewellery, but she does have one or two gold rings.
jumper (n)	I got hot during the lesson so I took my jumper off.
necklace (n)	In the shop window, there was a gold necklace with a large letter S on it.
pocket (n)	I like this jacket because it's got a pocket for my phone.
sandals (n)	Sandals are much more comfortable than shoes on the beach.
shorts (n)	When I'm on holiday, I usually wear a pair of shorts and a T-shirt.
sleeve (n)	Don't reach across the table or you'll get ketchup on your sleeve!
socks (n)	Change your socks every day or your feet will smell.
suit (n)	At his wedding, my cousin was wearing a nice blue suit.
sweatshirt (n)	I need a new sweatshirt to wear at the gym.
trainers (n)	You can run faster in trainers than in ordinary shoes.
wristband (n)	My best friend gave me a wristband that said 'Friends forever'.

PHRASAL VERBS

Phrasal verb	Meaning	Example sentence
have on (Type 1)	be wearing	When I got to the wedding, everyone had a hat on!
hang up (Type 1)	put (clothes) on a hook or hanger	Why don't you hang your clothes up instead of leaving them on the floor?
do up (Type 1)	fasten	Can you help me do the zip up on my coat, please?
dress up (Type 2)	wear formal or smart clothes	The party on Friday will be a great chance to dress up!
take off (Type 1)	remove, stop wearing	Take that ridiculous hat off!
put on (Type 1)	start wearing	It was raining so I put my coat on before leaving the house.
try on (Type 1)	wear to see if it fits or suits you	In the clothes shop, I tried on six pairs of jeans but didn't like any of them.
wear out (Type 2)	be used a lot and become old and useless	When your shoes start to wear out, it's time to get a new pair.

WORD FORMATION | Adjectives/nouns/verbs

Core word	Derivatives
amaze (v)	amazing (adj), amazed (adj), amazement (n), amazingly (adv)
appear (v)	appearance (n), disappear (v), disappearance (n), apparent (adj), apparently (adv)
beauty (n)	beautiful (adj), beautifully (adv)
cloth (n)	clothes (n), clothing (n)
create (v)	creator (n), creative (adj), creatively (adj)
design (v/n)	designer (n), designed (adj)
fashion (n)	(un)fashionable (adj), old-fashioned (adj), (un)fashionably (adv)
trend (n)	trendsetter (n), trendy (adj)

UNIT 9

TOPIC VOCABULARY | Words connected with *people in sport*

Word	Example sentence
acrobat (n)	It takes years of training to become a circus acrobat.
athlete (n)	The world's best athletes compete in the Olympic Games.
captain (n)	Greg is the captain of our football team this season.
climber (n)	Two climbers were rescued from the mountain by helicopter.
cyclist (n)	You need strong legs to be a professional cyclist.
gamer (n)	I play video games online with gamers from all around the world.
gymnast (n)	You need very good balance to be a gymnast.
player (n)	How many players are there in a football team?
referee (n)	The referee blew the whistle and the match began.
rider (n)	Two riders fell off their bikes during the race.

PHRASAL VERBS

Phrasal verb	Meaning	Example sentence
be knocked out (of) (Type 1)	have to leave a competition because you lose	In the first round, the loser of each match is knocked out of the competition.
catch on (Type 2)	become popular	*Pokemon Go* caught on extremely quickly.
join in (with) (Type 2/4)	take part	We're going to play a board game – do you want to join in?
pull out (of) (Type 2/4)	leave a game/ competition because of a problem or accident	My sister had to pull out of the swimming competition when she broke her leg.
put away (Type 1)	store something in its usual place	Please put the equipment away after you've finished using it.
put off (Type 1)	delay, postpone	The match has been put off until next week because of the bad weather.
send off (Type 1)	make sb leave a game because they broke the rules	The referee sent Jake off because he shouted at another player.
set up (Type 1)	prepare equipment	You set up the board and I'll get the money ready.

COLLOCATIONS | Collocations with *do, play* and *go*

Collocation	Example sentence
do athletics/gymnastics/yoga	We do athletics at school in the summer term.
go for a bike ride	Let's go for a bike ride tomorrow.
go swimming /windsurfing/ water-skiing/skiing/ice-skating/ surfing/horse-riding	My mum used to go horse-riding when she was younger.
play tennis/football/basketball/ golf	Have you ever played golf?

UNIT 10

TOPIC VOCABULARY | Words connected with *people in the media*

Word	Example sentence
actor (n)	Ana's an excellent actor – I hope she gets the main part in the play.
author (n)	The author of *The Hobbit* is J. R. R. Tolkien.
celebrity (n)	Most of the people they interview on chat shows are celebrities.
cinema (n)	Let's go to the cinema on Saturday to see the new Tom Cruise film.
DJ (n)	My cousin's a DJ on a local radio station.
festival (n)	There's a three-day music festival near here every summer.
gallery (n)	All the paintings in the gallery are for sale.
journalist (n)	My aunt works as a journalist for a local newspaper.
museum (n)	It's a fantastic museum – some of the exhibits are thousands of years old.
musician (n)	A big orchestra has between 70 and 100 musicians.
performer (n)	All the performers have to do an audition in front of the judges.
presenter (n)	Who's the presenter of the quiz show on Channel 5?
stage (n)	All the actors came back onto the stage at the end of the show.
studio (n)	They record the show in a studio in London.
theatre (n)	We're going to the theatre to see a play on Friday evening.
venue (n)	The Merton Centre is the perfect venue for weddings, parties and business meetings.

PHRASAL VERBS

Phrasal verb	Meaning	Example sentence
come out (Type 2)	become available (books, magazines, films, etc.)	The magazine I get comes out every Friday.
log onto/into (Type 3)	enter (a website, app, etc.)	You need your email address and password to log into Facebook.
log out of (Type 2/4)	leave (a website, app, etc.)	Log out of Gmail when you finish or someone else will be able to see your emails.
put on (Type 1)	hold (a show, event, etc.)	We're going to put on a school play at the end of term.
shut up (Type 2)	stop talking (often considered rude or very informal)	Shut up, Leo – I'm trying to watch a film!
turn down (Type 1)	decrease volume	Turn down the TV please – I'm on the phone.
turn up (Type 1)	increase volume	Turn up this song – it's my favourite!
write back (Type 2)	reply	I got an email from my cousin in Australia so I'm going to write back this evening.

WORD PATTERNS

Core words	Example sentence
allow sb to (do sth)	Many parents don't allow their children to use computers in bed.
be able to (do sth)	I'll be able to join you after six o'clock.
be allowed to (do sth)	Many children aren't allowed to use computers in bed.
be capable of (doing sth)	I'm not capable of swimming two lengths underwater.
chance to (do sth)	I'd love to have the chance to visit Antarctica.
chances of (doing sth)	What are my chances of passing the exam?
let sb (do sth)	Many parents don't let their children use computers in bed.
manage to (do st)	I managed to swim a length underwater!

UNIT 11

TOPIC VOCABULARY | Words connected with *studying*

Word	Example sentence
lesson (n)	It was such an interesting lesson that the time seemed to fly by!
pass (v)	Joe was so pleased when he passed the English test.
primary (adj)	I've still got lots of friends from primary school.
pupil (n)	There are 30 pupils in my class.
read (v)	I've been reading an interesting book about music.
secondary (adj)	When I was 11, I started at my local secondary school.
student (n)	I'd love to be a student at a large university.
study (v)	We've been studying the Ancient Romans in history at school.
subject (n)	My favourite subject at school is history.
take (v)	If you fail the exam, you can take it again next year.

PHRASAL VERBS

Phrasal verb	Meaning	Example sentence
copy out (Type 1)	write something again exactly as it's been written	Please copy out the first sentence on page 57.
break up (Type 2)	stop going to school for the holidays	We break up on Friday and then we can relax!
hand in (Type 1)	give to someone in authority	When you have finished your exam, hand your paper in to the examiner.
go over (Type 3)	repeat to make something clear	Let's go over the definition one more time.
drop out (Type 2)	leave (a course) before the end	Max hated college and he dropped out after only a few weeks.
fall behind (Type 2)	not be at the same level as	You need to work hard or you'll fall behind the others.

IDIOMS | Idioms for *education and learning*

Idiom	Example sentence
have your nose in a book	Tyler loves reading, he always has his nose in a book.
learn sth by heart	When I find a poem I really like, I try to learn it by heart.
learn the ropes	Once you've learnt the ropes, this job is quite easy.
pass with flying colours	You're good at maths so I'm sure you'll pass the test with flying colours.
put your thinking cap on	Put your thinking cap on and you'll find a solution to the problem.
teach sb a lesson	It's time somebody taught that bully a lesson!

WORD FORMATION | Irregular forms

Core word	Derivatives
believer (n)	believe (v), (un)believable (adj), (dis)belief (n), unbelievably (adv)
choice (n)	choose (v), chosen (adj), choosy (adj)
day (n)	daily (adj/adv), everyday (adj)
depth (n)	deepen (v), deep (adj), deeply (adv)
length (n)	lengthen (v), long (adj)
loss (n)	lose (v), loser (n), losing (adj)
proof (n)	prove (v), disprove (v), (un)proven (adj)
solution (n)	solve (v), (un)solvable (adj)
speech (n)	speak (v), speaker (n), spoken (adj)
success (n)	succeed (v), successful (adj), successfully (adv)
thought (n)	think (v), (un)thinkable (adj), thoughtful (adj), thoughtfully (adv)
width (n)	widen (v), wide (adj), widely (adv)

UNIT 12

TOPIC VOCABULARY | Words connected with *natural habitats*

Word	Example sentence
camel (n)	Camels can live for a long time without water.
desert (n)	Take lots of water if you're going out into the desert.
dolphin (n)	Dolphins don't enjoy performing or doing tricks.
elephant (n)	They say that elephants never forget!
giraffe (n)	Giraffes have long necks to reach the tops of trees.
gorilla (n)	Did you know gorillas make a new nest every night?
grassland (n)	Many animals live in the grasslands in Africa.
lion (n)	When we were on safari, we could hear the lions roaring.
lizard (n)	A small lizard ran across the hot rock.
monkey (n)	Monkeys can use their tails to hold onto branches.
ocean (n)	Does anything live at the bottom of the ocean?
rainforest (n)	Sadly, the rainforests are disappearing.
shark (n)	There aren't any sharks in the sea here, are there?
snake (n)	Watch you don't stand on that snake!
tiger (n)	Most tigers are orange and black, but I've seen white tigers.
whale (n)	We were all scared when a whale appeared beside our boat.
zebra (n)	Is it possible to ride a zebra like you can ride a horse?

PHRASAL VERBS

Phrasal verb	Meaning	Example sentence
bring up (Type 1)	raise a child	I was brought up by my grandparents.
cut up (Type 1)	break something down into pieces	He cut the vegetables up and started making the soup.
end up (Type 3)	the result of a past action or event	We're travelling across the USA and planning to end up in San Francisco.
fill up (Type 1/3)	make something full	Before a long drive, I always fill up the car with petrol.
grow up (Type 3)	grow older / become an adult	My best friend grew up in Spain, so she's fluent in Spanish.
keep up (type 1)	continue to do something	Our basketball team won the league last year, so hopefully we can keep up the winning ways this year!
split up (type 3)	to end a relationship	Apparently, 5% of animals are together for life and don't split up.
wake up (Type 1/3)	stop sleeping or feel energetic	The noisy traffic outside the hotel woke him up really early.

WORD FORMATION | Adjectives and nouns

Core word	Derivatives
explain (v)	explanation (n), unexplained (adj)
nature (n)	(un)natural (adj), (un)naturally (adv)
poison (n)	poisonous (adj)
scene (n)	scenery (n), scenic (adj)
science (n)	scientist (n), (un)scientific (adj), scientifically (adv)
sun (n)	sunshine (n), sunny (adj)
tropic (n)	tropical (adj)

WRITING REFERENCE

A SHORT MESSAGE | Example tasks

Your friend Ali recently moved to another school. Write a short email to him. In your email you should:

- tell Ali what school is like without him.
- ask him about his new school.
- tell him when you can visit him.

Write your short message.

You are going to go on holiday but your camera is broken. Write a note to your friend Lauren. In your note you should:

- explain how your camera broke.
- ask to borrow Lauren's camera.
- say when you will need it.

Write your short message.

Use an informal greeting with your friend's first name.

Cover the first point from the task in one or two sentences.

Cover the second point from the task in one or two sentences.

Cover the third point from the task in one or two sentences.

Hi Ali!

Everyone at school misses you! It feels a bit boring without you! What's your new school like? I hope you're enjoying it and you've made new friends. I could come and visit you next weekend. What do you think?

Bye for now!

Sam

Use your imagination for the details.

Use exclamation marks to create an informal style.

Ask your friend any questions mentioned in the instructions.

Dear Lauren,

I'm going on holiday and I've broken my camera! I dropped it on the floor when I was packing. Could I please borrow your camera for a week? I'll look after it! I need it tomorrow morning.

Let me know!

Love,

Amy

USEFUL PHRASES			
Opening	**Describing**	**Asking questions**	**Closing**
Hi Charlie!, Dear Grace,	*It is/was interesting/boring/fun/ enjoyable/wonderful, etc.* *It happened when …, I feel/felt happy/sad/excited/etc.*	*What's (your new school) like?, Could I please …? Do you think I could …? Is it OK if I …? Can I …?*	*Bye for now!, Love, Lots of love, All my love, Let me know! Call me!*

AN ARTICLE | Example task

You have seen this announcement in a travel magazine:

> **Win a free holiday!**
>
> We want articles on how to plan the perfect holiday. What advice do you have? Send us an article and you could win a week's holiday for you and your family!

Write your article.

Give your article a title.

Ask your readers a question to interest them.

Give your opinion where appropriate.

Use exclamation marks to create an informal style.

Use a connecting phrase to introduce your points in order.

Use imperatives to give advice in an informal way.

Use a connecting phrase to introduce your next point.

Use different ways of making suggestions, such as questions.

Use a good connecting phrase to introduce your final point.

Give examples where appropriate.

HOW TO PLAN THE PERFECT HOLIDAY

Have you ever had a terrible holiday? With a little planning, I believe you can make sure that you have a wonderful time instead!

First of all, only pack the things you need. Most of us take too much luggage on holiday. Just take one bag each and it'll make your life easier.

Apart from packing, you need to think about what you are going to do on holiday. Why not plan activities that all the family will enjoy, such as going on a boat trip or visiting a theme park?

Finally, don't forget to relax and enjoy it. Don't plan too many activities and remember to spend some time doing nothing!

USEFUL PHRASES

Rhetorical questions	Introducing points in order	Giving your opinion	Giving advice	Giving examples
Have you ever …? Do you ever …? What do you think about …?	*First, Firstly, First of all, To begin with, Second, Secondly, Third, Thirdly, What's more, Apart from that, Finally*	*I believe (that) …, I think (that) …, In my opinion, In my view, To my mind, Personally, It seems to me (that) …*	*You should …, Think about …, One thing to remember is …, Why don't you …?, Why not …? How about …?*	*for example, such as, for instance*

A REVIEW | Example task

You have seen this advert on a website for teenagers:

> ## Reviews wanted!
> We want your reviews of restaurants. Write a review of a restaurant in your area and we might publish it on the website! Tell us about the place, the food and the service. Explain why you would or wouldn't recommend it.

Write your review.

Always give your review a title.

The Olive Tree

In a quiet corner of my neighbourhood, there's a small restaurant called The Olive Tree. It's very popular with local people because of the tasty food and the relaxing atmosphere.

Use good vocabulary to describe what you are reviewing.

Give examples where appropriate.

The restaurant serves Italian dishes, such as spaghetti Bolognese and pizza. The food is always very well cooked and delicious. What's more, the prices are not too high, so anyone can afford to eat here.

Introduce additional points with connecting phrases.

Provide further details to explain.

The staff are friendly and helpful. If you are not sure about anything on the menu, they will explain the dishes to you.

Give your recommendations where appropriate.

I would definitely recommend The Olive Tree to anyone who likes simple, classic food at a low price.

Explain the reasons for your recommendation.

USEFUL PHRASES

Listing points	Giving examples	Making recommendations
First, Firstly, First of all, To begin with, Second, Secondly, Third, Thirdly, What's more, Apart from that, Finally	*for example, such as, for instance*	*I would (definitely) recommend this to …, I wouldn't recommend this because …*

A STORY | Example task

Your English teacher has asked you to write a story.

Your story must begin with this sentence:
Greg knew he was late so he started running.

Write your story.

Give your story a title.

If you are given the first sentence, you can't change it in any way.

Don't start writing until you've worked out the plot. Here, the writer noted this down before starting on the second sentence: late for important audition – main part in school play – just gets there in time – does audition – gets the part – very happy.

Use verbs such as tell *and* ask *for indirect speech.*

Use adverbs such as carefully, angrily, *etc. to give more detail.*

If you have a conversation in direct speech, start each speaker on a new line. Even though it's a new line, it's still part of the same paragraph.

Where appropriate/ necessary, show who said something.

Try to include some direct speech in your story if you can. Use speech marks. Remember that direct speech is usually informal.

Use appropriate tenses such as past simple, past continuous and past perfect, and a range of grammatical structures, such as relative clauses.

The Audition

Greg knew he was late so he started running. This was an important audition, and he didn't want to miss it. He wanted to get the main part in the school play.

When he arrived at the school hall, he was hot and tired. 'You're late, Greg,' said Mr Serhan angrily. 'I've been waiting.'

Mr Serhan told Greg about the part, and asked him to act in a scene. Greg, who was a bit nervous, listened carefully. Then he started acting.

'You're a very good actor, Greg,' said Mr Serhan. 'If you can promise not to be late again, you've got the part.'
'I promise! I won't let you down!' said Greg. He was the happiest boy in the world.

USEFUL PHRASES

Time phrases	Creating drama	Verbs with direct/indirect speech	Concluding
Soon afterwards, Some time later, Eventually, Finally, In the end	*Suddenly, At that moment, Without warning*	*ask, cry, lie, promise, say, scream, shout, tell, think, whisper, wonder*	*In the end, When it was all over, Afterwards, Later*

AN INFORMAL EMAIL | Example task

Read part of an email you received from an English friend and the notes you have made.

For my project at school I have to write about transport in a city in a different country. You live in a big city! Can you tell me about the different means of transport? How do people usually travel around the city? Which means of transport do you prefer using?

Interesting! (project)

Say which one (city)

Explain (different means of transport)

Decide (prefer)

Write your email.

Use an informal greeting with your friend's first name.

Don't start giving information immediately. Be polite and refer to something that has happened to or is connected to your friend. Use your imagination. Here, the writer imagined that Caroline attached a photo of her new puppy to the email.

From: Amber

To: Caroline

Hi Caroline,

Thanks for your email! I loved the photo of your puppy!

Use informal language, including contractions and exclamation marks where appropriate.

Introduce your answer to the questions in the second paragraph.

Your school project sounds interesting. I'll tell you about transport here in Athens.

The quickest and easiest way to travel around the city is by metro. That's my favourite! Many people also take buses – and there's also a tram, which goes down to the coast. It's quite slow, though! We also have lots of yellow taxis. If you want to leave Athens and go to an island, you can take a ferry.

Give details in the third paragraph.

Give your personal opinion if the question asks for it.

Mention something about your life to finish the email.

I hope that helps! Let me know if you need any more information. And wish me luck because I've got a flute exam tomorrow!

Use informal closing expressions.

Bye for now!

Love,

Amber

End the email with your first name.

USEFUL PHRASES

Starting the email	Thanking	Asking about health	Referring to someone's news	Introducing points	Final paragraph	Ending the email
Hi Laura!, Dear Carl,	*Thanks (a lot) for …*	*How are you? I hope you're well. How are things?*	*I'm so glad to hear you …, Congratulations on …, Well done on …, Great news about your …, I loved the photo of your …*	*You asked about …, Your … sounds interesting., I'd say that …, I'll tell you about …, First of all, Firstly, Also, Oh, and another thing!, By the way, Guess what!*	*I hope that helps! Let me know …, Wish me luck because …, I have to go now because …*	*Bye for now!, Take care! Write soon! Love, Lots of love, All my love, Best wishes, All the best, Yours,*

AN ESSAY | Example task

In your English class you have been talking about animals. Now your English teacher has asked you to write an essay for homework.

'Every family should have a dog.' Do you agree?

Write your essay.

Introduce the topic in the first paragraph. Create a serious and formal tone by using formal grammar, vocabulary and punctuation. This is not an article for your friends. It's a piece of academic writing for your teacher.

It is fine to ask a rhetorical question, but this is not an article or review, so don't address the reader directly.

Many families have dogs as pets. Should every family have a dog?

Give reasons for your opinion, and introduce them with appropriate phrases.

There are many reasons why dogs make great pets for families. Firstly, they are loving and loyal. Secondly, they are playful and great fun.

Make a number of points, and use appropriate phrases to do so.

Make contrasts, and use appropriate phrases to do so.

However, it is hard work to look after a dog properly. For example, you have to take it for a walk several times a day. Moreover, many dogs do not like being left alone at home.

Give examples, and use appropriate phrases to do so.

In conclusion, dogs are perfect pets for some families, but not for others. I personally believe that a family should only have a dog if they are sure they can take care of it.

Express your personal opinion, and use appropriate phrases to do so.

Come to a conclusion, and use an appropriate phrase to do so, in the final paragraph.

USEFUL PHRASES

Listing points	Giving examples	Expressing contrast	Expressing results, giving reasons, drawing conclusions	Expressing your opinion	Concluding and summarising
First, Firstly, First of all, To begin with, Second, Secondly, Third, Thirdly, What's more, Additionally, In addition (to this), Apart from that, Moreover, Furthermore	*such as, like, for example, for instance*	*However, In contrast, Having said that, but, although, even though, in spite of, despite, On the one hand …, On the other hand …*	*There are many reasons why …, Because of this, Consequently, For this reason, As a result, so, Therefore, This is the main reason why …*	*In my opinion, In my view, To my mind, Personally, It seems to me (that) …, It is my view (that) …, I personally believe (that) …*	*To conclude, In conclusion, To summarise, To sum up, In summary*

IRREGULAR VERBS REFERENCE

Bare infinitive	Past simple	Past participle
be	was/were	been
beat	beat	beaten
become	became	become
begin	began	begun
bend	bent	bent
bite	bit	bitten
blow	blew	blown
break	broke	broken
bring	brought	brought
build	built	built
buy	bought	bought
catch	caught	caught
choose	chose	chosen
come	came	come
cost	cost	cost
cut	cut	cut
deal	dealt	dealt
do	did	done
drink	drank	drunk
drive	drove	driven
eat	ate	eaten
fall	fell	fallen
feed	fed	fed
feel	felt	felt
fight	fought	fought
find	found	found
forget	forgot	forgotten
get	got	got
give	gave	given
go	went	gone
grow	grew	grown
hang	hung	hung
have	had	had
hear	heard	heard
hit	hit	hit
hold	held	held
hurt	hurt	hurt
keep	kept	kept
know	knew	known
lead	led	led

Bare infinitive	Past simple	Past participle
leave	left	left
lend	lent	lent
let	let	let
lie	lay	lain
lose	lost	lost
make	made	made
mean	meant	meant
meet	met	met
pay	paid	paid
put	put	put
read	read	read
ride	rode	ridden
ring	rang	rung
run	ran	run
say	said	said
see	saw	seen
sell	sold	sold
send	sent	sent
set	set	set
shine	shone	shone
show	showed	shown
sit	sat	sat
sleep	slept	slept
speak	spoke	spoken
spend	spent	spent
spring	sprang	sprung
stand	stood	stood
steal	stole	stolen
stick	stuck	stuck
swim	swam	swum
take	took	taken
teach	taught	taught
tell	told	told
think	thought	thought
tread	trod	trodden
understand	understood	understood
wear	wore	worn
win	won	won
write	wrote	written

Macmillan Education
4 Crinan Street
London N1 9XW
A division of Springer Nature Limited

Companies and representatives throughout the world

Optimise B1 Student's Book ISBN 978-1-380-03000-9

Written by Malcolm Mann and Steve Taylore-Knowles
Additional material by Ursula Mallows

This edition published 2019
First edition entitled "Optimise B1 Student's Book" published 2017 by Springer Nature Limited.

Concept and text design by Designers Collective
Design and page make-up for this edition by emc design ltd
Illustrated by David Belmonte/Beehive Illustration,
Dani Geremia/Beehive Illustration and Andrew Painter
Cover design by Designers Collective
Cover photographs by Shutterstock/Happetr, Shutterstock/Machalski, Shutterstock/Syda Productions and Shuttertsock/XiXinXing
Picture research by Penelope Bowden, Proudfoot Pictures, and Emily Taylor

Authors' acknowledgements
Malcolm and Steve would like to thank the team at Macmillan Education and all the many teachers and students around the world who helped make this wonderful project possible.

The author and publishers would like to thank the following for permission to reproduce their photographs
Alamy/Aflo Co. Ltd p16, Alamy/Jason Batterham 2 p85, Alamy/Blen Images p42(b), Alamy/Blickwinkel p127(tr), Alamy/Onnie Chua p75, Alamy/Thomas Cockrem p18(bcl), Alamy/Cultura pp98(cl), 132(cl), 146(a), Alamy/Iulian Dragomir p121(r), Alamy/Sarah Edwards/WENN Ltd p82, Alamy/Encore p70(tcr, bl), Alamy/F1online p97, Alamy/Paul Glendell pp94, 131(l), Alamy/Manfred Grebler p41(l), Alamy/Hemis p129, Alamy/ Hero Images p125, Alamy/imageBROKER p53(cr), Alamy/ITAR-TASS Photo Agency p107, Alamy/Juice Images p64(r), Alamy/Rastislav Kolesar p18(tl), Alamy/Gerard Koudenburg p96(r), Alamy/Liquid Light p18(cl), Alamy/Mint Images Limited p64(l), Alamy/Moodboard p121(l), Alamy/ Mr Pics p60, Alamy/Stuart Pearce p31, Alamy/Mervyn Rees p87, Alamy/ Borges Samuel p108(inset), Getty Images/Chris Schmidt p22, Alamy/ Robert Seeberg/Agencja Fotograficzna Caro p5(bcr), Alamy/Skim New Media Limited p26(cr), Alamy/Dariusz Szwangruber p132(t), Alamy/ Thye Gn p63(bl), Alamy/Galyna Tymonko p66(br), Alamy/Villorejo p131(r), Alamy/Franz Walter/imageBROKER p100, Alamy/Wavebreak Media p4, Alamy/Jan Wlodarczyk p21, Alamy/Hongqi Zhang p50; **Array** p71(br); **Costa Rica Animal Rescue Centre** p49(tr); **Getty Images** p146(b), Getty Images/Ababsolutum p139(), Getty Images/The Asahi Shimbun p103, Getty Images/Asiseeit p86(lcb), Getty Images/Christian Aslund p26(tr), Getty Images/AzmanL p83, Getty Images/Barcroft Media p33(r), Getty Images/Thomas Barwick pp12, 56, Getty Imagers/ Alistair Berg p95(cl), Getty Images/Ed Bock p54(l), Getty Images/Retales Botijero p70(tcl, br), Getty Images/BrandX p30, Getty Images/Jeff Cadge p77(t), Getty Images/Caiaimage p40(bl), Getty Images/Caiaimage/Tom Merton p110(t), Getty Images/Caiaimage/Chris Ryan pp86(lct), 118(tl), Getty Images/Compassionate Eye Foundation/Martin Barraud p119, Getty Images/Comstock p19(c), Getty Images/Corbis p40(tl), Getty Images/Cultura p122, Getty Images/Nick David p116, Getty Images/ Danita Delimont p124(bcl), Getty Images/Claudia Dewald p115(2), Getty Images/Kevin Dodge p32(r), Getty Images/Emmanuel Dunand p93, Getty Images/Emyerson p76(l), Getty Images/EyeEm pp44(b), 52(bl), 124(r), Getty Images/Fatihhoca p55(b), Getty Images/Floortje p62(r), Getty Images/Noam Galai p107(inset), Getty Images/Alan Graf p115(4), Getty Images/Grandriver p66(cr), Getty Images/Daniel Grill p37(2), Getty Images/Jamie Grill pp81(tr), 98(c), Getty Images/Hadynyah p26(l), Getty Images/HASLOO p58, Getty Images/David G Hemmings p124(tcr), Getty Images/Hero Images pp37(4), 137(3), Getty Images/Adam Hester p15(tl), Getty Images/Hill Street Studios pp106, 120(tr), Getty Images/ Tony Hopewell p70(brc, tl), Getty Images/Jeremy Hudson p62(rc), Getty Images/Nathan Hutchinson p33(l), Getty Images/ImageBroker p49(d), Getty Images/Image Source pp120(l), 146(b), Getty Images/iStockphoto pp95(tl), 103(penguin), Getty Images/iStockphoto/Magda p139(), Getty Images/Jimsilva p137(2), Getty Images/John Wood Photography p128(tl), Getty Images/Juice Images pp54(r), 114, Getty Images/Sean Justice p32(l), Getty Images/Ronnie Kaufman/Larry Hirshowitz p137(1), Getty Images/Kolesnikovserg p63(sweets), Getty Images/Laflor pp51, 53(bc), Getty Images/Liquorice p37(3), Getty Images/Holger Leue p34, Getty Images/Maskot p41(r), Getty Images/Alex Mares-Manton p20(l), Getty Images/Maskot p108(l), Getty Images/Peter Mason p70(c, tr), Getty Images/Minden Pictures p124(cr), Getty Images/Monkey Business Images p115(5), Getty Images/Mtreasure pp53(lc), 110(cr), Getty Images/ Richard Newstead p26(tm), Getty Images/Kristal O'Neal p115(3), Getty Images/Pete Oxford p127(forest), Getty Images/Jose Luis Pelaez Inc p115(1), Getty Images/PhotoAlto/Odilon Dimier p84(tr), Getty Images/ PhotoScenics/Terry Cartwright p26(c), Getty Images/Javier Pierini p11, Getty Images/Praetorianphoto p109(t), Getty Images/Monty Rakusen p146(c), Getty Images/Shironosov p140, Getty Images/Starcevic p71(br), Getty Images/Paul Starosta p63(br), Getty Images/Stock4B p37(1), Getty Images/Les Stocker p49(tl), Shutterstock/Boris Stroujko p14, Getty Images/Sturti p53(tc), Getty Images/Svetikd pp19(r), 20(r), Getty Images/ Technotr p44(tl), Getty Images/UpperCut Images pp29, 74(t), Getty Images/ValeriKimbro p27(map), Getty Images/Werner Van Steen 124(tcl), Getty Images/Klaus Vedfelt p120(br), Getty Images/Vgajic p10(lc), Getty Images/VikaRayu p49(c), Getty Images/VisualCommunications p43, Getty Images/Wellglad p105, Getty Images/Westend61 pp96(l), 99, 100(r), Getty Images/Westend65 p42(lc), Getty Images/Yoh4nn p36, Getty Images/Lisa F. Young p52(tl), Getty Images/Zero Creatives pp126(tr), 130(c); **Glow Images**/Deposit Photos p130(cl); **Paul Hameister** p104; **Hyperloop Transportation Technologies**/By kind permission of Hyperloop Transportation Technologies p27(tl,r); **MTJ Media** pp145, 146(br); **Natphotos** p126(br); **PlainPicture**/Cavan Images p80, PlainPicture/Fogstock/Oscar Knott p109(b), PlainPicture/Willing Holtz p48; **Rex Features**/Ciro De Luca/SIPA/Shutterstock p62(tl), Rex Features/M & Y Agency Ltd/Shutterstock p128(br,cat); **Robert Harding**/Craig Easton p72(c); **Science Photo Library**/Michael Donne/ University of Manchester p5(tr), Science Photo Library/Tek Image p52(tr); **Shutterstock**/Alexeysun p59(t), Shutterstock/Anky 124(l), Shutterstock/Assimofusaro p100(l), Shutterstock/Catwalk Photos p88, Shutterstock/Ilyshev Dmitry p127(desert), Shutterstock/Dream79 p81(tl), Shutterstock/GreenArt Photography p61, Shutterstock/I Believe I Can Fly p8(tl), Shutterstock/JMiks p78, Shutterstock/Andrzej Kubik p127(grassland), Shutterstock/Andrey Kuzmin p63(onion), Shutterstock/ Jacob Lund p84(tl), Shutterstock/Armin Staudt p70(bcl), Shutterstock/ Tischenko Irina p63(tree), Shutterstock /Jeka p7, Shutterstock/ Philip Lange p28, Shutterstock/Mangostock p77(cr), Shutterstock/ Melnikofd p92, Shutterstock/Michelangeloop p5(cr), Shutterstock/ Gui Jun Peng p127(ocean), Shutterstock/Sarsmis p66(tl), Shutterstock/ Thai Soriano p37(5), Shutterstock/Tetra Images p81(c), Shutterstock/ Elya Vatel p44(tr), Shutterstock/VGstockstudio p95(bl), Shutterstock/ Wavebreakmedia p55(t). **The Teenage Market** p71(l,r); **Thinkstock Images** p72(r); **Tulsa World**/James Gibbard p58(rc); **UpperCut Images** p74; **Zooner RF** p27(tr).

Printed and bound in Great Britain

2023 2022 2021 2020 2019
11 10 9 8 7 6 5 4 3